THE NORTHUMBRIANS

DAN JACKSON

The Northumbrians

North-East England and Its People

A NEW HISTORY

HURST & COMPANY, LONDON

First published in the United Kingdom in 2019 by
C. Hurst & Co. (Publishers) Ltd.,
41 Great Russell Street, London, WC1B 3PL
© Dan Jackson, 2019

Fifth impression 2020

Printed in Great Britain by Bell and Bain Ltd, Glasgow

Distributed in the United States, Canada and Latin America by
Oxford University Press, 198 Madison Avenue, New York, NY 10016,
United States of America.

A Cataloguing-in-Publication data record for this book
is available from the British Library.

ISBN: 9781787381940

This book is printed using paper from registered sustainable
and managed sources.

www.hurstpublishers.com

CONTENTS

PREFACE AND ACKNOWLEDGEMENTS

This is a book about Northumbrians, and what makes them distinct. Northumbrians are those people from the two historic counties of Durham and Northumberland (which included the City and County of Newcastle upon Tyne) as they existed from the Middle Ages until 1974, a territory that roughly covers the Bernician heartlands of the ancient kingdom of Northumbria. Although the name is now only used officially by a handful of local institutions—a regional police force, the former Newcastle polytechnic, and a local water company—I will use the term Northumbria and Northumbrians throughout this book as a shorthand for the lands and people of what was known in the Middle Ages as either 'Northumberland,' or, in official documents, *comitatus Northumbriae*: a single royal county that began at the Tees (eighty miles to the north of the Humber) and then ran all the way north from the Tees to the Tweed. This is an area of land that now encompasses the post-1974 local authority boundaries of Northumberland and County Durham, Newcastle and Gateshead, North and South Tyneside, Sunderland, Hartlepool, Stockton-on-Tees and Darlington.

Using the more inclusive term 'Northumbrians' avoids bogging us down in the imprecise demarcation of Geordies and Mackems, the two feuding tribes of Tyne and Wear whose modern rivalry has obscured how much they share in common. In their seminal collection of essays, *Geordies: Roots of Regionalism*, the great duo Bill Lancaster and Robert Colls made a strong case to reclaim 'Geordies' to include everyone within Northumberland and Durham (or at least the industrial parts of those historic counties), as had been commonplace until the 1980s. Enduring local rivalries have unfortunately ruled this out, although I use the term where it makes sense. However, a history of the *Northumbrian* people allows us to tell a rich and compelling story—of deep-rooted and almost unchanging cultural mores that have persisted over centuries, alongside world-changing intellectual and technical innovation. And all within a sliver of land smaller than the island of Corsica.

PREFACE AND ACKNOWLEDGEMENTS

Nor is this book a study of identity, which has always struck me as a fruitless and anachronistic pursuit. Instead, I trace the roots of the Northumbrian people, and, by looking at how they have thought and behaved down the centuries, try to help the reader understand why the North East remains one of the most distinctive parts of England; a place described by *The Economist* in 1962 as 'consisting of slag heaps ... and hearty barbarians.'[1] As we shall see, the heartiness of the locals is well attested; yet to understand Northumbrian history is to realise that describing the Northumbrians as barbarians would be a grave misapprehension.

But I should declare my own biases here: I am a Northumbrian, born on the banks of the Tyne to parents from pit village Northumberland and the West End of Newcastle. I count among my ancestors Durham pitmen, Berwick fisherfolk, and Byker publicans. And it was this family background that first sparked my interest in the culture of the place that shaped me— especially when I left home and realised that not everywhere was like this. Why were the pit villages so close-knit, and where did that instinctive warmth and kindness come from? Why did my grandparents say of their tough interwar childhoods, 'we had nowt, but we were happy'; and were they kidding themselves? Why did my forebears and so many of my school pals end up in the military? Why were we so obsessed with football? Why do we love drinking so much, and why did the pub-chat of my father and his pals invariably get around to discussing local hard men, like 'Billy One Punch' and that bloke at Smiths Dock who could twist nails with his fingers? Indeed, why was working hard seen as so essential to earning and maintaining one's self-respect? And, last of all, why was everyone so funny?

The answer to these questions is located deep within the emphatically working-class culture that emerged so strongly in Northumbria's industrial age, but one that shared important continuities with previous eras in Northumbrian history. It was the Victorians who first noticed and articulated these connections, and they stirred a powerful sense of Northumbrian patriotism. Writing in the 1880s, the Gateshead solicitor Robert Spence Watson— solicitor, reformer and Secretary of the Literary and Philosophical Society of Newcastle upon Tyne—surveyed the past of North East England and wrote something approaching a Northumbrian credo:

> I am a devoted Northumbrian, with an intimate love for and belief in the Northumbria of old and the Northumberland of today. I have wandered through every nook and into every cranny of the grand old county since I was a little child, and still visit with ever renewed delight the hills and vales, the peles and castles, which are so abundant, so varied, and so full of interest for

us all ... Northumbria was, in many a great emergency, the saviour of England. Northumbria was the cradle of its religion and decided the form of its religious faith. Northumbria strikes the keynote of the poetic song which is one of England's greatest glories. Northumbria led the van of Christendom in learning as in art. And what Northumbria did Northumberland has continued to do in some measure, and will continue to do in full measure when we all fully recognise and live up to the privilege and responsibility which are implied in the proud boast, 'I am a Northumbrian.'[2]

Statements as beguiling as this can be hard to resist, so I offer this in mitigation to any reader who finds the litany of Northumbrian achievements in these pages a little overweening. But as that scion of Wallington Hall in Northumberland (and the sixth Chancellor of Durham University) George Macaulay Trevelyan noted in his essay 'Bias in History' (on his histories of the Italian *Risorgimento*), 'Without bias, I should never have written them at all. For I was moved to write them by a poetical sympathy with the passions of the Italian patriots of the period, which I retrospectively shared.'[3] When it comes to Northumbrian patriots I certainly share some of their passions, and a sense that North East England is a place whose story has maybe been misunderstood, and its people underestimated—a feeling addressed head on in Northumbria University's 'Global Geordies' online course: 'this is one of Britain's most fascinating, influential and misunderstood regions ... not a remote, isolated and parochial part of the United Kingdom.' Northumbria is all of those things, but the factors that once made it so distinctive—for good and bad—are fast slipping away. For as Frank Atkinson, the founder of Beamish (the North of England Open Air Museum in County Durham) once explained: 'the people of north-east England ... tended to have a chip on their shoulder about their past, proud of it and yet feeling that it was undervalued. The museum was for them.'[4] This book is written for the Northumbrian people too, and for anyone who wants to understand why they are the way they are.

Any writing project would be impossible without the support of family and friends, and I must record my thanks to the many people who have helped me so much over the past two years. Firstly, to Michael Dwyer and his team at Hurst, for commissioning this book. Michael is a gentleman and a scholar, and has provided constant support and encouragement. I am grateful to Judy Greenway, and the Trustees of Wilfred Gibson's Estate for allowing me to quote from her grandfather's poem, 'The Watch on the Wall.' My special thanks to Johnny Handle for permission to quote from his song 'The Collier Lad', and to Ed Pickford for the verses from 'Ah Cud Hew', and to Sam

PREFACE AND ACKNOWLEDGEMENTS

Slatcher for allowing me to reference his song 'City of Sanctuary'. Thanks to Bloodaxe Books for the use of extracts from Basil Bunting's Complete Poems, edited by Richard Caddell (Bloodaxe Books, 2000) and U. A. Fanthorpe's Beginner's Luck (Bloodaxe Books, 2019); and, finally, to Tom Pickard, and his publisher Flood Editions, for the extract from Hole in the Wall: New & Selected Poems (Flood Editions, 2002).

The distractions of social media can be a curse for any writer, but, in my case, Twitter has provided a rich source of information and guidance, and I'm pleased to recall the help of Dr Alan Allport, Marina Amaral, Janis Blower, Paul Brown, Bill Corcoran, Gillian Darley, Tom Draper, Rachel Dwyer, Steve Ellwood, Hilary Fawcett, Katherine Fidler, Dr Christopher Goulding, John Griffiths, Tony Henderson, Tom Holland, Anton Howes, Richard Kelly, Anthea Lang, Dave Morton, Kathryn Rix, Max Roberts, Kathryn Tickell, Tony Veitch, Ed West, Brad Wight, and Jonathan Wilson.

I must also thank Dorothy Rand for her insights into the life of Jack Lawson, and to Ross Forbes of the Durham Miners' Association for sharing his knowledge of that fascinating organisation. My dear friends Alice and Anthony Smithson generously let me treat their wonderful Keel Row Bookshop in North Shields as a personal research library, and I relied too on my oldest pals Jonathan Tully and Michael Dodds for their (often sardonic) advice and motivational trips to the pub. Particular thanks must go to the doyen of Northumbrian history Professor Bill Lancaster for his wise guidance and the brilliant, painstaking and ground-breaking research both he and Professor Robert Colls carried out on the history of North East England. Theirs are the foundation stones on which this book seeks to build. I am also deeply grateful to Professor John Tomaney whose generosity and encyclopaedic knowledge of the region helped shape my thoughts on how to write this book. Likewise, my friend Alan Fidler did a great job in reading my incoherent initial drafts with great forbearance and acuity. It would be remiss of me not to mention here my former history teacher, Byker's own Rob Cunningham, who inspired so many generations of pupils at Astley High School in Seaton Delaval with a love of history; and to the inestimable Professor Don MacRaild who supervised my PhD and at whose feet I learned my craft as a young historian.

I must add too my love and thanks to my wonderful family who have had to put up with a distracted son, husband and father for two years. My parents Mike and Teresa have always been wonderful supporters, as have my parents-in-law Karen and Phil, and their practical help has been utterly invaluable throughout this process—especially my mother who has been a brilliant researcher, transcribing tens of thousands of words from sketchy notes and without which this book simply would not have been possible. Finally, the patient and loving support of my wife Naima has been an unfailing source of encouragement when the going has got tough, and I will be forever grateful for the additional parenting she had to take on for our beautiful, kind and intelligent daughters Rose and Poppy. This book is dedicated to them.

Dan Jackson, Monkseaton   *April 2019*

LITERARY PERMISSIONS

For Tom Pickard's 'The Devil's Destroying Angel Exploded' we thank him and his publishers, Carcanet Press and Flood Editions (*Hole in the Wall: New and Selected Poems*, 2002).

For extracts from Basil Bunting's *Complete Poems*, ed. Richard Caddell (2000), and from U. A. Fanthorpe's, *Beginner's Luck* (2019), we thank their publisher, Bloodaxe Books, www.bloodaxebooks.com.

For Jonny Handle's ballad, 'The Collier Lad', we thank the author for his kind permission to reproduce a verse.

For Ed Pickford's 'Ah Cud Hew', we thank the author for his kind permission to reproduce a verse.

LIST OF ILLUSTRATIONS AND PERMISSIONS

between pp. 14–15

Lindisfarne Gospels via Wikimedia Commons.

Anthony Bek, Bishop of Durham, via Wikimedia Commons.

The Battle of Neville's Cross, via Wikimedia Commons.

A Brank Scold's bride, via Wikimedia Commons.

'Northumberland and Durham', photo by SSPL/Getty Images.

Sandhill Wine Pant, © Civic Centre & Mansion House, Newcastle-upon-Tyne.

The Lit & Phil, photo © Dan Jackson.

Northumberland House on the Strand, via Wikimedia Commons.

Theatre Royal Newcastle, photo © Dan Jackson.

Statue of Hugh Percy, photo © Dan Jackson.

Trafalgar Square almshouses, photo © Dan Jackson.

Penshaw Monument, photo © Dan Jackson.

Joseph Swan/George Stephenson, photo © Dan Jackson.

Thomas Oliver's 1833 map of Newcastle, via Flickr.

Geological Map of Northumberland and Durham 1867, via Wikimedia Commons.

Stephen's Rocket, photo © Dan Jackson.

between pp. 78–79

'Keelmen Heaving in Coals by Moonlight' (Photo by The Print Collector/Getty Images).

London Coal Exchange, Heritage Image Partnership Ltd/Alamy Stock Photo.

'Barge Day', Laing Art Gallery, Newcastle-upon-Tyne, © Tyne & Wear Archives & Museums, Bridgeman Images.

LIST OF ILLUSTRATIONS AND PERMISSIONS

Belsay Hall, photo © Dan Jackson.

Yashima at Jarrow, © Tyne & Wear Archives & Museums, Bridgeman Images.

Theatre Royal Newcastle, photo © Dan Jackson.

'Going Home', Laing Art Gallery, Newcastle-upon-Tyne, © Tyne & Wear Archives & Museums, Bridgeman Images.

Fawcett St Sunderland, Daniel Whiteley Marshall, Sunderland Museum & Winter Gardens, Tyne & Wear, Bridgeman Images.

View of Sunderland (Photo by Universal History Archive/Getty Images).

High Main coal seam, photo © Dan Jackson.

'The Women', Laing Art Gallery, Newcastle-upon-Tyne, UK / © Tyne & Wear Archives & Museums / Bridgeman Images.

Sunderland v Aston Villa, via Wikimedia Commons.

Permanent Relief Fund, Northumberland and Durham Miners' Permanent Relief Fund, courtesy Tyne & Wear Archives.

HMS *Opal*, via Wikimedia Commons.

'Out of Work or Doing Nothing', Google Cultural Institute. Discovery Museum. The Picture Art Collection/Alamy Stock Photo.

Finishing big guns, via Wikimedia Commons.

between pp. 110–111

Warkworth Castle, via Wikimedia Commons.

Chillingham Bull, via Wikimedia Commons.

Lord Collingwood full page, via Wikimedia Commons.

Lord Londonderry, via Wikimedia Commons (Tim Green).

Durham Cathedral from the southeast, via Wikimedia Commons.

'Iron and Coal', via Wikimedia Commons.

Sodom and Gomorrah, via Wikimedia Commons.

'The Response, 1914', via Wikimedia Commons.

Wearmouth Bridge, photo © Dan Jackson.

Working men's club, photo © Dan Jackson.

Fisherfolk on Cullercoats Beach, Historic Images /Alamy Stock Photo.

Wives, daughters, relatives and friends of the victims of the Easington Colliery, Trinity Mirror/ Mirrorpix/ Alamy Stock Photo.

LIST OF ILLUSTRATIONS AND PERMISSIONS

between pp. 142–143

HMS *Superb*, via Wikimedia Commons.

The *Mauretania*, via Wikimedia Commons.

Seaton Delaval, © *Country Life*, Bridgeman Images.

Gertrude Bell, © AF archive / Alamy Stock Photo.

Town Hall South Shields, Private Collection, *Look and Learn*, Elgar Collection, Bridgeman Images.

Building of the Tyne Bridge, © Tyne & Wear Archives & Museums, Bridgeman Images.

Durham Miners Pitmen's Parliament, photo © Dan Jackson.

The largest railway crossing in the world, Alamy Stock Photo.

'Under the Coal', courtesy of The North of England Institute of Mining and Mechanical Engineers.

'The Fighting Fifth', Lebrecht History / Bridgeman Images.

Tyneside Industrial Heritage stained glass, photo © Dan Jackson.

Edwardian view of Grey Street, Infinity Images / Alamy Stock Photo.

'Weel May the Keel Row', by Ralph Hedley, photo courtesy of Anderson & Garland Auction House, Newcastle.

Tynemouth Castle, photo © Dan Jackson.

Exhibition Park, Newcastle-upon-Tyne, Historic England Archive/Heritage Images/Alamy.

between pp. 206–207

Patrick McCormack in his coal mining 'duds', photo © Dan Jackson.

Map of World War 1 Deaths Tynemouth Borough, image courtesy of Steve Young who produced the map for the Northumbria WW1 Commemoration Project http://northumbriaworldwarone.co.uk/.

King George V with General Sir Julian Byng, via Wikimedia Commons.

Miss Ellen Wilkinson MP, with the Jarrow Marchers, Trinity Mirror / Mirrorpix /.

Alamy Stock Photo.

Newcastle United in their dressing room at Wembley, Trinity Mirror / Mirrorpix / Alamy Stock Photo.

Martin Luther King, by kind permission of Newcastle University Archives.

LIST OF ILLUSTRATIONS AND PERMISSIONS

The Animals, © Trinity Mirror / Mirrorpix / Alamy Stock Photo.

The Charltons return to Ashington, Trinity Mirror / Mirrorpix / Alamy Stock Photo.

My Plot, photo © Dan Jackson.

'Whippets', photo courtesy of the Ashington Group Trustees.

'Gordon in the Water' courtesy and © Chris Killip.

'The Angel of the North', © Edifice / Bridgeman Images.

The Northumbrian Riviera, photo © Dan Jackson.

1

UNDERSTANDING THE NORTHUMBRIANS

Are they always like this?—living in the past?
Well, we've had a bigger ration of the past here than in most places.

Alan Plater, 'Close the Coalhouse Door,' 1968

Whisht! lads, haad yor gobs,
An' aa'll tell ye aall an aaful story

Clarence Leumane, 'The Lambton Worm,' 1867

In October 1914 the Morpeth Troop of the Northumberland Hussars found themselves in Flanders. Their direct forebears, Lord Dacre's 'border prick-ers,' had covered this same ground 400 years earlier, screening Henry VIII's army before it routed the French at the Battle of the Spurs. As the first British yeomanry unit sent to the continent in 1914, Northumbrian light-horsemen were again the spearhead of an army from across the Channel; this time as part of a British Expeditionary Force struggling to hold the line against the *feldgrau* columns of German infantry scything through Belgium on route to Paris. The Northumberland Hussars were first raised in the Napoleonic Wars and comprised an odd combination of Northumbrian gentry and miners from the Great Northern Coalfield. They'd left Newcastle in August 1914—a pho-tograph shows them clip-clopping past the Durham Ox pub to the Central Station through a cheering throng of schoolboys—and in the melee around Ypres on the Franco-Belgian border, where the pavé roads had forced them to dismount, a pretty girl had waved her handkerchief and shouted 'Vivent les Anglais.' Private Daglish, one of the troopers marching along on the road, bridle in hand, heard this greeting and made his comrades laugh by returning the compliment with 'vary canny, hoos yorsel?'[1]

No doubt this local lass would not have understood that snippet of Northumbrian dialect—'I'm very well, how are you?'—yet this vignette illuminates some enduring characteristics of the people of North East England. First, that we find Northumbrians in the vanguard of an army is absolutely typical, and a constant in the long sweep of the region's history. Likewise, the distinctive speech and cheerful bonhomie of this private trooper also reveals something of the characteristic outlook of the Northumbrians. The word 'canny,' however, is ambiguous. Its definition shares a sense with the German *gemütlichkeit* evoking a genial mood or temper, and with the Danish word *hygge* too, that sense of wellness and contentment brought on by the warmth of good company. In a 1929 book, *Canny Newcastle*, one author commented that

> by all Newcastle people the word 'canny' is perfectly understood. It is however an adjective which, to the Southerner presents difficulties. To him its many, apparently contradictory applications are puzzling. It is said that it first made its appearance in literature in the Seventeenth Century but the with men of Tyneside it has been current coin from time immemorial. In 'Canny' Newcastle' this very *multum in parvo* among words expresses as none other could, the true Novocastrian's love for and pride in his birthplace.[2]

This goes some way towards arriving at a definition—although its usage, in North East England, extends beyond the confines of Newcastle upon Tyne. An online guide from Newcastle University muses that canny is 'possibly a variation on the Scots word 'ken'—meaning to know' (as in, one assumes, wise or wary); but the Newcastle *Evening Chronicle* claims that 'by the late 1700s canny had begun to be used to mean 'agreeable,' 'appropriate,' or 'good.' And it's from there that all the positive connotations we associate with canny today first came about.'[3] More often than not, and speaking from experience, canny is used to describe agreeable social situations—'we had a canny night out'—or congenial individuals—'their lass is dead canny' (that man's significant other is most agreeable), or 'he's a canny auld fella.' That the attributes most praised by Northumbrians are the social and the convivial, and that they have a special term for that awareness, tells us a lot about them. As the medieval Islamic scholar Ibn Khaldun described in his *Muqaddimah* of 1377, the bond of cohesion among any group of humans—what he called *asabiyyah*—is the basic motive force of all history. The County Durham poet William Martin even coined the term 'Marradharma' to describe the spiritual force that animated the culture of the North East, a compound word he derived from the pit village socialism that thrived among the coalfield 'marras' (the Northumbrian dialect term for close friends and workmates), and 'dharma', a concept meaning a universal truth, or 'the way', that he discovered during his Second World War encounters with the religions of the sub-continent.[4] As we shall see, the history of the Northumbrian people is one where mutuality has always been more cherished than individualism.

The North East of England has been well served by historians. Newcastle is home to the oldest provincial antiquarian society in Britain, and Northumberland is the only county not to have a volume in the *Victoria County History* series as local scholars had already produced a fifteen-volume history—itself based on centuries of scholarship—in the 1940s. But as the founders of the *Annales* school of history noticed, historians tend to be chroniclers of events (*l'histoire événementielle*), those 'brief, rapid, nervous oscillations,' and specialists in noticing change.[5] Yet such traditional approaches tend to obscure deeper continuities and regularities. In the preface to his classic *Annales* study, *La Méditerranée et le Monde méditerranéen à l'époque de Philippe II*, Fernand Braudel described his work as 'the history of long, even of very long duration' (*l'histoire de longue, même de très longue durée*).[6] This book is a modest attempt to follow W.B. Yeats' dictum that 'the history of a nation is not in parliaments and battlefields but in what the people say to each other on fair-days and high days, and in how they farm, and quarrel, and go on pilgrimage.' For it is possible to detect on the shores of the North Sea—just as it was in the Mediterranean, '*une histoire quasi-immobile*,' the deep continuities of humans in their physical environment.

So, what can one observe in the *longue durée* of North East England's history? I contend that a distinctive Northumbrian culture is discernible, one that has always relied upon—and celebrated—toughness and hard work—firstly in a dangerous frontier zone which, after centuries of violence, transformed into a great crucible of the Industrial Revolution where the same qualities of endurance were relied upon and celebrated. This in turn bred an almost instinctive solidarity and friendly (but often claustrophobic) communalism, with offshoots in dry humour and treacly sentimentality. For despite the hardship, this was a people that remained cheerful and gregarious, or at least made a point of appearing so. The philosopher Professor John Gray, himself the son of a Tyneside shipyard joiner, has described the ethic of the South Shields community in which he grew up as a mix of 'stoicism and assertiveness,' and one is reminded here of the contrast between the beaten-down stickmen of L.S. Lowry's Salford and the warmth and joviality of the Durham folk that appear in Norman Cornish's artwork, who he always refused to portray as 'cowed and defeated.'[7]

Autodidacts like Gray and Cornish were by no means untypical, and will be a key part of this story, but the intellectual tradition of the region is often

3

overlooked. Inquisitiveness has been a hallmark of Northumbria since the days of St Bede and in the early modern period it was arguably the most literate part of England. This created fertile ground for subsequent generations of world-changing Northumbrian Enlighteners—think of Stephenson, Swan and Armstrong. Moreover, literacy and industry, and the nexus of Christian nonconformity and trade unionism, meant that there was a deep respect for learning throughout Northumbrian society, especially in the empirical fields of science and engineering.

While other parts of Britain share some of these characteristics, Northumbria has long been considered distinctively different: England's Ultima Thule or freezing Extremadura, where the wind from the steppes rolls across the North Sea to refrigerate the fells of Coldlaw, Coldside and Coldmartin, and blast the marshland of Coldstrother and the hilltop at Cold Hesledon. Much of that definition is grounded in the first fact of Northumbria: that it was a contested military frontier since the Emperor Hadrian built his wall from Wallsend to the Solway Firth. This colossal structure left enduring psychological as well as physical remains. To the Saxons it was 'the work of giants' and was remembered in what was left of the Empire, as the Roman world shrank back towards the Mediterranean, as a metaphysical frontier with the land of the dead.[8] Procopius of Caesarea captured this belief better than anyone else before or since.

> Now in this island of Britain the men of ancient times built a long wall, cutting off a large part of it; and the climate and the soil and everything else is not alike on the two sides of it. For to the south of the wall there is a salubrious air, changing with the seasons, being moderately warm in summer and cool in winter. But on the north side everything is the reverse of this, so that it is actually impossible for a man to survive there even a half-hour, but countless snakes and serpents and every other kind of wild creature occupy this area as their own. And, strangest of all, the inhabitants say that if a man crosses this wall and goes to the other side, he dies straightway. They say, then, that the souls of men who die are always conveyed to this place.[9]

The native Britons themselves had similar feelings about the Wall's role in delineating civilisation. In the words of the British monk Gildas, one of the last voices of Roman Britain, we learn that:

> As the Romans went back home, there eagerly emerged from the coracles that had carried them across the sea-valleys the foul hordes of Scots and Picts, like dark throngs of worms who wriggle out of narrow fissures in the rock when the sun is high and the weather grows warm ... they seized the

whole of the extreme north of the island from its inhabitants, right up to the Wall. ... They were readier to cover their faces with hair than their private parts with clothes.

Ed West has written of the obvious parallels between the far north of England and the lands north of Westeros in George R. R. Martin's fantasy novels, where the landscape and people who live there are 'like its Warden: stark, unforgiving, masculine and wild.'[10] In Peter Davidson's view two opposing ideas of North repeat from European antiquity down to the age of the Arctic explorers: 'that the north is a place of darkness and dearth, the seat of evil. Or, conversely, that it is a place of austere felicity where virtuous peoples live behind the north wind and are happy.'[11] Northumbria typifies this contradiction, where William of Malmesbury could describe the people of the far north as hard and granite-like, but twenty-first century commentators like Stuart Maconie could write that the people of the North East are widely seen as 'kindly, roguish, tough but not nasty, bluff but warm.'[12]

In 1924 the sociologist Henry Mess came to the North East to carry out an official survey of its depressed industrial areas. In the preamble to his final report he felt it important to describe the distinctiveness of the people he encountered:

It will be felt by any stranger who comes to live on Tyneside that it is one of the districts of England with the most marked characteristics in custom, character, manners and speech. It is difficult to set down in words local characteristics, which are so easily felt. There is a curious abruptness of manner, which is very disconcerting until one has got used to it. There is a marked clannishness of the old families. Hospitality is generous when once a newcomer has been admitted to it, but he may be kept a long time waiting in the cold. There is a great love of outdoor sport; an unusual knowledge of wild life; [and] a great deal of interest in local history and antiquarianism.[13]

Fifty years later, in *A Tale of Five Cities: Life in Provincial Europe Today*, the journalist John Ardagh described the North East in patronising terms, 'no longer quite so much the Marrakesh or Palermo of the North,' but nevertheless captured the otherness of the region in the eyes of a Southern Englishman:

one of the few areas in Britain where true regional tradition survives. It is at least as real and self-aware as Languedoc [and Newcastle] has a stronger personality than any other big English town. But there are things I find objectionable, even frightening ... language I could not follow ...felt something of that angst in the presence of an alien, vaguely menacing culture that I have felt in Muslim lands such as Iran and Algeria.[14]

5

Some Northumbrian stereotypes, as understood by the rest of the country—the beery hedonism and the performative masculinity—are undeniably grounded in reality. One thinks here of Reeves and Mortimer's 'Geordie of the Antarctic' sketch, where our football shirt clad-hero is revealed to have provisioned his dog-sled with only crisps, lager and Newcastle Brown Ale; or the 'Geordie Haka' that went viral on social media in 2016, a war dance that celebrates beer, tabs [cigarettes] and hard work with blood-curdling shouts of 'geet fat knacka!' (seek it out, it's a genuinely useful anthropological text). The more interesting question though is *why* these stereotypes are accurate, and where do they come from? There are few more insightful writers on North East England than Bill Lancaster, and in one essay, while musing on the twenty-first century equivalents of the 'bonnie pit laddie and lassie' that now roam the fleshpots of Newcastle, he observed that his pursuit was essentially one of 'cultural archaeology,' a search for those threads 'that link the present-day noise, banter, affability and exuberant sense of social ownership of the city's central area, with previous periods and generations.'[15] This book is an archaeological dig into the deep and interlocking strata of history that explain why Northumbrians are still so distinctive. It is largely based on my observations of the circumambient culture that I grew up in, but also my own reading of Northumbrian history.

A good place to start is to study the language. This makes the Northumbrians distinctive, but it is the things that this language is pre-occupied with that really helps us to understand the characteristics of the Northumbrian people and what they value. As Noam Chomsky once observed of the Native Americans of New England, 'a language is not just words. It's a culture, a tradition, a unification of a community, a whole history that creates what a community is. It's all embodied in a language.'[16] This is no less true of the Northumbrians, some of whose best-known dialect terms reveal the qualities that they most esteem. Consider 'ha'way (or howay) the lads,' an expression most associated with the football terrace (it's even spelled out on the seating behind the goal at the Stadium of Light, home of Sunderland AFC). Yet ha'way is a multi-purpose term of encouragement, close to the French *allez*, and usually meaning 'come along' or 'hurry up,' a very useful phrase in industrial contexts. Much as the varying intonations of 'sir!' in the British Army can mean anything from 'I'll carry out that order,' to 'are you sure that's wise?', ha'way—especially when teamed with 'man!'—can express frustration with slackers and dawdlers, but it can also signify reassurance, as in 'ha'way, don't be daft, it'll be alreet.' (A more stinging variation: 'hadaway'—often coupled with an emphatic 'and shite'—expresses complete disbelief in a far-fetched yarn or an impractical suggestion.) One could also mention here the words that derive from notions of masculinity or violence, such as 'belta,' meaning outstanding or impressive, a word deriving from the verb to belt, or to strike a heavy blow or punch; likewise 'radge' and 'radgie,' where to 'gan radge' means an aggressive outburst; the earthiness of 'hacky'—a bronchial description of unpleasant workplace or domestic grime, and 'stotting'—which has a root in an old Scandinavian word meaning 'to thrust' or 'to push'—can describe both torrential rain or abject drunkenness. Or there's the surprising way that otherwise heterosexual Northumbrian men greet each other as 'bonny lad' in celebration of the *beau ideal* of Northern masculinity. This is a similar salutation to the Italian 'ciao bello,' and echoes that well-known Northumbrian 'dandling song' for children, a hymn to a bountiful County Durham MP:

> *Bobby Shafto's gone to sea,*
> *Silver buckles at his knee;*
> *He'll come back and marry me,*
> *Bonny Bobby Shafto!*

All these terms share a certain vigour and bluntness, but this is matched by Northumbrian terms that reveal an unexpected *tendresse*, like the ubiquitous 'bairn' for children, originally an ancient Anglo-Saxon word to mean a descendent; the friendly unisex term 'hinny,' denoting the sweetness of honey; and 'marra' itself derives from the Northumbrian pronunciation of marrow—in other words an associate whose companionship has a meaning so deep and essential that it's felt in the bones.

The accent itself is ancient too and is immediately distinctive. This may be because there are an unusually high proportion of Northumbrian dialect words that retain a clearly Anglo-Saxon phonology compared to everyday English: words like deed (dead), coo (cow), hoos (house), wrang (wrong), strang (strong) and lang (long).[17] This repelled as much as it endeared: from Ranulph Higden in the 1300s—'the language of the Northumbrians is so sharp, rasping, piercing and unformed that we Southerners can rarely under-stand it'—to that pompous Yorkshireman J. B. Priestley in the 1930s of Tyneside's 'barbarous, monotonous and irritating twang.' You can even hear it in its written form, as in the gruff voice of the Northumbrian frontiersman Sir John Forster in a letter to Francis Walsingham:

> For we that inhabit Northumberland are not acquainted with any lerned and rare frazes, but sure I am I have uttered myt mynde truly and playnely ... where as I am wonderfully charged with aboundance of catell fedinge and bredinge upon the Borders, as is aledged—I assure your honour I never solde non.[18]

In 'The Reeve's Tale,' Chaucer gives the two students from the North, Alan and John, a northern accent (and they swear by St Cuthbert of Northumbria, not by St Thomas of Canterbury). George MacDonald Fraser thought that Hotspur's lines in *Henry IV, Part 1*—especially his 'I remember when the fight was done' speech—seemed designed to emphasise Northumbrian vocal peculiarities as might be heard in 'perfumed like a milliner,' 'guns and drums and wounds,' 'untaught knaves, unmannerly,' and so on.[19] (It helps to say them out loud, and will remind any Northumbrian of having their patience tested by Southern colleagues, or university pals, to say certain words for their amusement—'snooker ... photocopier ... conjunctivitis'; although I think Greek foodstuffs work best here: ouzo, tzatziki, taramasalata ...). This is not to say that accents within modern Northumbria are identical, far from it. There are stock jokes about Ashington speech—a man walks into a hairdresser's and asks for a perm. 'Certainly sir: ah wandered lurrnly as a cloud,' and Newcastle fans are known to taunt their Sunderland rivals with 'wheeyze keyze are theyze keyze?' (who do these keys belong to?) in imitation of the Wearside drawl. Nevertheless, it is hard for outsiders to detect these variations, although any Northumbrian can instantly tell by the way a person pronounces, say, the word 'beetroot' whether they come from North or South of a line that runs from Whitburn north of Washington and between Birtley and Chester-le-Street. Whatever the variant, you can hear the accent down the ages, and it encapsulates a certain direct and boisterous quality, such as in this verse that children would chant as they went door to door on New Year's Eve in the country districts of eighteenth-century Northumberland:

> Get up, aad [old] wife, and shake your feathers,
> Dinna think that we are beggars;
> We are but bairns come oot to play,
> Get up and gie's wor [our] Hogmanay.[20]

* * *

So, what were the origins of Northumbria? The story of Hadrian's arrival with his legions in the year 122 is well known, but his purpose in building his great wall remains obscure. Was it to defend the Empire from barbarians? Or to monitor the population and gather taxes? Or was it simply to reflect the power and prestige of Rome by throwing up such a great barrier from coast to coast? Whatever the rationale, its enduring effect was to establish the northern part of what became Northern England—which the Romans knew as *Britannia Inferior*—as a militarised frontier, and one that would not see lasting peace until the union of the English and Scottish crowns a full fifteen centuries later.

The earliest records we have of the indigenous population come via the 1st and 2nd century Vindolanda tablets (the oldest surviving handwritten documents in Britain) which record the names and professions of some local men. It sounds almost too good to be true (given what we know of the subsequent pre-occupations of this part of the world), but one of these natives was a man called Metto who sold locally-made parts for wheeled vehicles—hubs, axles, spokes and seats—to the Roman garrison; mention is also made of two other local entrepreneurs: a general dealer called Gavo, and Atrectus, a brewer of cervesa—in other words, beer.[21]

When the legions finally evacuated Britain in the early fifth century, the local people seem, for a time, to have maintained some of the Roman traditions and ways of life.[22] However, this was only a brief interlude before Angles and Saxons poured across the North Sea and gradually imposed themselves upon the region in the sixth century. The Angles came from Angeln in the southern part of the Jutland peninsula, where the borders of Germany and Denmark now meet, and to this day, the linguistic roots of Northumbrian dialects are arguably much closer to German than any of the Scandinavian languages. In the north, the Angles established the kingdoms of Deira (centred in what is now Yorkshire), and then Bernicia (in modern Northumberland and Durham). These would eventually merge in the reign of Aethelfrith, 'the ravening wolf,' as joint ruler of Bernicia and Deira—possibly the first united kingdom in these Isles, and one that would, in time, develop into a new kingdom of 'Northumbria'—a realm that would stretch on the east coast from the Humber in the south to the Firth of Forth in the north. But this new kingdom was seldom stable. Violent turf-wars erupted regularly between Bernicians and Deirans to determine overlordship in Northumbria. And between Oswiu, who is considered the first King of Northumbria proper in 654, and the death of Eric Bloodaxe in 954, there were forty-five kings, with an average reign of only six and a half years.

The greatness of Northumbria in the Dark Ages was based less on its political power—although it was blessed with a succession of kings of outstanding ability (some were saints, some were warriors, and some, like Oswin, were both)—than on the distinctive Christian culture which flowered there in art and learning and religious piety. After King Oswald gained the throne of Northumbria after his victory at the Battle of Heavenfield in 634 he sent to Iona (where he had lived in exile among the Irish monks) for Celtic missionaries to preach Christianity to the Northumbrians. The greatest of these was St Aidan who built his first monastery, a handful of simple huts, on Lindisfarne within sight of the royal capital of Bamburgh. The new religion spread quickly, and Northumbria became the stronghold of Anglo-Saxon Christianity. The decision by King Oswiu at the Synod of Whitby in 664 to adhere to the Roman practice of dating Easter favoured by the Northumbrian churchman Wilfrid, rather than the Celtic custom argued for by Colmán, Bishop of Lindisfarne, would be both a watershed for English Christianity and evidence of the extraordinary connections between Northumbria and the wider Christian world.

The Northumbrian church generated an embarrassment of riches, with the Lindisfarne Gospels and the *Codex Amiatinus*, the ancient churches and libraries at Monkwearmouth-Jarrow, Hexham and Corbridge, the glorious sculptured crosses at Bewcastle and Ruthwell, and Caedmon's Song of Creation— 'Now we must honour the guardian of heaven, the might of the architect, the father of glory'—all telling of the richness of that Northumbrian culture. Their monasteries were adorned with gifted and urbane men and women like St Benedict Biscop (who travelled to Rome and back six times in the seventh century to buy books for his library, which was probably the largest in Europe at the time), and the Abbess St Hilda. In St Bede Northumbria gave England its first historian and writer of English prose, its only native Doctor of the Church, and the only Englishman to be named in Dante's *Paradiso*. His celebrated *Historia Ecclesiastica Gentis Anglorum (the History of the English Church and People)*, recorded the spread of Christianity in England, and left us with a metaphor for human life—'like the flight of a sparrow through a lighted hall, from darkness into darkness'—which can still stop us in our tracks with its unsparing clarity.

Yet the golden age of Northumbria did not last long. The Anglo-Saxon Chronicle records that the terrifying Viking raids, that began in 793, came with a 'dreadful forewarning':

> these were immense sheets of light rushing through the air, and whirlwinds, and fiery dragons flying across the firmament. These tremendous tokens were soon followed by a great famine; and not long after, on the sixth day before the ides of January in the same year, the harrowing inroads of heathen men made lamentable havoc in the church of God in Holy-island, by rapine and slaughter.

The Northumbrian monasteries at Lindisfarne and elsewhere, with their wooden outbuildings and heather roofs, were as vulnerable to flaming torches as they were to axe-wielding Vikings. These raids set in train a period of weakness and decline in Northumbria's fortunes that culminated with the arrival of the 'Great Heathen Army' from Scandinavia in 865 that barrelled across the four kingdoms that constituted England, settling and seizing control or exacting 'Danegeld' tribute. As the unifying English kingdom in the South under Alfred the Great and his successors systematically reconquered the 'Danelaw,' and the Scottish kingdoms to the North similarly coalesced, then it was inevitable that the strategically vital lands that separated them would become a battlefield. Indeed, some of the latest scholarship on the location of the great Battle of Brunanburh, the English King Athelstan's victory over the Kings of Dublin, Alba and Strathclyde in 937 that secured England's northern and western flanks, suggests that it was fought at Lanchester in County Durham, near to Longovicium, an auxiliary fort on Dere Street, the Roman road that led north to Corbridge.[23]

Although the Danes had occupied and gained control of southern Northumbria, from the Humber to the Tees, and installed a series of puppet rulers as Kings of York (the last of these being Eric Bloodaxe, killed by rival Norsemen on the slopes of Stainmore in 954), the crucial fact for the subsequent development and distinctiveness of North East England was that, unlike Yorkshire, the Vikings raided, *but did not settle* Northumbria north of the Tees. The most obvious evidence of this is the absence of Scandinavian place names—all those '-thorpes,' '-thwaites' and '-bys' scattered across maps of Yorkshire and Lincolnshire peter out at the Tees. In contrast, Anglo-Saxon '-worth' endings predominate in Northumbria, such as Backworth, Killingworth, Heworth, Usworth, and Hunstanworth. Bernicia re-emerged as an Anglo-Saxon stronghold where the Danes had no jurisdiction, and thus, despite the widespread misapprehension that endures to this day, Northumbrian distinctiveness derives not from any Viking DNA, but from their German ancestry.

The history of Northumbria in the ninth and tenth centuries is poorly recorded, but we do know that the Anglo-Saxon Northumbrian elite that held on in Bamburgh called themselves either 'Kings of the North Saxons' or Earls of Bamburgh. They were joined by a 'Community of St Cuthbert'—the monks who had fled from Lindisfarne in fear of Danish raids and then wandered in Northumbria until settling first in Chester-le-Street and then Durham, which became known as the 'Haliwerfolklond,' 'the land of the holy people.' Cuthbert was a simple shepherd and hermit from Doddington in Glendale, and would become the most popular saint in England from his death in 687 to the canonisation of Thomas Becket in 1175. The mighty cathedral at Durham, the grandest Romanesque building in Europe, was first built as his shrine. In death, St Cuthbert gained a reputation as a fierce protector of his 'haliwerfolc' (the holy people of the saint), and he was invoked whenever battle was joined with the Scots and was appealed to as a guarantor of local privileges well into the later Middle Ages.

In 883 the Danish King of York, Guthred, a pious Christian convert, had granted the lands from the Tees to the Tyne—the former patrimony of the Monastery of Monkwearmouth-Jarrow—to the Community of St Cuthbert. In return for their fealty, they were conferred significant juridical autonomy, including a right of sanctuary in Durham for anyone who fled there from north or south (a right that existed until 1624). Writing of the Northumbrian defeat by the Scots at the Battle of Carham in 1018, Symeon of Durham described it as a campaign waged by the 'people of St Cuthbert,' which he defined as 'the whole people between the river Tees and the river Tweed.'[24] It was to the haliwerfolc that King John granted a charter of liberties in 1208, and in 1433, when a faction challenged Bishop Langley's authority, it was done in the names of 'Goddes Kirk and Saint Cuthbert of Duresme,' the ever-reliable protector of his people. This patrimony was the basis for what would become the quasi-regal power of the Prince Bishops of Durham—a unique office in England—whose custodianship of Saint Cuthbert's relics added a holiness to their temporal authority over the 'liberty of Durham' (one of several such 'liberties' within Northumberland's boundary that were subject to powers other than the crown—with Hexhamshire, for example, belonging to the Archbishop of York, and Tynedale to the King of the Scots).

St Cuthbert remained totemic to the Northumbrians, and was thought to intercede for his people at times of peril; as in 1346 when the saint haunted the dreams of the invading Scots King, David II, and 'disturbed his evening slumbers, and threatened him with direst vengeance if he continued in his evil course' (he was subsequently captured at the Battle of Neville's Cross). Or in the Second World War where some Northumbrians believed that 'St Cuthbert's Mist' had shielded Durham and Newcastle from Luftwaffe bombing raids.[25]

The rise and fall of Northumbria left more than just an intellectual and religious legacy—as dazzling as they were. They left a sense of a loss, of a great civilisation once having the dignity of a kingdom being snuffed out by barbarian invaders. As the thirteenth century monk John of Wallingford's *Chronicle* observed: 'From that time to the present, Northumbria has been grieving for want of a king of its own, and for the liberty they once enjoyed.'[26] As English royal power burgeoned in the south of England, with the court centred on London, the very remoteness of Northumbria became an important factor in its otherness. From 1000 until the Treaty of York in 1237 was agreed between Henry III of England and Alexander II of Scotland, where the Scots king relinquished his claim to 'comitatu Northumbrie, Cumbrie et

Westmerland,' it was not certain whether the modern counties of Northumberland and Durham would become part of the kingdom of England or of Scotland. This gave them a 'particular and uncertain status in Britain' which foreshadowed our modern understanding of North East England as a distinctive region.[27]

North East England remains a most unusually well-defined region. It was first described by Symeon of Durham in the eleventh century as being 'between the brine and the high ground and the fresh stream water'—in other words, the North Sea, the Cheviots, Pennines, and Cleveland Hills, and the rivers Tweed and Tees. But then the very real topographical boundaries and barriers within England are not well understood in English history. The heart of medieval England was always London and the wide and fertile southern plain, which was bounded in the west by the rivers Exe and Severn and in the north by the Trent and a fringe of hills and high moorland. As Sydney Middlebrook described in his classic history of Newcastle upon Tyne, north of this frontier

> formed a unity, cut off from Scotland by the Solway and the Cheviots and separated from the rest of England by the 'mosses' of South Lancashire, the hills and moors of Derbyshire, the great forest of Sherwood, and the marshes of the Isle of Axholme and the Humber. Remote from the centre of government as from the Continent; wild, bleak and poor in yield compared with the South; and backed by still more rugged country in Scotland, it was difficult to conquer and to hold, as both the Romans and Normans found.[28]

To this day, many will argue where the North starts, and yet this was settled centuries ago by the simple facts of geography which defined the limits of juridical circuits, military commands, and indeed the jurisdiction of the King's Council in the North which reached from the Trent to the Tweed. The North then was well defined, firstly by major rivers, and then by a ridge of Jurassic limestone that runs through England, which separates a Highland zone of older, harder rocks forming a landscape more suitable to pastoral agriculture, from the low-lying and more fertile plains of Southern England. From this division, of North and South, England still retains the ecclesiastical provinces of Canterbury and York, demarcated along a sinuous line that stretches from the Mersey to the Humber via the Trent, and the jurisdiction of the two royal heralds: Clarenceaux and Norroy (a corruption of 'Nord Roi'—North King) in the College of Arms. Even Shakespeare has his rebels in *Henry IV, Part 1* carve up England along these lines, with Mortimer taking 'England … south and east of Trent and Severn'; to Glendower, Wales; and to Harry Hotspur, 'the remainder northward, lying off from Trent.'

This division of England further isolated Northumbria, doubly-immured as it was from the centres of wealth and royal government, behind both the Mersey-Humber line—permeable in only a few places, including Dore (which literally means door or entrance) outside Sheffield—and the narrow gap between the Pennines and the Cleveland Hills. This remoteness from the English heartlands was well captured by John Cleveland, who wrote in 1653 that 'England's a perfect world, hath Indies too; Correct your map, Newcastle is Peru!' This has meant that Northumbria can often be excluded even from conceptions of the North in our national discourse—consider the Poet Laureate Simon Armitage who argues that the 'true north' is in the Yorkshire Dales, or in other books by men of Lancashire and Cheshire where the North East appears as an afterthought, if it features at all.[29] This sort of thing makes Northumbrians roll their eyes at what they see as bumptious Midlanders, but these are futile debates, and need not detain us beyond noting that 'the North' is always relative, as Alexander Pope put it in his poem 'Essay on Man':

> Ask where's the North? At York 'tis on the Tweed
> On Tweed 'tis on the Orcades, and there
> At Greenland, Zembla or the Lord knows where …

In 1989, the French geographer Roger Brunet developed the concept of a West European 'backbone', a consistently industrious and prosperous urban corridor of industry stretching from southern England through the Low Countries and the Rhineland to northern Italy. In this sense, it was the 'Southumbrians' who lived in what we might call core Europe, whilst in historical terms the region's two golden ages—the Northumbrian Renaissance of the seventh to the mid-eighth centuries, and the industrial pre-eminence of the 'long nineteenth century'—went against the grain of British and European history. At the time of the Norman Conquest in 1066 the English population stood at about 1.7 million, but only around 20,000 of those lived North of the Tees, scattered thinly across the region with only a handful of major settlements other than Bamburgh and Durham. By 1290 the population of England had grown to 4.75 million and that of the North East to 223,600, but the English population plummeted after the Black Death in 1348 to 1.9 million, recovering only gradually to 2.35 million by 1522.[30] In the same period the North East suffered both from plague and the devastating raids by King Robert I of Scotland between 1307 and 1329. This caused the population to shrivel to just 55,000 in 1377, recovering to 149,400 by 1600.[31]

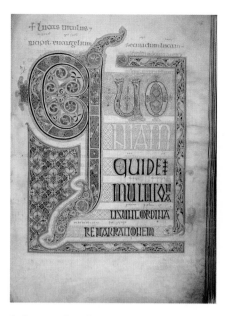

The opening of St Luke's Gospel in the Lindisfarne Gospels (715–720 AD). 'Quoniam quidem multi conati sunt ordinare narrationem …' (Since, indeed, many have attempted to set in order a narrative).

THE BISHOP OF DURHAM'S CHARGE AT FALKIRK (*see page* 34).

Anthony Bek, Prince Bishop of Durham, who led an English division at the Battle of Falkirk in 1298.

The Battle of Neville's Cross, 1346, from Jean Froissart's *Chronicles*. David II, King of Scots can be seen on the left in the red lion tabard.

'A brank [sometime's known as a 'scold's bridle'] and a drunkard's cloak at Newcastle-on-Tyne', from *Old-time punishments* by William Andrews (1890).

'Northumberland and Durham', LNER poster, 1923–1947, by Montague B. Black.

'Sandhill Wine Pant, Coronation of King George IV', Henry Perlee Parker (1795–1873).

An embarrassment of riches: the first eleven presidents of the Literary & Philosophical Society of Newcastle upon Tyne.

The Strand front of Northumberland House, London palazzo of the Percies, as painted by Canaletto in 1752.

Theatre Royal and Grey Street, Newcastle upon Tyne.

Statue of Hugh Percy, 3rd Duke of Northumberland, in front of the Master Mariners Homes (1838) at Tynemouth.

Trafalgar Square (1840) Merchant Seamen's Almshouses at Sunderland.

Penshaw Monument (1844), a memorial to 'Radical Jack' Lambton, 1st Earl of Durham, photo.

Memorial to Sir Joseph Swan on Carliol House, Newcastle upon Tyne (1928), and a memorial at York Railway Museum from 'the railwaymen of Italy' to George Stephenson (1925).

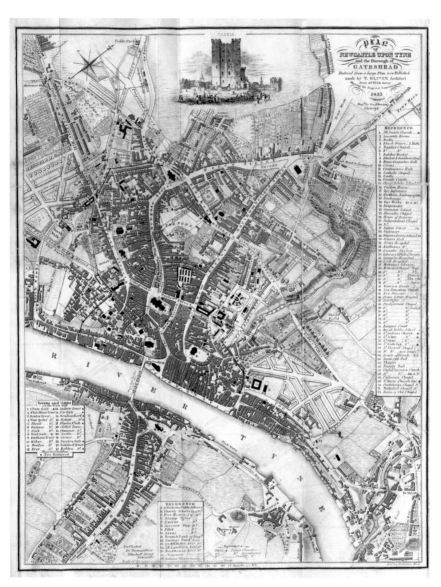

Thomas Oliver's 1833 Map of Newcastle upon Tyne and Gateshead.

Geological Map of Northumberland and Durham 1867.

They changed the world: George Stephenson's 'Rocket', which won the Rainhill Trials in 1829, and Sir Charles Parsons' 'Turbinia' (1894) the world's first steam turbine powered steamship.

Even after the Industrial Revolution the population of the North East did not keep pace with the rest of the North, growing from 262,500 in 1761 to 332,000 in 1801, a fact usually attributed to the remoteness of the region.[32] What overcame this isolation was the exponential growth of coal mining, especially from the nineteenth century onwards, an industry that came to define the whole North East. 'Coals to Newcastle, Hoare's to Paris' was King George V's laconic response to Sir Samuel Hoare's appointment as Ambassador to France in the 1930s, and the identification of the region with coal-production was well-founded. Output had soared from 1.56 million tons in 1750 to 3.2 million tons in 1801, and 15.4 million tons by 1854.[33] This drew in workers to the coalfields from all over Northumbria, and from as far afield as Cornwall and Ireland. County Durham's population increased almost tenfold between 1801 and 1901, with a population of 150,000 leaping to 1.2 million, while Northumberland grew from 170,000 to 600,000 during the same period. This population growth in the industrial period was anomalous for such a peripheral region, and the stagnant population growth of the twentieth century is the inevitable consequence of the decline of coal-mining and other heavy industries.

What further helps us understand Northumbrian difference from the rest of Britain is that in defensible terms the North of England had a southern 'inner bailey' south of the Tees and an 'outer bailey' north of that point guarding the Northern perimeter. For the far northern counties were expected to provide a buffer zone against Scottish invasion (it is noteworthy that whenever the Scots successfully invaded England they would pull up sharply at the river Tees, as they did as late as 1644 when the Earl of Leven's army occupied Northumberland and Durham). Indeed, it was the centuries of conflict with the Scots that really set the Northumbrians apart from the rest of England, which had long since beaten their swords into ploughshares. As the geographer C. B. Fawcett put it in 1919:

> For several centuries, while the rest of England was a peaceful agricultural country, this border region was its fight frontier, a land of savage guerrilla warfare of mingled heroism and barbarity. In every ancient village there are traditions of the border raids. For long after the cessation of that warfare the then poor region of the north was an unimportant part of the realm, except for the fact that the road from England to Scotland passed through it for a hundred miles. It was too poor and barbarous to attract settlers from the more fertile lands to the south, and hence maintained its distinctive character.[34]

Curiously enough those centuries of border warfare have left little or no bitterness, unlike, say in the Balkans, and the Northumbrians' relationship with their Scottish neighbours has long been very cordial. To some in the South of England Northumbria's distinctiveness derives from being little more than the overlapping section in a Venn diagram of England and Scotland. As Thomas Carlyle observed of the inhabitants, they are 'Scotch in features, in character and dialect,' and this echoed the view of Tudor officials who saw the Northumbrians as not really 'civil Englishmen' at all.[35] These similarities were observed in George MacDonald Fraser's classic *The Steel Bonnets* where the people on both sides of the nominal border were seen as

> barbarous, crafty, vengeful, crooked, quarrelsome, tough, perverse, active, deceitful—there is a harmony about the adjectives to be found in travellers' descriptions and official letters. In general, it is conceded that the Borderers, English and Scottish, were much alike, that they made excellent soldiers if disciplined, but that the raw material was hard, wild, and ill to tame.[36]

In Linda Colley's seminal *Britons: Forging the Nation* she records how the poor in the North East consumed oatmeal like the Scots and 'to pass from the borders of Scotland into Northumberland,' a Scottish clergyman wrote at the end of the eighteenth century, 'was rather like going into another parish than into another kingdom,' an observation that John Buchan would note a century later as he passed into England from his beloved Tweeddale.[37] The symbiotic Scoto-Northumbrian relationship was reinforced by large scale migration into Northumbria from as early as the 1500s when there were hundreds of Scots living in Newcastle, including John Knox who was appointed a preacher at St Nicholas's Church in 1550. Many of the coal miners recorded on Tyneside in 1637 came from Scotland, and of the keel-men working on the Tyne in 1740 a majority came from 'Fife, Stirling and Lothian.' By the time of the 1745 rebellion so many Scots had made Tyneside their home that the native Northumbrians differentiated what they saw as 'the savage Highlanders' from the more civilised Lowland Scots. The path northward was well-trodden too: much of classical Edinburgh is built with Northumbrian sandstone, and it became common for the gentry and bourgeoisie of the North East to send their sons to Edinburgh University; its alumni included noted Northumbrians like the poet and royal physician Mark Akenside, the mathematician George Walker, the industrial tycoons Robert Stephenson and Sir Lowthian Bell, and the Northumberland shepherd boy Thomas Kirkup whose *History of Socialism* was such an influence on Mao Tse-tung. (Edinburgh returned the favour through Burke and Hare who robbed graves on Tyneside as they did in 'Auld Reekie.') The unusually high levels of literacy in Northumbria owed much to an appreciation for the neighbouring system of parish education in Scotland, and Northumbrians shared many other traits with the Scots including a taste for classical architecture, an obsession with football, and a debilitating enthusiasm for alcoholic beverages.

That Northumbria was the cockpit of the British Isles for almost two millennia has added a note of drama and romance that has long excited historians and can still beguile the modern reader. 'The history of Northumberland is essentially a drum and trumpet history,' wrote the Victorian antiquarian Cadwallader J Bates, 'from the time when the buccina of the Batavian cohort first rang out over the moors of Procolitia down to the proclamation of James III at Warkworth Cross.'[38] Swashbuckling stories of moonlight raids and jousting knights was the central thrust of the 'Ballad of Chevy Chase' ('Chevy' here refers to the Cheviot Hills) and moved the Elizabethan courtier Sir Philip Sydney to declare that 'I never heard the old song of Percie [sic] and Douglas, that I found not my heart moved more than with a trumpet.' And how could one not be moved by the lament for the Northumbrian Jacobite Sir James Radclyffe, 3rd Earl of Derwentwater, beheaded for treason on Tower Hill in 1715:

> *Albeit that, here in London town*
> *It is my fate to die,*
> *Oh! carry me to Northumberland,*
> *In my father's grave to lie;*
> *There chant my solemn requiem*
> *In Hexham's holy towers,*
> *And let six maids from fair Tynedale*
> *Scatter my grave with flowers.*

Many of these old tales were amplified first by Sir Walter Scott in the nineteenth century, who added the Earl of Northumberland—'a formidable name to Scotland'—to his roll of chivalric heroes, and his *Minstrelsy of the Scottish Border* (1802–03), *Marmion* (1808) and *Rob Roy* (1818), introduced, and to an extent, invented an epic Northumbrian history for public consumption:

> *And now the vessel skirts the strand*
> *Of mountainous Northumberland;*
> *Towns, towers, and halls, successive rise,*
> *And catch the nuns' delighted eyes...*
> *And Warkworth, proud of Percy's name;*
> *And next, they cross'd themselves, to hear*
> *The whitening breakers sound so near,*

Where, boiling through the rocks, they roar,
On Dunstanborough's caverned shore.

This in turn built upon Arthurian Legend; Sir Thomas Malory, the author of *Le Morte D'Arthur*, has Merlin's master, the hermit Blaise, dwelling in the forests of Northumberland and locates 'the Joyous Gard,' Sir Lancelot's castle, somewhere in the north, probably at Bamburgh, where Tristram holds Isoud—a theme picked up by Algernon Swinburne in his *Tristram and Iseult*, where he recounts that there

They saw the strength and help of Joyous Gard.
Within the full deep glorious tower that stands
Between the wild sea and the broad wild lands.

Such thrilling drama occurs too in the dragon stories that proliferate in Northumbrian folklore.[39] These monsters are known locally as 'worms' (derived from the Norse '*ormr*,' for serpent or dragon), and typically feature a knight errant returning from distant wars to grapple with these creatures and save their kinsfolk, as in the Laidly Worm of Bamburgh, the Sockburn Worm of South Durham (which inspired Lewis Carroll's Jabberwocky after a stay at Croft-on-Tees), and, most famously, the Lambton Worm. The story as recounted in the song is interesting because it tells of our hero Sir John Lambton who having caught a strange beast in the River Wear, threw it down a well and then left to 'gan and fight' in the Crusades. While he's gone the worm burgeons and wreaks havoc, feeding on livestock and 'swally[ing] little bairns alive when they laid doon to sleep.' To this day, Northumbrians learn the song from childhood, and its chorus 'whisht lads haad ya gobs' (quiet boys, hold your tongues and listen in) speaks of the communal and allegorical purpose of retelling these folk tales: in this case the virtue of defending your people, and confronting danger—as Sir John does when he smites the worm:

So noo ye knaa hoo aall the foaks
On byeth sides ov the Wear
Lost lots o' sheep an' lots o' sleep
An' leeved i' mortal feor.
So let's hev one te brave Sor John
That kept the bairns frae harm,
Saved coos an' caalves by myekin' haalves
O' the famis Lambton Worm.

Penshaw Hill—round which the famous worm coiled itself—dominates the lower Wear valley, and the landscape of Northumbria is thick with such dramatic features, whether topographical, historical or industrial. The apocalyptic canvasses of the nineteenth-century painter John Martin, such as *The Destruction of Sodom and Gomorrah*, or *The Great Day of His Wrath*, were heavily influenced by his native Tyne Valley, where the remains of Hadrian's Wall and Border strongholds lay close to the heat and smoke of industry and what appeared to him as the infernal bowels of local lead mines. These were undoubted influences on his re-creation of the world of Moses, Joshua and Satan:

> He used to get up at 2 o'clock in the morning and stand in the dark waiting to see the miners' lamps bobbing along the horizontal dark tunnels. He mentions the terror of the open pits, how once, as they played blindfolded, his sister saved him from folly. It was a landscape of extremes that became a theme for his work. Perhaps we can see through him the mining area as hell.[40]

Isolated it may have been, but it was emphatically not a sleepy backwater—as Daniel Defoe wrote on his tour through Northumbria in 1724, 'here is abundant business for an antiquary; every place shews you ruin'd castles, Roman altars, inscriptions, monuments of battles, of heroes killed, and armies routed.' (Even now one can stumble across places like Vespasian Avenue in South Shields, the unpronounceable Ecgfrid Terrace in Jarrow, or even no-smoking signs in Latin—'nolle fumare'—at Wallsend Metro Station.) This sense of a place steeped in history was perhaps best captured by the Newcastle-based Scottish artist William Bell Scott in his series of eight frescoes at Wallington Hall in Northumberland. Rather like the ceiling of the Sistine Chapel told the story of Creation, Bell Scott's cycle of paintings recounts the birth of Northumbria from the building of the Roman Wall, through Cuthbert, Bede and the Border wars to culminate in the much-reproduced final image of a squad of workmen hammering out a gun barrel at Armstrong's factory on the Tyne—while a locomotive passes by on Robert Stephenson's High Level Bridge—above the legend 'In the nineteenth century the Northumbrians show the world what can be done with iron and coal.' Scott clearly saw these men as the continuation of a key theme in Northumbrian history, that of violence and masculinity that began with the Roman Legions and had now been merely recast into a sort of industrial combat in the service of the British Empire. This was certainly the view of the Northumbrian intelligentsia of the later nineteenth century who imagined that the 'swords of moss troopers had been turned into iron ships' and Armstrong's field guns were said to stand in unbroken line with 'Roman javelins and Hotspur's spear.'[41]

* * *

There are, of course, risks to taking all this self-congratulatory regional jingo-ism at face value. Historians have noted (in the grandiloquent claims that accompanied the North East Coast Exhibition in 1929) 'Selective reimagining of the ancient Northumbrian past ... to bolster Tyneside industrial confidence with reference to another heroic age' has only ever had limited efficacy.[42] Whether they are true or not these are the stories that Northumbrians have told themselves, in which their morals are encoded in a history of victories and defeats, of courage and toil, of communalism and solidarity where the past is a source of pride and resilience in the face of adversity. For authors like Joe Sharkey the key pillars of North East identity are cruder still: 'class, accent, drink and football,' and the boorishness of their cultural expression— which, paradoxically, seem to incorporate both friendliness and aggression— engender the same mixed feelings as the eighteenth-century poet, and son of Newcastle, Mark Akenside, who was 'said to be ashamed of his native place.'[43] Others have summed up the modern history of the North East as a trinity of labour, industry and decline, which in turn has engendered emotions of 'pride, regret, nostalgia and solidarity,' and a sense of a 'hard-worked past, whose marks evoke not only bitterness and poverty, but the greatness, too, of industrial achievement and the pride that went with it.[44]

Although it is true to say that traditional approaches to British history can often miss the nuances of regional difference, there is a danger that accounts of the North East, as with any other part of the country, can become exclu-sively a search for variations from the national historical norm.[45] In an attempt to redress that balance too many studies of the North of England can take on a tiresomely rhapsodic tone. We should be wary of a sort of regional jingo-ism—lest we turn into a pastiche of the character from the BBC comedy series 'Goodness Gracious Me' who claims everything of any worth is Indian—Locomotive engines, Northumbrian! Lucozade, Northumbrian! I can be guilty of that feeling myself: a certain chippiness, a sense of being overlooked, underestimated and occasionally patronised. The sense that in its industrial heyday Northumbria's was a great civilisation, that has now gone with the wind, was summed up by the South Shields miner Tommy Turnbull who described the Northumbrian proletariat as 'a great tribe of people, now decimated, degraded and dispersed' and their demise has left the country 'forever as impoverished by this loss as have the Americas by the loss of their Apaches and their Incas.'[46]

The Yorkshireman Frank Atkinson, the founder of the North of England Open Air Museum at Beamish in County Durham, wrote that he built the Museum to 'inculcate pride,' for the people of the region 'have a curiously sad chip on the shoulder ('we lack the benefits that the people of the south have'), mixed illogically with the belief that 'we have a marvellous, self-reliant region.' Quite remarkably these conflicting views are almost true.'[47] As a result, Northumbrians can be as tediously chauvinistic as the most boring Yorkshireman, though as the Teessider Harry Pearson put it in a piece on the charms of Tyneside, 'its atmosphere of almost pathological friendliness and good humour' stems from 'one simple thing: all Geordies believe themselves blessed to have been born here.'[48] And Northumbrians always seize eagerly on any account of local friendliness. The Scottish football writer Neil Cameron concluded that Tynesiders are 'good folk, slightly mad,' but 'you will struggle to find a nicer population in England.'[49] In *Pies and Prejudice*, Stuart Maconie observed that British people have been conditioned to see the people of the North East as 'kindly, funny, roguish, tough but not nasty, bluff but warm,' and that call centres and the Samaritans 'love Geordie volunteers because their down-to-earth but quietly reassuring tones are proven to turn people's minds away from the gas oven and tablets.'[50]

The instinctive sociability of Northumbrians is as much a popular stereotype as Yorkshire dourness, or Mancunian swagger, and seems to have been one factor which allowed for the relatively friendly welcome that immigrants to the North East received in the nineteenth century. There is an inscription from 1802 on a sundial at Frenchman's Row near Heddon-on-the-Wall that records the gratitude of emigres who spent their exile from France in the Tyne Valley: '*Quam signare piis gaudes, gens hospital, donis, prospera sit semper quaelibet hora tibi*' (May each hour which you, hospitable race, delight to mark with affectionate gifts, be always fortunate for you.) Consider too the former slave Olaudah Equiano—who wrote to the *Newcastle Chronicle* in 1792, giving, as he put it, 'his warmest thanks of heart glowing with gratitude to all of the people of Newcastle for their fellow feelings for the Africans and their cause'—and Frederick Douglass who made a special visit to the town in 1846 to meet 'the two ladies who were mainly instrumental in giving me the chance to devoting my life to the cause of freedom. These were Ellen and Anna Richardson, of Newcastle-upon-Tyne.' And yet when Equiano visited Tyneside in the 1790s he was acutely aware that some of the manacles and neck collars used to shackle slaves in the Americas were made at Crowley's Iron Works at Gateshead. If there's a temptation towards self-congratulation in the North East then the horrible racist bullying and abuse endured by the historian David Olusoga, who grew up on a Tyneside council estate in the 1970s and 1980s, may be more typical than Northumbrians might wish to admit.[51]

There is another risk here, that of self-flattery, even communal narcissism, of which I was reminded by a tweet in 2018 from 'Fans Supporting Foodbanks' ahead of the Liverpool versus Newcastle United fixture, which claimed that 'our actions define who and what we are. Scousers and Geordies are caring, thoughtful, loyal, generous, compassionate, community spirited, humanitarian.'[52] That's part of the story, but as Simon Donald, one of the co-creators of that famous Tyneside organ, *The Viz* once remarked, 'a whole life of witnessing violence,' in schools, pubs and bus-stops in Newcastle played a key part in the creative impulse behind some of the comic's most famous characters, from 'Biffa Bacon' and his 'Mutha and Fatha' 'are yee looking at wor lass?', to 'Raffles the Gentleman Thug,' 'are you scrutinising the aesthetic exteriority of my bird?'

There is a North East tradition of self-mythologising on the stage too, with only perhaps London, Glasgow and Liverpool having the equivalent of the populist 'Geordierama' theatrical singalongs. Northumbrian working-class endurance in the face of adversity has been a leitmotif in 'Billy Elliot,' 'The Pitmen Painters' and Sting's tribute to his own home-town of Wallsend in 'The Last Ship.' The Jarrow-born playwright Alan Plater may have launched this conceit with the 1968 musical 'Close the Coalhouse Door,' an unashamed celebration of Northumbrian stoicism. In the introduction to the published version of its libretto he wrote that

> The soul of the piece is unchanging. We originally described it as 'a hymn of unqualified praise to the miners—who created a revolutionary weapon without having a revolutionary intent.' If, today, the hymn is more in the nature of an elegy, it is a strain that haunts the dreams of everyone with roots in the North East.

However, when the South Shields-born historian Robert Colls saw the musical in the early 1970s he was wary of its varnished history, and feared that:

> It did not celebrate a history so much as a mythology ... it presented to the audience an image which was self-congratulatory; that their enjoyment, and my enjoyment, and my motive to understand history all basked in the same self-indulgence. This 'Geordieism' has truly known hard times, but with humour and togetherness has won through. Out of the past struggle has emerged a heroic sensibility made in our own image: to be proud of it is to be proud of ourselves.[53]

This is not to say that all has been laudable; for all the communalism and conviviality that have been the hallmark of this place since time immemorial, many native Northumbrians have been equally repelled by the claustrophobia and conformity of those same communities, and the sometimes-aggressive inebriation that is too often the corollary of a distinctive North East sociability. Likewise, the almost genetic impulse towards belligerence—which is hard to avoid tracing back to the millennia and a half of border warfare—may once have been a useful trait on the battlefield, but has also been at the root of a decidedly macho culture. The latter has not always been pleasant to live with for Northumbrian families who have to contend with some of the highest levels of domestic violence in England. Even the political and trade union traditions of the North East, which have played such an undoubted part in improving living standards and safety at work for generations of people, seemed to ossify a long time ago into complacent voting patterns, too often taken for granted and easily ignored.

In this book I return to five recurring themes in Northumbrian culture that have historically made the place so distinctive, but are sometimes overlooked or at least underplayed. The following chapter will delve into the deep past to understand the extraordinary longevity of the Northumbrian martial tradition, and its enduring cultural legacy; Chapter 3 covers the Northumbrian Enlightenment and the centuries-long search for illumination and innovation that emerged from this most literate part of England; Chapter 4 explores the landscape and architecture of North East England and what it tells us about the people who have lived here; Chapter 5 will describe the native traditions of sociability that grew out of the symbiosis between hard work and heavy drinking; Chapter 6 takes us back in time to understand how the interplay of feudalism and industry helped to shape the characteristic political outlook of the region; and, finally, Chapter 7 will attempt to draw these strands together to try and make sense of where North East England has been, and where it might be going next.

In attempting such a wide-ranging study, I am reminded of Basil Bunting's epic poem *Briggflatts* which he composed while working as a toiling sub-editor on the *Newcastle Chronicle*, and which was first read in the Morden Tower, a turret on the old town wall, in 1965. Bunting was a genius at combining the contradictory strands of this place's past: weaving the war-like and visceral with the irenic and intellectual. In one memorable passage he uses the intricacy of Anglo-Saxon metalwork as a metaphor for the unfathomability of life and the universe, whilst still conveying the epic arc of Northumbrian history. To attempt this last, at least, is my purpose too.

Columba, Columbanus, as the soil shifts its vest,
Aidan and Cuthbert put on daylight,

wires of sharp western metal entangled in its soft
web, many shuttles as midges darting;
not for bodily welfare nor pauper theorems
but splendour to splendour, excepting nothing that is.
Let the fox have his fill, patient leech and weevil,
cattle refer the rising of Sirius to their hedge horizon,
runts murder the sacred calves of the sea by rule
heedless of herring gull, surf and the text carved by waves
on the skerry. Can you trace shuttles thrown
like drops from a fountain, spray, mist of spiderlines
bearing the rainbow, quoits round the draped moon;
shuttles like random dust desert whirlwinds hoy at their tormenting sun?
Follow the clue patiently and you will understand nothing.

2

BLOOD AND IRON

The Scots, their neighbouring enemies, hath made the inhabitants of Northumberland fierce and hardy … being a most warre-like Nation.

William Gray, *Chorographia*, 1642

When England sets her banner forth, and bids her armour shine
She'll not forget the famous North, the lads of Moor and Tyne.

Sir Henry Newbolt, 'The Old and Bold,' 1905

If the Battle of Waterloo was won 'on the playing fields of Eton,' then it could also be said that the British victories of 1918 and 1945 owed as much to the men and materiel from the coalfields of Northumberland and Durham. The world wars of the twentieth century saw something like an apotheosis of a Northumbrian martial tradition, which has had a rich and interlocking history since the far north of England became a seat of Mars in the reign of the Caesars, and then a forge of Vulcan in the era of the great Victorian armourers. It was Otto von Bismarck's view that disputes between states are settled 'durch Eisen und Blut,' and the blood and iron of Northumbria have long been pivotal, but usually overlooked, factors in British military history. It is perhaps well known that the stupendous output of coal, armaments and shipping from North East England were decisive in both the world wars of the twentieth century; what is less understood is the symbiosis between this industrial output and the fighting record of the Northumbrian working classes. As Harold Macmillan put it, in his maiden speech in the House of Lords during the 1984 Miners' Strike, the miners were 'the best men in the world, who beat the Kaiser and Hitler's armies and never gave in.'[1]

That Tyneside and Wearside took up arms in the Great War with an enthusiasm unmatched in any of the nation's other great conurbations, and that the

50th Northumbrian Division was the most experienced battle-fighting division in the British Army in the Second World War, with a formidable combat record, can be seen as the fulfilment of centuries of a native militarism that was exceptional in England. It is clear that the reputation of the 50th—who were called upon time and again from Dunkirk to North Africa, Italy and Normandy—was built as much on their origins in the martial North of England as it was on their tenacity and endurance. As General Sir Brian Horrocks noted in his introduction to the official history of the Royal Northumberland Fusiliers (a component unit of the 50th), the regiment:

> has always consisted of the following types of men: tough Northumbrian yeo-
> men whose ancestors regarded border clashes as a normal way of life, and
> Geordies from the northern collieries, whom I have always regarded as the
> finest infantry in the world.[2]

Of course such claims to martial prowess are impossible to prove, and can, when a Northumbrian makes them, sound gauche and vainglorious—'my dad's harder than your dad'—a tone I detected in a recent history of Northumberland's military heritage, which claimed that anyone who has spent time in the military 'will almost certainly have had a comrade known to all as Geordie ... the backbone of the British armed forces for centuries.'[3] But the facts are that no other part of England is more fortified with castles or soaked in blood. This left a lasting legacy, one that helps us to understand why a peculiarly martial culture endured and shaped Northumbrian identity well into the twentieth century.

It is certainly true that all regions like to claim to be particularly tough and war-like, and that traditions of military service usually follow from the absence of alternative careers in economically depressed regions. Think of Elvis Costello's line in 'Oliver's Army' about 'the boys from the Mersey and the Thames and the Tyne.' And yet, if we take the long view, violence was the dominant factor in Northumbrian lives in a way that was absent elsewhere in the rest of England. It has been written that 'a Scots raid down toward the Tyneside often did as much killing in relation to the local population as the plague did nearly everywhere else,' and that 'until after 1745, the region never enjoyed fifty consecutive years of quiet.'[4] The readers of George S. Surrey's *A Northumbrian in Arms* (1910) would have understood why the main character, a warrior called Harald, is so sanguine about death, as bravery in battle is seen as typical of the 'Northumbrian race,' allowing the reader to understand Northumbrians as 'helpfully, even quaintly, fierce and aggressive,' stereotypes that persist to this day.[5] 'For if there are qualities in the Border people which are less than amiable, it must be understood that they were shaped by the kind of continuous ordeal that has passed most of Britain by,' wrote George MacDonald Fraser in his unforgettable study *The Steel Bonnets*, and 'if the Borderer is closer and tougher and dourer than his fellow-countrymen, it is because he is the descendant of men and women who lived by and in the shadow of raid and theft and bloody murder.'[6]

Martial exploits were celebrated in local culture, as the eighteenth-century engraver Thomas Bewick recalled of his childhood: 'the winter evenings were often spent in listening to the traditionary tales and songs, relating to men who had been eminent for their prowess and bravery in the border wars.'[7] This violence and bloodshed were powerfully evoked by the Northumbrian poet Wilfred Gibson in 'The Watch on the Wall':

Of light on Broomlee Lough; and thinks of all
The fighting and the fury and the fear
These Northern wastes have known since time began—
Forgotten tribes of prehistoric man
Warring with wolves and their own wolf-like kind:
Through the ensuing centuries till the last
Forlorn adventure of the Jacobites:
And, always, startling the dark Northern nights
With fiery forays, the Border reiving clans. And, recollecting how these fells have been
Bloodsoaked so often and how these hills have seen
Defeat and victory and foes put to rout
Or vanquished in a last heroic stand
Times out of mind; and wondering at man's
Insatiable lust for killing, his heart is filled,
As in the haunted night he watches alone,
With dire despair, to think that now the whole
World seethes in insensate slaughter fiercer far
Than even these border battlefields have known
Through their long history of futile strife.

Simple geography made such violence inevitable. As discussed in the preceding chapter, the lands north of the Tees were never settled by the Vikings (even after their conquest of southern Northumbria); when that same Norse kingdom of Northumbria was absorbed by the new English kingdom those loose ends remained untied. And with powerful neighbours to the North with designs on the lands south of the Tees it became inescapable that the rump of Northumbria would become a battle ground separating the Kingdoms of Scotland and England—'the ring in which the champions met.'[8]

The twelfth century author of the *Gesta Stephani* (the Deeds of King Stephen) concluded that the 'root and origin of all evil arose in that part of England called Northumbria to produce plunder and arson, strife and war.'[9] Much of what is distinctive in Northumbrian culture derives from the simple fact that living in a warzone made it prudent to huddle together for warmth and safety, and in this bloody land it was inevitable that martial prowess would become much esteemed. From this root grew a whole ethical framework that partly explains why 'hardness' is still much-prized in Northumbrian culture. Henry Mess thought this background was important enough to cover at length in his study of social conditions in 1920s Tyneside.

> Tyneside is—we will not say militarist—exceptionally interested and proud with regard to all that concerns armies and navies. It is easily understood when one looks at its history. There is, first of all, the Border tradition; for centuries there was watchfulness against the Scot, and the great leaders of Northumberland were, above all, leaders in war. In the second place, Newcastle and Tynemouth are barracks-towns, and the former is a great recruiting depot; the officers take a prominent place in local society. And in the third place, Tyneside grew and thrived on the race in armaments. Battleships and big guns meant wealth to the captains of industry, work to the rank and file, and dividends to thousands of local investors. Men love what they create, and the Tynesider followed the fortunes of his craftsmanship all over the world. When the Japanese fleet blew the Russian fleet to pieces at Tsushima, it was remembered with pride on Tyneside that most of the victor's ships came from their river. Scotswood and Jarrow, in particular, lived on materials of war. Naturally, they found it hard to be enthusiastic about disarmament.[10]

There is now a growing literature that explains how inclinations towards military service are highly genetically heritable.[11] A review published in *Advances in Genetics* in 2011 found that roughly half the variance in aggressive behaviour among both males and females is attributable to genetic factors.[12] Importantly, however, there is also evidence for significant gene-environment interactions affecting violent behaviour.[13] Some of the most interesting applications of such analytical frameworks have been in studies of the Southern USA, and how a propensity for local men to resort to violence in the face of social, personal, or political conflict contributed to the outbreak of the Civil War in 1861. As we shall see, much of the Deep South's virile, aggressive culture originated in the Anglo-Scottish borderlands.[14] Nevertheless we should be wary of a sort of geographical determinism that claims that a rugged landscape or society automatically makes all the local inhabitants similarly robust. However, scholars have noted that European frontier societies all share common traits of militarism—indeed, Northumberland has the greatest number of recognised battle sites in England—and unlike most other parts of the British Isles, Northumbrian history is one of violence and conflict for at least a millennium and a half.[15]

* * *

As far as we can tell from the limited traces that they left to posterity, the Celtic tribes that occupied Northumbria before the Romans arrived—the Votadini and the Brigantes—probably lived precarious lives, hunkering down in hill forts such as the 'Traprain Law'—'the fort of the spear shafts'—in modern East Lothian. Rome's impression of this territory was of quarrelsome tribes and petty kingdoms that nevertheless resisted colonisation. Hadrian's policy, upon his accession as Emperor in 117, was to strengthen the borders of the Empire, hence he despatched his legions to northern Britannia to quell the remaining native resistance. The VI Legion, which embarked from Germany in 122 accompanied by Hadrian himself and the new governor of Britain, A. Platorius Nepos, sailed up the Tyne and landed at a site eight miles inland where the Legions would build a crossing—'Pons Aelius' (the only bridge outside Rome named after a Roman Emperor)—that would eventually grow into the city of Newcastle. Such a dangerous sea-journey from the Rhine to the Tyne was still a daunting enterprise for Roman sailors, and demanded the protection of Neptune and Oceanus. In 1875 an altar decorated with a trident and a dolphin was found in the riverbed with the thankful inscription *Neptuno le(gio) / VIVi(ctrix) / P(ia) F(idelis)* ('To Neptune, dedicated by the Sixth Legion Victrix'). There were already major military installations in the north—including Vinovium / Binchester near Bishop Auckland, one of the largest Roman forts in Britain. It was on this visit in 122 that Hadrian decided to construct a wall between the Tyne and the Solway to sustain the peace, and this massive structure, fully eighty-four miles long, was completed by the Roman Army in just six years.

Eighteenth-century commentators tried to locate the origins of the British martial spirit and love of liberty in Northern Britain. According to William Stukeley the North Britons were 'a bold and hardy people ... strong and hardy in body, fierce in manners who refused subjection,' while William Hutchinson would write that the Brigantes 'were esteemed the bravest race of Britons, and consisted of those heroes who would not submit to the invaders as they advanced in conquest, but with a true patriotic virtue strove to retain their native liberty.'[16] The only extant text from Vindolanda which refers explicitly to the native Britons is a military memorandum describing the fighting prowess of the 'Brittunculi,' a derogatory term meaning something akin to 'nasty little Britons' which the legions in Northern Britain used to describe the locals:

> the Britons are unprotected by armour (?). There are very many cavalry. The cavalry does not use swords nor do the wretched Britons mount in order to throw javelins.[17]

The Roman troops stationed on the Wall itself were called *Limitanei*, and thus Northumbria under Roman rule became one large military camp, with drafts of legionaries and auxiliaries arriving from all over the empire. These included the IX Legion 'Hispana' from Iberia, and later in 175 a 5,500 strong force of Sarmatian cavalry from the Ukrainian steppe sent to put down unrecorded uprisings. For all the cold winds and the restless locals, there was a flourishing military life along the Wall. Rudyard Kipling in his 'Roman Centurion's Song' has the protagonist plea to remain in Britain and not be recalled to Rome:

> Some Western camp (I know the Pict) or granite border keep
> Mid seas of heather derelict, where our old messmates sleep.

In the year 180 the Wall was breached by the Picts and the commanding officer killed in what the historian Cassius Dio described as the most serious war of the reign of the Emperor Commodus, and one of the most interesting monuments found at Corbridge was one dedicated to 'Mars the Avenger,' recording the name of a governor who had quelled a local revolt. The Roman occupation did not last, and by the late fourth century a string of military coups, economic decline and the barbarian encroachment into the Empire's Mediterranean heartlands concentrated attention away from Britain, and by 410 the last of the legions were gone.

The kingdoms that gradually emerged in this Roman militarised zone—Bernicia and Deira, and then Northumbria itself—would also be characterised by conflict and bloodshed. One of the earliest Northumbrian kings, Oswald, was 'a remarkable member of the Northumbrian aristocratic warrior caste who appears to have been as schooled in the Gospels as he was in sword play.'[18] His victory over a Welsh army at Heavenfield near Hexham was exploited by St Bede to exalt Northumbrian prestige and stimulate devotion to their warlike king and northern saints, like Columba, who appeared to Oswald in a vision before the battle. But the instability and violence of Northumbria, and its vulnerability to sea-borne invaders and to the burgeoning kingdoms to its north and south, would be its downfall. Indeed, the ten kings that ruled Northumbria between 737 and 806 were all either murdered, deposed, exiled, or became monks. Only four of the last twenty-five Northumbrian Kings before the Danes arrived in the ninth century died of natural causes, and of those that were killed it was King Ælla who met the most gruesome end. Ælla himself was ruthless, and Scandinavian sources have it that he had the Viking leader Ragnar Lodbrok put to death in a pit of venomous snakes (this is obviously unlikely given what we know of the fauna of northern Europe). The invasion of Northumbria that followed in 866 was instigated in retaliation for Ragnar's execution, and according to *Ragnarssona þáttr* ('The Tale of Ragnar's Sons'), Ælla was captured by the Vikings after a battle for York and then tortured to death in a method known as the 'blood eagle':

> They caused the bloody eagle to be carved on the back of Ælla, and they cut away all of the ribs from the spine, and then they ripped out his lungs.[19]

Despite the Norse takeover of Southern Northumbria, the regular Viking raids on the coast, and the arrival in 875 of Halfdan's fleet, which anchored at the mouth of the Teams, a tributary of the Tyne, Northumbria north of the Tees remained unconquered. Were the Northumbrians particularly ferocious? We can say that although rebellions against Danish rule in the Deiran end of Northumbria were crushed, Bernicia remained unconquered (or at least not settled), and may even have become a centre of Northumbrian resistance. Nevertheless, it is telling that in one of the earliest Ango-Saxon poems, 'The Battle of Maldon' of 991, the martial characteristics of Northumbrians are described in some detail:

> Then their hostage helped eagerly:
> he was of sturdy stock from Northumbria,
> Ecglaf's son, he was named Æscferth.
> He did not flinch back at all at the war-play,
> but he sent forth arrows very frequently;
> sometimes he shot into a shield, sometimes he skewered a warrior,
> more than once in a while he gave someone a wound,
> so long as he wielded weapons.

Perhaps the last successful rearguard action of a quasi-independent Northumbria came in 1006, when a Scots army crossed the Tweed and then the Tyne, burning villages and slaughtering the population. They were then met at Durham by Uhtred, the son of Waltheof, Earl of Northumbria, who rallied an army of Northumbrians there and routed the Scots. One chronicler, writing of this event sixty years after Uhtred's death, tells of what followed:

> Uhtred had the heads of the dead made more presentable with their hair braided, as was then the custom, and transported to Durham; there they were washed by four women and fixed on stakes round the ramparts. They gave the women who had washed the heads a cow each in payment.[20]

Such brutality did not abate in the eleventh century. While it had been commonplace for tussling warlords to join in battle for the overlordship of Northumbria, it was William the Conqueror's 'harrying of the North' that had the most devastating effect on the Northumbrian population. In response to massacres of his garrisons at York and Durham in 1069, and then the later murder of the Norman bishop of Durham at Gateshead in 1080, William's forces wreaked bloody vengeance on the land north of the Humber, destroying villages and killing the inhabitants without mercy. Herds of animals were slaughtered, crops were burned, and the land was salted, so that thousands then starved to death. Some even turned to cannibalism. Many of the entries for the North Riding of Yorkshire in the Domesday Book simply recorded *wasteas est* or *hoc est vast*—'it is a waste' (as the northern border of England was not then settled the Domesday surveyors did not record anything north of the Tees or the Ribble). The twelfth century monk Simeon of Durham recorded the empty villages and the 'extensive solitude' that followed William's campaign of devastation.

> It was horrific to behold human corpses decaying in the houses, in the streets and the road, swarming with worms, while they were consuming in corruption with an abominable stench. For no one was left to bury them in earth, all being cut off by the sword or by famine. Meanwhile, the land being thus deprived of anyone to cultivate it for nine years, an extensive solitude prevailed all around. There was no village inhabited between York and Durham; they became lurking places to wild beasts and robbers and were a great dread to travellers.

Some estimate that 100,000 people in the North were either killed or starved to death, but Northumbria north of the Tees was doubly unfortunate as it was caught in a pincer by both William I and Malcolm III, King of Scots, who exploited the upheaval to invade from the North, wreaking havoc and even taking men and women back to Scotland and into slavery. The Anglo-Saxon Chronicle for 1079 records that Malcolm ravaged Northumberland as far as the Tyne and 'killed many hundreds and took home much money and people into captivity.' Malcolm III was killed at Alnwick (and buried at Tynemouth) and an uneasy peace was brokered between the King of Scots and the King of England. However, the overlordship of Northumbria would not be settled for some time.

* * *

The Anglo-Scottish Borders derived their cultural character from the simple fact that the kings of Scotland and England could not agree who owned it, and constantly transgressed each other's territory. As David Hackett Fischer pointed out, 'from the year 1040 to 1745, every English monarch, but three, suffered a Scottish invasion, or became an invader in his turn,' while in the same period, most Scottish kings went to war against England, and many 'died with their boots on' as the border saying went.[21] Scotland's first king, Duncan (1034–40), was slain by Macbeth after losing a war to the Northumbrians; and then in 1057 Macbeth himself was murdered after being defeated by another English army in the forest of Dunsinane. In the twelfth century most towns on both sides of the border were sacked and burned, and the countryside ravaged from the Tyne to the Forth. As in the Viking period, churches and monasteries were targeted, and the soldiers of one Scottish army even drowned in the River Eden such was the weight of the ecclesiastical loot that they carried with them. The brutality was unrelenting. At the capture of Berwick in 1215 the Scottish townsfolk were put to death by torture (with King John himself setting fire to their houses with his own hand); and in 1297, when William Wallace ravaged Northern England, his soldiers flayed the bodies of English knights who fell into their hands. There's a reason why no purely domestic medieval buildings survive in Northumberland, so it is no wonder then that after Wallace's own brutal execution in London's Smithfield, one quarter of his body was sent to Newcastle to be hung on the old Tyne Bridge, as well as an 'unmentioned part' which was put on display in the castle keep.

King Henry III of England and King Alexander III of Scotland signed a treaty in 1249 that delineated six 'marches'—a west, middle and east march on each side of the border—as quasi-autonomous and legally distinct jurisdictions, creating a buffer zone between their two kingdoms. This had a major cultural influence on the peoples who lived there. For the population of the medieval Northern Marches there was a clearly recognised and accepted obligation to contribute to the defence of the border; indeed this was the basis of land tenure.[22] From at least the late Middle Ages, the people of Northumberland had 'prided themselves on being different from other English folk, projecting their menfolk as a warrior elite'—most notably in ballads that venerated their chivalrous heroism on the borders.[23] Even Bishops of Durham were known to gird their loins—as Anthony Bek did when he led an English division into battle against the Scots at Falkirk in 1298.

There are echoes of this in Malory's two knightly brothers from Balan and Balen. In the *Tale of Balen* (1896), the nineteenth-century Northumbrian poet Algernon Swinburne describes them as lusty and impetuous knights errant— 'His brother Balan, hard at hand/Twin flower of bright Northumberland'— sallying forth to Camelot. But this chivalric ideal of old Northumbria was first expressed in the fifteenth-century *Ballad of Chevy Chase* where a hunting expedition is taken as a declaration of war:

> *The stout Earl of Northumberland*
> *A vow to God did make,*
> *His pleasure in the Scottish woods*
> *Three summer's days to take.*
>
> *The chiefest harts in Chevy Chase*
> *To kill and bear away.*
> *These tidings to Earl Douglas came,*
> *In Scotland where he lay ...*

It was in the wake of disturbances of the later eleventh century that William began building a string of formidable Norman castles at York, Richmond, Durham and the 'New Castle' constructed above the site of Pons Aelius. When the Norman keep was strengthened by Henry II in the later twelfth century he called upon 'Maurice the Engineer,' the architect of Dover Castle, so that formidable stone sentinels guarded both the southern and northern extremities of his kingdom. From 1265 a stupendous wall was then built around the burgeoning town of Newcastle, fully two miles in extent, up to thirty feet high and studded with seventeen towers. The strength of these walls acted as a formidable deterrent to Scottish arms who tended to skirt round the west of the town if ever they wanted to cross the Tyne (although in 1388 the townsfolk were able to watch from the battlements as Harry Hotspur fought the Earl of Douglas at Barras Bridge). John Leland, writing in 1533, observed that in their strength and magnificence the walls of Newcastle 'far passith all the waulls of the cities of England and most of the cities of Europe'; and a century later the Scotsman William Lithgow wrote that

The walls about the town are both high and strong, built both without and within with saxoquadrato [square blocks]; and maynely fenced with dungeon towres, interlarded also with turrets, And alongst with them a large and defensive battlement, having eight sundry ports and four parochial churches, the which walls, the defendants within had marveilously fortified, rampiering them with interlinings and mountagnes of earth … The walls here of Newcastle are a great deal stronger than those of Yorke, and not unlike to the walls of Avineon, but especially of Jerusalem.[24]

The epic wars with Scotland made Newcastle the usual mustering ground for English armies marching north (typically on the 'Shield Field' to the east of the town). The Tyne was long considered the 'the meetest place to mount the sea' against the Scots—as in 1333 when an expedition of Newcastle seamen sacked and burned Dundee, carrying off their great bell, or in 1542 when an English army was despatched from the Tyne to the Forth. Yet the status of Northumbria as a buffer zone meant that it could be abandoned if necessary. This may explain why when King John invested £25,000 on twenty-five castles in the North, only £670 was spent on the expendable first line of defence: the three border castles at Norham, Wark, and Newcastle.[25]

In many ways the trade of the town was war, and armed men and supply trains would have been constantly passing through, requiring arms and provisions, entertainment for the soldiers and care for the wounded. When the house of Trinitarian friars was established in Newcastle in 1360, one third of its revenues was routinely devoted to ransoming prisoners from Scotland. By 1400 it is recorded that nightly watches of a hundred men were being organised by the burgesses who also maintained the wall and the castle in repair. The King himself was a regular visitor to the King's Manor (now the site of Manors Metro Station) 'whenever he came with an Army Royal against Scotland' as Henry Bourne wrote in 1736, as too were the Kings of Scotland who kept the 'Scottish Inne' in the Bigg Market (Newcastle is unique in having held both Kings of Scots and a King of England captive within its walls).

In two of the most celebrated English victories over the Scots the sense of Northumbrian martial identity emerges strongly. In 1346 King Philip of France had pleaded with King David II of Scotland to launch an invasion, describing northern England as 'a defenceless void.'[26] But David's crushing defeat at Neville's Cross in the shadow of Durham cathedral was inflicted by troops recruited from the North and commanded by men typical of a Northumbrian samurai class in Lord Henry Percy and Lord Ralph Neville, whose families owned vast swathes of Northern England. Indeed, after the battle—where the prior of Durham and his monks bore the 'holy cloth' (the corporal which St Cuthbert was said to have used when celebrating mass), an exhausted and wounded King David was captured by a Northumbrian knight, John Copeland, hiding beneath a bridge, and the Scottish royal regalia (including the 'black rood,' a supposed fragment of the true cross) were placed in triumph on St Cuthbert's shrine.[27] This invocation of St Cuthbert by Northumbrian troops was repeated in the recapture of Berwick in 1482, when the Durham contingents took with them the banner of their saint, and most famously at Flodden Field in 1513, where the English commander Lord Surrey made sure to pray first at the shrine of St Cuthbert in Durham Cathedral before collecting the same sacred banner to inspire the Northumbrians and their fellow North-countrymen gathering at Newcastle.[16] At the battle itself the banner flew over the soldiers of Northumberland and Durham in the centre of the English line, and after the Scots were routed and the body of James IV was found by Lord Dacre, the border lord who commanded the English border horse, the Scottish king's body was taken to Newcastle, and, just as in 1346, James's sword and armour were placed on Saint Cuthbert's shrine at Durham.

One study has described how the Tudor state used the 'militarised society of Northumberland as a means of subduing Scotland,' and relied on Northumbrian light cavalry—known as 'hobelars'—who were masters at the art of ambush and skirmish.[28] Every part of Northumbrian society furnished suitably horsed and harnessed soldiers for military service, from the burgesses of Newcastle and Berwick, and the rural gentry and their tenants, to the 'surnames,' those English clans who lived in the wilds of North Tynedale and Redesdale, each of which were led by their own 'heidsmen,' or chieftain. The Bishop of Durham described the plain workmanlike weapons and gear of these men as 'a steel cap, a coat of plate, stockings of plate, bootes and spurres; a skottish short sworde and a dagger, a horsemans staffe and case of pistolls.'[29] By the 1540s Henry VIII had 25,000 of these border horsemen in his service, as lance-wielding skirmishers—'prickers'—scouts and freebooters. They were amongst the most effective cavalry in Europe, but they were not always disciplined. In the campaign in Scotland in 1547 they were witnessed bargaining for ransoms from the Scots Borderers rather than engaging them in combat and one witness saw them 'right often, talking with the Scottish prickers within less than length asunder, and when they perceived that they had been aspied, they have begun to run at one another … they strike a few strokes but by assent and appointment.'[30]

36

The Anglo-Scottish wars made the borderlands constantly volatile, but in the fifteenth century the land was reduced to extremes of violent anarchy, and places like Redesdale and upper Tynedale became the Helmand province of medieval England (and it's strangely fitting that Otterburn is now home to the Ministry of Defence's live firing ranges). As a young diplomat, the future Pope Pius II travelled the borderlands between England and Scotland in 1435 and upon arrival in Newcastle—'which,' he noted 'is said to have been built by Caesar'—he recorded that here for the first time was 'a familiar world and a habitable country; for Scotland and the part of England nearest it are utterly unlike the country we inhabit, being rude, uncultivated, and unvisited by the winter sun.'

The hardness of the people who lived in this forbidding place has been much commented on, and even if it is not possible to corroborate the truth of that descriptor, the very fact that their bloody recreations of the 'Border Reivers' who lived there were so often remarked upon is striking and helps us to understand why their military capabilities were in such high demand. The feuding 'surnames' that roamed this ill-defined border were notorious and shared in a unified upland culture where raids on livestock and property and disputes over grazing rights could trigger open warfare and feuds that lasted generations. In 1550, Sir Robert Bowes notes that the dwellers of North Tynedale 'were wild and misdemeanoured people much inclined to disorder and given to theft and must be kept continually in dread of justice under their keepers.'[31] When the antiquary William Camden visited the 'wastes' of Northumberland in 1599 he contended that it was the county's landscape and situation which had shaped the war-like temperament of the people, being 'for the most part rough,' which 'seemed to harden the inhabitants, whom the Scots their neighbours also made more fierce and hardy, adding that here you may see 'the ancient nomads, a martiall kinde of men ... who ride on horse-back with a fresh turf for saddle and twisted straw for girth.'[32]

The dangers of ambush were an ever-present. On one Sunday in 1483 the Northumbrian heidsman Robert Loraine was 'bushwhacked' by a Scottish raiding party on his way home from church to his Pele Tower in Kirkharle, then butchered into pieces and packed into the saddlebags of his own horse. The Rutherford and Hall families were so violent that in 1598 royal officials ordered that no quarter be given to anyone bearing those names, and the Johnston clan became notorious for decorating their houses with the flayed skins of their Maxwell enemies.[33] In 1599 it was even recorded that during a six-a-side football match involving the Armstrongs at Bewcastle, west of

Kielder, they were interrupted by a gang of Reivers who cut the throats of two of the players. The martial culture of upland Northumbria expressed itself in the colourful names of the Reivers themselves, so we find 'Fingerless Will Nixon' and 'Nebless Clem Croser' (body parts presumably lost in border clashes), or Armstrongs called 'Skinabake' and 'Bangtail.' Names that commemorate violent exploits were also common including 'Ill-drowned Geordie,' 'Archie Fire-the-Braes,' 'Out-with-the sword,' 'Crack-spear,' and 'Cleave-the-crune,' and it's noticeable how similar these nicknames are to the famous fighters of the American Plains, such as 'Alligator-Stands-Up,' 'Thunder-Rolling-over-the-Mountain,' and 'Crazy Horse,'[34] And for some of the most interesting evidence of the persistence of the belligerent outlook of the Northumbrians we must look to eighteenth-century America.

* * *

In *Albion's Seed: Four British Folkways in America*, David Hackett Fischer explains how the regional patterns of emigration to the American colonies help us to understand the very different social and political outlook of the peoples who live in the modern United States. While the the Puritans from East Anglia established communities in New England, the Quakers went to Pennsylvania, and what he calls the 'Cavaliers' made the valley of the Delaware their home; the dangerous Appalachian back-country was settled by a group he refers to as the 'Borderers.' In an American context this latter group are often misleadingly termed the 'Scots-Irish,' but as Hackett Fischer pointed out, this obscures the 'Border English' ancestry of a group more often known today as the Hillbillies. The Northern English origins of these people was noticed too by the English folklorist Cecil Sharp, who left his Warwickshire home early in the twentieth century to spend several months in the Appalachian highlands, observing and collecting the songs and dances of the people who lived there. After a careful study of the local inhabitants he concluded from an analysis of their traditional songs, ballads, dances and singing-games that they came from a part of England 'where the civilization was least developed—probably the North of England, or the Border country between Scotland and England.'[35]

This was true, for in North Carolina alone, there is a *Durham Branch*, several *Durham Creeks, Durham County* and *Durham Township* as well as the city of *Durham* while in nearby Pennsylvania there are the counties of *Westmoreland* [sic] and *Northumberland*, as well as all those places named after Cumberland (either the English county or the royal scourge of the Jacobites). The durability of border culture amongst these settlers was striking. Firstly, American backcountry speech was descended directly from that spoken in the lowlands of Scotland and in the border counties of England during the seventeenth and early eighteenth century. For example, the use of *man* was—and is—commonly used in Northumberland by a wife to refer to her husband, as in the Tammy Wynette classic 'stand by your man' (and in the North East still to this day 'wife' is often used to mean woman, whether their marital status is known or not); similarly *honey* as a term of endearment was transplanted from North Britain, as well as *let on* for tell, *nigh* for near, and *lowp* for jump. The distinctive pronunciation of Appalachian and Southern US speech also had its roots in North Britain: *sartin* for certain, *deef* for deaf, *widder* for widow, and so on.[36] Even the famous American log-cabin derives directly from the building traditions of the British borderlands (there is a record of a soldier from the south of England marching over the river Tweed in the eighteenth century and noting that the 'husbandmen's houses ... resemble our swine coates, few or none of them have more storeys than one, and that very low and covered usually with clods of earth, the people and their habits are suitable to the dwellings').[37]

The outlook of the Anglo-Scottish borderlands profoundly shaped the culture of the Southern United States in several important ways. First, the lawlessness of their North British homeland had created opportunities for theft and plunder on a massive scale, and a prominent feature of border reiving was the endemic theft of livestock, with marauding gangs of professional rustlers operating 'on a scale more reminiscent of the traditional American model than any English equivalent.'[38] The need to patrol these grazing lands, and launch retaliatory raids against trespassers when necessary, created a very different, and much more violent society than the rest of England, with societal structures more akin to warlordism than the usual manorial system. Here forms of tenancy were designed to maintain large bodies of fighting men, as Lord Burghley noted ('there is no lease in that country, but with provision to find horse and arms, to be held by an able man'), and in the Crown's great manors of Wark and Harbottle in Northumberland secure tenure was offered to ensure that fighting men had enough land for subsistence.[39]

This dangerous world had implications for patterns of association, with blood relationships becoming extremely important—especially when families grew into clans. Feuding was commonplace, for if one man took a backward step in a confrontation the entire clan's honour was forfeit, or if one of their women was seduced and abandoned all of her menfolk would feel the humiliation keenly and usually seek bloody vengeance.[40] The famous feud of Hatfields versus McCoys that raged for almost thirty years across Kentucky and Virginia, and was triggered by either the theft of a hog or an illicit relationship between offspring of the two families, was typical of the sort of vendettas that were so common among the clans of the Anglo-Scottish border. For these Borderers placed very little trust in legal institutions, preferring instead to settle their disputes via 'the *lex talionis* of feud violence and blood money'; they even invented the concept of 'blackmail' (from the French *mail*, meaning rent), a system of paying protection money to powerful families, and defined by the *OED* as 'a tribute formerly exacted from farmers and small owners in the border counties of England and Scotland ... in return for protection or immunity from plunder.' And when robbers were pursued—in what was known as a 'hot trod' or posse (a shortening of *posse comitatus* 'the force of the county')—those that were caught could expect no mercy and blood was usually spilled, hence the expression 'caught red-handed.'

This honour culture was transplanted wholesale to the New World, where as a North Carolina proverb had it—in a phrase that came directly from the borderlands of North Britain—'every man should be sheriff on his own hearth.'[41] These borderers found the North American frontier strangely familiar, with its wooded, hilly fastnesses, emerging ranching culture and regular confrontations with hostile neighbours. Sometimes these clashes would be with Native Americans, but more often than not these would be skirmishes with fellow 'backsettlers' in contested territory similar to the contested lands that separated England from Scotland. These conditions were ideally suited to what Hackett Fischer described as 'their family system, their warrior ethic, their farming and herding economy, their attitudes toward land and wealth and their ideas of work and power.'[42]

These attributes of hardiness and aggression had contributed to their complete cultural hegemony in this region by the time of the American War of Independence, and they would go on to dominate the leadership of the new Continental Army and make names for themselves as formidable politicians. Hackett Fischer notes how the baleful faces of backcountry leaders often bear striking resemblance to the descriptions of the North British borderers who settled the Appalachian highlands. 'Contemporary observers described these men as tall, lean and sinewy, with hard, angry, weather-beaten features,' men like John Caldwell Calhoun and Andrew Jackson, who both shared Border ancestry.[43] It is striking how much this physiognomy recalls the description in Linda Colley's *Britons: Forging the Nation* of 'Northumbrians and Lowland Scots [tending] to look alike, with the same raw, high-boned faces and the same thin angular physiques' (for a good example look to Nathaniel Dance's portrait of the Northumbrian gardener Lancelot Brown), or even George MacDonald

Fraser's vivid description of that moment in 1969 when the descendants of 'three notable Anglo-Scottish Border tribes' gathered for the US Presidential Inauguration in Washington DC, with Lyndon Johnson handing over to Richard Nixon in the presence of Billy Graham. Johnson with his 'lined, leathery Northern head and rangy, rather loose-jointed frame,' and Nixon's 'blunt, heavy features, the dark complexion, the burly body, and the whole air of dour hardness [which] are as typical of the Anglo-Scottish frontier as the Roman Wall.'[44]

* * *

The union of the English and Scottish Crowns in 1603 brought almost immediate stability and order to the borderlands: 'the Border problem melted like snow on the Cheviots in spring.'[45] The year 1606 opened with the hanging of five Borderers at Carlisle and seventeen at Newcastle, and the aftermath of the last significant Border foray in 1611, an attack on the Robsons of Teviotdale by the Elliots and Armstrongs, showed how little toleration there now was for Border Reiving—all of its leaders were arrested and promptly executed. Newcastle began to thrive in the peaceful first decades of the seventeenth century, and threats from Scotland were so remote that Anthony Errington even had the confidence to build an *un*fortified manor house in the Jacobean style west of the town at East Denton. But the martial capacity of Northumbria still remained potent, and there is a record from 1615 of a general muster at Spennymoor 'of all men able to bear arms within the bishopric [of Durham], between the ages of 15 and 60,' a gathering that amounted to 8,320 men. The 'Trained Bands of Durham' would go on to form one of the most famous regiments of the English Civil War: the Marquess of Newcastle's Royalist 'whitecoats' (so named for their distinctive lambswool tunics), who distinguished themselves as a hard-fighting unit throughout the war until their final demise at Marston Moor in 1644, where, after arriving late—Prince Rupert accused them of being drunk—they refused quarter when surrounded and fought to the last man.[46] (On the Parliamentarian side that day was the Sunderland-born firebrand Lieutenant Colonel John Lilburne—whose father was the last man in England to insist that he should be allowed to settle a legal dispute with a trial by combat.)

The Civil War may have had different causes from the wars that had engulfed Northumbria in the past, but as was customary the land was fought over by English and Scottish armies—with the growing importance of securing coal resources only increasing the strategic importance of North East

England (that the Royalists first controlled Newcastle, and Parliament there-fore turned to Sunderland to get the coal out marks the origins of the ongo-ing Tyne-Wear rivalry). Newcastle was besieged twice: once briefly in 1640 after a Scottish victory at Newburn, and then over ten weeks in 1644 a gar-rison of fifteen hundred men—trained bands alongside 'volunteers, prest men, colliers, keillmen, and poore tradesmen'—withstood an army of twenty thousand.[47] When a breach was finally made in the west walls (with the help of some sympathetic local coalminers) the Scottish army poured into Newcastle fighting street by street—as recorded by a Scottish eyewitness, William Lithgow:

> The thundering cannon roaring from our batteries without, and theirs rebounding from the castle within; the thousands of musket balls flyeing at other's faces like to the droving aylestones from septentrion blasts; the clan-gour and carving of naked and unsheathed swords; the pushing of brangling pykes crying for blood.

It is from these events, one of the last sieges of an English walled city, that Newcastle adopted the motto *Fortiter Defendit Triumphans* (she triumphs by a brave defence). But the capitulation of Newcastle was not the final act of the Wars of the Three Kingdoms in Northern England, for after Cromwell's crushing victory at Dunbar thousands of Scottish Covenanters were 'driven like Turkeys to Newcastle … where about 1,600 of them were starv'd, having nothing to eat but green cabbage leaves, and oats in a small Proportion.'[48] And from there to Durham where 3,500 of these Scottish soldiers were impris-oned in the then redundant cathedral, with 1,700 of them dying in captivity (their remains were only rediscovered, buried in a mass grave at Palace Green, in 2015).

Warfare and instability returned to Northumbria in the early eighteenth century via the first and second Jacobite rebellions. It's an interesting footnote that 'White Sorrel,' the horse that caused the death of William III when it stumbled on a molehill at Hampton Court (throwing the king and breaking his collarbone) had been confiscated from the Northumbrian Jacobite Sir John Fenwick MP. Sympathies for the Stuarts died hard—in rural Northumberland at least where the Earl of Derwentwater raised the Old Pretender's standard at Warkworth and his cousin, General Tom Forster commanded the Jacobite army which was defeated at Preston, the last battle fought on English soil. When the Young Pretender marched South thirty years later he avoided Newcastle, whose walls and garrison had been strengthened in anticipation. While the townsfolk fretted about Highlanders arriving down the Great

North Road, John Wesley, then living in the town, found time to worry about the language, manners and behaviour of the redcoats who were sent to defend Newcastle, writing to the commander of the city of his horror at the 'shameless wickedness, the ignorant profaneness, of the poor men to whom our lives are entrusted. The continual cursing and swearing, the wanton blasphemy of the soldiers in general, must needs be a torture to the sober ear.'[49] In fact, it was not just the army who rallied to defend the town: the local justices made sure that Jacobite suspects were arrested, that hundreds of volunteers were enrolled, and over 200 cannon were mounted on the old towers and ramparts, with old property being pulled down to give a clear field of fire against an enemy that never came.

That the town had once again supported a King George over the rival Stuarts is one of the more popular explanations for the origins of Geordie as synonymous with Newcastle, and it is undeniable that the *Pax Hanoveriensis* ushered in a period of security and prosperity for Tyneside. There is a monument in St Nicholas's Cathedral to Matthew Ridley, the Mayor of Newcastle who had refortified its ancient walls. It bears an inscription celebrating his role in opposing the 'Enemies of the House of Brunswick' and a panel showing him as a warrior defending a cringing female figure of Newcastle against 'Rebellion,' bearing the 'flame of sedition.'[50] During the 1745 rebellion the stones of the Roman Wall were used as a foundation for the new 'Military Road' across Northumberland, but road-building was often violently resisted. In 1712, for example, a powerful coal cartel in the North of England exhorted their tenants to 'cut-up a wagonway' that belonged to commercial rivals, and 'pulling up the ways' was a common form of rural protest against encroaching civilization; the standing army was called out to suppress road riots along the border.[51] (In rural Durham it was still customary, well into the nineteenth century, for brides to be accompanied to church by escorts of men with guns, which would be fired continually as the procession advanced).[52] Indeed, travelling in the countryside was still unsafe: the Newcastle mail-coach would be guarded by a man riding ahead with a drawn sword and behind by another man with a blunderbuss, to repel the sorts of cut-throats that would still descend from the hills, and in 1752 seventeen of these brigands were transported from Newcastle to the Carolinas.

That sense of volatility is well-illustrated by the violence that followed the balloting for the Militia in 1761. Unrest spread throughout Northumberland and Durham, with mobs of pitmen, waggon-men, and labourers seizing and burning militia lists before a crowd of 5,000 gathered in Hexham, where two battalions of Yorkshire militia received their insults for close on three hours until one of the crowd seized a soldier's musket and shot him dead with it.

The militia then opened fire and eighteen of the rioters were killed and six seriously wounded. Forcible conscription into the armed forces was undoubtedly a cause of discontent, but nonetheless patriotic feelings still ran high and local histories give prominence to the burning of effigies of Admiral Byng (the naval officer who was court-martialled and shot in 1757 for losing Minorca) in the Newcastle Flesh Market where a mob carried his 'guy' on an ass through the streets, with the label 'This is the villain who would not fight.'

If we wind forward to the Napoleonic wars, Northumberland was the county with the highest proportion of men volunteering for military service in England at a staggering 75 per cent of eligible males, and Newcastle even established a military logistics unit of 160 waggons and carts, the only regular establishment of its kind in the country except the royal waggon-train.[53] At the King's birthday celebrations in 1804, Newcastle Corporation mustered 8,000 uniformed men and Northumberland and Durham had thirteen troops of yeomanry in 1816. This extraordinary growth of various local militias and regular forces continually in movement across the country is well evoked by the Tyneside folk lament 'Dol-li-a' (one of Philip Larkin's *Desert Island Discs* selections in 1976), where the regiments come and go like the changing seasons:

> Green Cuffs is coming in, Dol-li, Dol-li
> And that'll make the lasses grin, Dol-li-a
> The Black Cuffs is gone away, Dol-li, Dol-li
> That'll be a crying day, Dol-li-o

It was on the high seas, however, where the Northumbrian martial tradition was manifest most clearly in the eighteenth century. Generally speaking the army was recruited from the gaols and the navy by the press gang, and it was the latter's cruel efficiency—separating men from their families and livelihoods for years at a time—that caused the greatest distress. Under the manpower levies of 1795 Newcastle and Sunderland together were second only to London, and by November 1800 the ports of Newcastle and Sunderland had lost 2,781 pressed men.[5] On one occasion in 1798 a regiment of marines was dispatched from Tynemouth to surround the port of North Shields so that the local men couldn't escape and hide in the fields as was customary. The marines then closed the cordon and rounded up 250 local seamen for service in the Royal Navy. One eighteenth-century folk song, 'Captain Bover,' records the fear of this naval officer and his Press Gang who operated on the Newcastle quayside with the answer to the question 'Where has ti' been maw canny hinny?', being 'Aw've been to the Norrard, cruising back and forrard, but daurna come ashore for Bover and his men.'

BLOOD AND IRON

The keelmen on the Tyne and Wear (who rowed the coal out to waiting collier ships) were considered a trained reserve, like the crews of the colliers themselves, to be drawn upon as required, and an elaborate system of obligations and levies were placed on to them to ensure they supplied enough men (with two landsmen considered an acceptable substitute for one prime seaman). Nevertheless, the popular songs of the time give us a sense of local pride in the men who served at sea, such as 'The Keelmen Volunteers' from 1812:

> With spirits heroic and sublime,
> Our lads are brought up on the Tyne;
> They will our foes with sorrow fill,
> When once they sail from Newcastle:
> Where bullets fly and cannons roar,
> They'll sweep the sea from shore to shore;
> And all the world their wonders tell:
> Huzza, Keel Lads of Newcastle!

The coal trade from the Tyne and Wear had long been considered one of the nurseries of the navy, and no less than Captain James Cook began his nautical career working on a collier ship between the Tyne and the Thames. This was a testing and dangerous journey down the east coast as French privateers often lurked around Flamborough Head, a favourite point for ambush, so colliers would often have black painted ports along their topsides to give the illusion of being armed.[54] This was the world that the future Vice-Admiral Cuthbert Collingwood knew when he joined the navy aged twelve in 1760. Collingwood came from an old Newcastle family, proud of its Northumbrian roots (he and his brother Wilfred were named for local saints), and he'd built a distinguished career in the navy before his moment of personal glory leading the British fleet into action at Trafalgar in 1805, engaging the Franco-Spanish fleet alone in his ship the *Royal Sovereign* for an hour until the other British ships caught up. Nelson had exclaimed on seeing this, 'See how that noble fellow Collingwood takes his ship into action,' and his conduct that day was one of extreme *sang froid*, with one sailor recalling:

> Dear old Cuddie (as we called him) was walking the break in the poop with his little triangular, gold-laced, cocked hat and wearing his silk stockings and buckled shoes. He was musing over the progress of the fight and munching on an apple. At length he went down to the quarterdeck and joined the men encouraging them not to 'fire a shot in waste.' Admiral Collingwood looked himself along the guns to see that they were properly pointed, and commend-

ing the sailors, particularly a black man, who was afterwards killed, but who, while the Admiral stood beside him, fired ten times directly into the porthole of the *Santa Anna*. It was like being in the heart of a volcano—with five ships around us—yet Collingwood had a single-handed coolness that he showed all day. A large part of the crew on board were men from the Tyne and they stood by their man.[55]

Collingwood was adored in the North East and considered to be the real victor of the battle. He was seriously injured too—with injuries to his back and shoulder, cuts to his face and deep lacerations on his legs—but as was typical of this modest and unassuming sailor, this was not widely known. His memorial in St Nicholas's Church in Newcastle lauds him as a 'pious, just and exemplary man,' and an enormous statue of Collingwood was erected at Tynemouth, guarding the approaches to the river like the Colossus of Rhodes. He was not the first naval hero celebrated in North East England however. The exploits of the former keelman Jack Crawford—the famous 'Sun'lan' lad,' as the folksongs have it, who shinned up the main mast of the British flagship during the Battle of Camperdown against the Dutch in 1797 to literally 'nail the colours to the mast,' as they had been shot away, was a favourite subject of folk song and poetry. He too has a statue, in Sunderland, not far from a group of alms-houses called Trafalgar Square, built to commemorate and accommodate the seventy-three men from the Wear who fought with Nelson and Collingwood.

Only London supplied more men for Nelson's Royal Navy than the towns of North and South Shields, Newcastle and Sunderland.[56] Indeed, military service in general was a common occupation—the well-known Northumbrian artist John Martin had one brother who fought with Wellington in Spain and another who served with Nelson at Copenhagen—and it was said at the time that nearly half of the sailors in the fleet were North Countrymen. The frequent appearance of former soldiers in tattered uniforms in Thomas Bewick's illustrations show us how common was service in the army.[57] Bewick—who was known to have made charitable donations for local men held prisoner in France—was fascinated by the old soldiers that tramped the roads of the North East. Many of these men had to rely on charity or draw on their expertise with firearms as gamekeepers or poachers, but their fierce nicknames that Bewick referred to—Hawk, Falcon, Wolf, Bloodhound, Raven, Gorfoot (carrion crow)—spoke of their descent from the old martial families from the borderlands.[58]

* * *

The sudden reduction of the Royal Navy at the end of the Napoleonic wars threw large numbers of seamen out of work at Sunderland, Shields and Blyth, and this was a factor in the growing unrest that began to spread in the region later in the 1810s. Throughout the early nineteenth century troops were regularly dispatched north to fight pitched battles with riotous keelmen and miners. In scenes more reminiscent of Reformation Germany than nineteenth-century England, the Bishop of Durham, Shute Barrington, deployed an armed posse twice: once to break a miners' strike at Chester-le-Street in 1812, and again in 1818 to prevent striking miners from poaching in his deer park at Stanhope. Even Walter Scott was worried by news from over the border, appealing to his neighbours in Tweeddale to

> sound the men, and mark down those who seem zealous. They will perhaps have to fight with the pitmen and colliers of Northumbria for defence of their firesides, for those literal blackguards are got beyond the management of their own people.[59]

After complaints were made to the Home Secretary that there were insufficient troops to deal with coal strikes, permanent barracks were built at Sunderland in 1794 and Newcastle in 1804, alongside the existing garrison at Tynemouth. This was of a piece with a century of draconian legislation which had seen a surge of capital statutes, mostly related to property, including statutes in 1736, 1769 and 1800 for the protection of collieries against arson, sabotage, and destruction. When this was found to be insufficient, 'the black cap majesty of the Law was replaced by the red coat terror of the army ... to frighten the Pitmen in a Return to their Duty.'[60]

Throughout the 1830s the British state waged a sort of war against the miners of Northumberland and Durham. It took the challenge so seriously because they knew the calibre of the men they were dealing with. In 1815 one North Shields shipowner complained directly to the Prime Minister that the North was 'country cover'd with Thousands of Pitmen, Keelmen, Waggonmen, & other labouring men [all] hardy fellows,' and in 1832 the officer in charge of the British Army's 'Northern Command,' Major-General Everard Bouverie wrote to the Home Department explaining why the miners of the North were a different proposition from the crowds they faced at Peterloo:

> If the Pit men continue refractory they will be awkward persons to deal with, one pit man being equal to three weavers at the least, and should the discontent spread to the Keelmen & Sailors it may become very serious and the force at present in Newcastle would be very soon harassed to death.[61]

In 1831 all the miners of Northumberland and Durham came out on strike for a general wage increase and shorter hours. This proved successful but it enraged the coal-owners who retaliated by refusing to take on any man at the annual 'hiring days' who was a member of the Miners Union. Pitiless evictions then followed of miners and their families from 'tied cottages' and blackleg labour was brought in from all parts of the British Isles. Huge unrest inevitably followed and throughout the year there were pitched battles and mass arrests along the Tyne. The authorities knew that pitmen could be intimidated by shows of military force, and the snatching of individual ringleaders. One man was shot dead by a policeman during a repulsed attack on a pit at Chirton on the Tyne, sabre-wielding dragoons clattered through the pit villages to intimidate and reassure in equal measure, and at Cowpen colliery near Blyth, where fortifications had been constructed, the striking miners were rushed by the 98th Regiment in full skirmishing order. After the murder of a magistrate at South Shields (ostensibly by a striking miner, although the case remains controversial), the body of the man found guilty and hanged for his murder, William Jobling, was tarred, hung in chains and bolted into a cage then toured through the colliery districts escorted by 100 soldiers. At Jarrow Slake, an area of tidal mudflats, it was then attached to a 21 feet high wooden post or 'gibbet' to swing in the river wind as a warning to all others (the penultimate gibbeting in British history). In the view of General Bouverie the pitmen's defeat by starvation and intimidation was only achieved by an 'almost military occupation.'[62]

Peace and security took longer to arrive in the North East than in any other part of England. It is ironic then that during the peaceful mid to late nineteenth century Tyneside should develop a specialism in manufacturing weapons of war. Such work had an established pedigree in Northumbria: the first recorded vessel built on the Tyne was a warship, the *Newcastle Galley*, commissioned by Edward I for his wars against the Scots (although the first recorded Northumbrian-made ship was the boat built on the Tees that Bishop Pudsey of Durham ordered to take him on Crusade to Palestine). There had been a colony of German sword-makers at Shotley Bridge since the sixteenth century, while the wooden walls of the Royal Navy would not have held together without the 108 varieties of nail supplied from Sir Ambrose Crowley's great ironworks in the Derwent Valley near Gateshead.[63] An account of the village of Bywell, on the Tyne, in 1569, described a long street, closed by gates at each end, inhabited by workers in metal, making arms and armour, bits, spurs and other horse trappings.[64] There had been some limited warship-building on the Tyne in the later eighteenth century (and there was a 175 feet tall 'shot tower' at Redheugh for the manufacture of lead projectiles), but it was the life and career of William Armstrong that was decisive in turning Tyneside into the arsenal of the British Empire.

Armstrong was a Newcastle-born solicitor-turned gentleman inventor, descended from the famous clan of Border Reivers (the name reputedly derives from an armour-bearer to a Scottish King who had lifted his sovereign onto a horse using one arm). His life served as a bridge between those older Northumbrian martial traditions and the mechanised industrial warfare of the nineteenth and twentieth centuries. The growth of his enterprises was extraordinary: initially focused on hydraulic cranes, and then artillery pieces, and then finally warships in staggering array. Between 1868 and 1927 Armstrong's company was responsible for 42% of all British warship production—from the daintily rigged Victorian ironclads to the all-steel behemoths of the twentieth century. He sold armaments to any government who could afford his products: he armed both sides in the American Civil War; Armstrong ships fired on and sunk each other at the Battle of the Yalu River in the Sino-Japanese War in 1894; and the Japanese crews of Armstrong-built cruisers even appeared on the terraces of St James' Park after annihilating the Russian fleet at Tshushima in 1905. When the Italian Navy took delivery of the *Europa*, complete with a 100-ton gun in 1876, the local antiquarian John Collingwood Bruce pointed out that

> In the second century, Rome exhibited on the banks of the Tyne the triumphs of her engineering skill, ... In the nineteenth century the chieftains of Tyneside showed Rome how largely Britain had profited by her instruction.[65]

The *Newcastle Chronicle* had noted with pride that 'Tyneside has become one of the world's greatest centres for the production of weapons of death' and from the 1880s it was the only place where a battleship could be built and armed from scratch on one site. The local press understood that the town was 'most prosperous at times of peril.' Armstrong's huge enterprise dominated Newcastle, and the pub names in his fiefdom of Scotswood spoke of his influence on the culture of Tyneside: the Rifle, the Gun, the Vulcan, the Blast Furnace, and the Ordnance Arms. Despite dealing in weapons of war, it seems that Armstrong experienced no pangs of conscience, unlike his almost exact contemporary, Alfred Nobel. To be sure, he was a great philanthropist and endowed the city with hospitals, schools, and parks, but during a speech in Newcastle Armstrong shrugged his shoulders at those who questioned the morality of his trade:

> We as a nation have few men to spare for war, and we have need of all the aid that
> science can give us to secure us against aggression—and to hold in subjection the
> vast and semi-barbarous population which we have to rule in the east.[66]

When he died in 1900, the black-bordered *Newcastle Chronicle* paid him fulsome tribute, but in a thoughtful obituary they noted that he was responsible for both 'the most wonderful machinery of production' and 'the most tremendous machinery of murder,' and that 'there is something that appalls the imagination in the application of a cool and temperate mind like Lord Armstrong's to the science of destruction.'[67] Could it be that the normality of such massive arms production influenced the ordinary Northumbrian's attitude towards conflict resolution? Some Victorian observers saw in the shipyards of Armstrong, and his rival Charles Mark Palmer at Jarrow, the ghosts of Ecgfrith's Saxon fleet or the serpent ships of the Norsemen.[68] But these were cutting-edge killing machines—the 'castles of steel' that Churchill saw putting to sea in 1914. The Tyne-built *HMS Agincourt*, for example, had the most twin gun turrets—seven—of any Royal Navy battleship ever built.

The naval blockade of Germany in the First World War was arguably as decisive as any action on the Western Front in winning the war, and between 1914 and 1918 Armstrongs alone built 47 warships, armed another 62 and repaired or refitted 521. By the war's end they were employing over 60,000 men and women on Tyneside—bigger than a whole British army corps—and that workforce had churned out over 13,000 heavy guns, 12,000 gun carriages and 14.5 million shells. Their output was just as stupendous in the Second World War, where Vickers-Armstrongs (as they were known by then) produced 33,000 guns, 1.25 million shells and bombs, 11 million cartridge cases, 16 million fuses, 39,000 high-pressure air and oxygen cylinders, 23,000 aircraft undercarriages and 3,500 tanks.'[69] So although Northumbria supplied prodigious amounts of materiel for Britain's war efforts in the twentieth century, it supplied the fighting men too—and in huge numbers.

* * *

The regimental reforms of the 1860s—where the old numbered infantry regiments were given county titles—had the consequence of making the names of Northumberland and Durham well known throughout the British Empire. In Conan Doyle's *A Study in Scarlet*, Dr Watson announces that he has recently returned from Afghanistan where he was serving with the '5th Northumberland Fusiliers.' The 5th of Foot, who had been associated with Northumberland since the eighteenth century, were unusually garlanded with praise: General Burgoyne at Bunker Hill observed that 'they behaved the best and suffered the most'; and Wellington, who relied upon them in the Peninsula War from the retreat at Corunna to the storming of Badajoz, described them as 'the ever fighting, often tried, but never failing Fifth.' In the Indian Raj of the 1880s, Rudyard Kipling knew the 'Fighting Fifth' as the best of all the British infantry regiments. He loved the raucousness and camaraderie of their mess, calling them the 'Tyneside Tail-Twisters,' and wrote of hearing the strains of the 'Keel Row' and seeing them march over the hill 'a thousand and eighty strong—smallish tough men [their stocky physique was often commented on], all of a size and most with a grateful Northumbrian burr.' In the military and popular discourse of Victorian Britain certain 'martial races' such as Scottish Highlanders, Punjabi Sikhs and Nepalese Gurkhas 'became linked as the British Empire's fiercest, most manly soldiers.'[70] Northumbrian militarism was similarly nurtured with the 'Fighting Fifth'—uniquely for an English regiment—having their own piper. In the Indian Rebellion of 1857, where the regiment fought throughout, it was a Scot, Sir Colin Campbell, and a Northumbrian, Sir Henry Havelock (the son of a Sunderland ship-owner and a man who was 'thoroughly persuaded in his own mind that war was righteous and carnage beautiful'), who were widely portrayed as the embodiment of British martial prowess.[71]

For the respectable working-classes a career in the ranks was not held in high esteem, and recruitment to those regiments from within a region of high employment was only sporadic in peacetime. Yet, when the Boer War broke out, recruiting sergeants were kept busy in the North East—and prominent 'pro-Boer' anti-war Liberals were given a rough ride in the 'khaki election' of 1900 by a Tyneside population enthusiastic for war and the military contracts that it usually led to. When war came in 1914, 'no area of Britain answered the call for recruits more enthusiastically than Tyneside.'[72] Indeed, by the end of the Great War the Northumberland Fusiliers alone had an astonishing fifty-three battalions—a record for the British Army.

The response of the North East is interesting because it is inexplicable by economic factors alone. Employment in the region was still relatively strong, and the miners of the Northern coalfield were among the highest paid proletarians in the world. To be sure, many men joined up because life was unremittingly tough, and a spell in uniform with fresh air and excitement was an appealing alternative to the drudgery of rolling armour plates or hewing coal in a two-foot seam. Nor should we forget that some 100,000 men were killed in British pits between 1850 and 1950, and many thousands more seriously injured. Although it would be wrong to say that these men were inured to

51

death, they were used to danger and to relying on their 'marras' for their own safety. As the South Shields miner Tommy Turnbull wrote:

> Because we were pitfolk we could probably accept our losses easier than other people. All our lives we had to deal with sudden and violent deaths of fathers, uncles, husbands, brothers, sons and friends. Not only men in their prime, like the young soldiers, seamen and airmen in the war, but also men past their prime and boys that had never reached it. One in every fifty Durham miners were expected to be killed in the pit and ten times that number would have a serious accident at some time.[73]

This was a world where masculinity was celebrated, and the industrial working classes were unusually vigorous and robust, and obsessed with strength and courage. This manifested itself in the obsession with hard work and sporting prowess that we will explore in later chapters, but it is not surprising that the pugilistic arts were also much feted, either in the ring—where the North East had the busiest fight scene outside London, and St James' Hall Newcastle was known as the 'graveyard of champions'—or in the back lanes of pit villages where score-settling fights were common-place.[74] The 1911 *Encyclopedia Britannica* noted that in 'physique the Northumbrian is stalwart and robust, and seldom corpulent,' and although this was hardly a scientific assessment it is difficult to avoid the conclusion that these men were robust and generally very fit. Indeed the army later discovered that, in England, the highest proportion of men with 'Grade I' physical fitness came from the 'Northern District'—of Northumberland, Durham, Cumberland and Westmorland.[75] The direct appeals made by Kitchener at the start of the war to the Northumberland miners were per-fectly calibrated to get a positive response.

> Tell them from me that I have often had occasion to thank Heaven that I had the Northumberland Fusiliers at my back. Tell them from me that I have often relied upon the Northumberland Fusiliers in the past and I know that I may need to do so in the future. I need their assistance and those who give their aid will have an opportunity of proving their worth.[76]

The numbers that came forward were astonishing. By November 1914 it was calculated that 20,000 men had been attested in Newcastle for Kitchener's Army; indeed the Lord Mayor rebuked the women handing out white feathers because there was 'no need to distribute white feathers amongst the young men of Tyneside.'[77] These recruiting figures were undoubt-edly spurred on by the economic slump that began in July 1914, so that within three months fully 18,000 men had taken the king's shilling in

Sunderland.[78] Such recruitment was spurred on by the opportunity to serve in the dashing Tyneside Scottish and Tyneside Irish Brigades, or the 'Tyneside Commercials' and 'Durham Pals.' Twenty-seven out of forty Newcastle United players had signed up by 1915, and 2,000 surplus infantrymen from North Country regiments had to be transferred to the Royal Naval Division in September 1914. The demand was such that so called 'bantam battalions' of otherwise ineligible shorter men were created after a Durham miner (who had been rejected for being too small) had walked 160 miles to Merseyside to enlist. When the recruiters in Birkenhead initially tried to turn him down, 'the disappointed man offered to fight anyone in the room.'[79]

The Northumbrian response to Kitchener's call was used to shame other places that were thought to be dodging their duties. At one meeting in Leicester (where low recruitment was a serious civic embarrassment) 'a speech pointed out that in Newcastle 18.5% of those eligible had joined the colours' compared to only 2.6% in Leicester.'[80] And when it came to buying war bonds the North East also led the way. The Jarrow-born author Catherine Cookson—whose uncle Jack signed up early from 'alcoholic bravado'—was told that two shillings' worth of saving stamps would pay to kill a German, but she worried that her tuppence contribution 'wouldn't have given him a limp.'[81] Adrian Gregory has written that it is 'bizarre that Newcastle should subscribe three times more heavily per head than Oxford,' but 'amongst the major provincial cities, Newcastle stands out, just as it had in the well-publicised recruiting contests of pals battalions in 1914–1915.'[82] In the first fourteen weeks of the campaign Newcastle gave on average £1 12s per head, per week, eventually raising £3,068,768 (including, it must be said, generous donations from armaments manufacturers). The perceived vulnerability of the East coast may well have been another factor behind the urge to enlist (the first shot of the war in Europe was fired by a Royal Marine from Gateshead called John Brown-King on 6 August 1914 from a mine-hunter in the North Sea) so it is perhaps not surprising that the eventual winner of the war bond campaign was West Hartlepool, which had been shelled by the German Navy in 1914, and would have the distinction in 1916 of being bombed by a Zeppelin captained by Marlene Dietrich's uncle.

Despite attempts by revisionist historians to develop a more nuanced reading of the purpose and legacy of the First World War, and the experiences of those who fought in it, the enduring Blackadder interpretation of the conflict as a futile and unrelenting slaughter has, perhaps, obscured the views of the 88 per cent of British soldiers who served and returned, the majority of whom may well have believed in the cause they were fighting for.

Nor should we overlook the considerable numbers of men who found in the trenches camaraderie and purpose, but also an aptitude for combat which they often found thrilling. George Orwell wrote of the men he knew in the 1920s who constantly talked of their wartime experiences 'with horror, of course, but also with a steadily growing nostalgia.'[83] The war had been terrible, but it had also been the most exciting times of most men's lives—no wonder that so many joined organisations like the British Legion or the Comrades of the Great War, in part to relive those experiences. Consider the much-reproduced picture of exhilarated Northumberland Fusiliers after their victory at St Eloi in 1915, or the Southern officer who joined the regiment in 1916 and recalled how as 'stunt troops' (those specially chosen for assaulting enemy positions) they were 'virulent ... callous about the dead and jeered at effete southerners.'[84]

Over 7,000 men from the North East served too in the Dominion armies of Canada, Australia and New Zealand—the elite shock troops of the British Empire in the First World War—and the archetypal ANZAC John Simpson Kirkpatrick, long considered the embodiment of Australian 'mateship,' for his role in rescuing the wounded at Gallipoli with a donkey (there are statues of him across Australia) was actually born and raised in South Shields. Even the white-collared men of the 'Tyneside Commercials'—shipping line clerks, solicitors and draughtsmen at Armstrong's works—reveled in the region's estimation of itself and celebrated their contribution in verse:

Just a company of penmen,
soldiers then of little worth,
but we set the ball-a-rolling
in the hard and fighting North.[85]

Any visit to the war cemeteries of Flanders is testament to Northumbria's grim share of the nation's butcher's bill. The badges of the Fusiliers and DLI are ubiquitous, and the lists of their dead dominate the granite slabs that record the missing at Thiepval and Ypres. Death did not discriminate by rank either; officers had a higher chance of being killed than other ranks, as was the case when Brigadier General Sir James Riddell—from one of those old Northumbrian Junker families—was shot and killed leading the Northumberland Infantry Brigade into action at St Julien in April 1915, or Brigadier General Roland Boys Bradford, VC, the son of a colliery engineer from Witton Park, who became, at twenty-five years old, the youngest general in the history of the British Army.

But the casualties still have the power to shock: on the first day of the Battle of the Somme 1,644 Northumberland Fusiliers were killed (most of them before noon), and in total over 17,000 from the regiment were killed in the war, while the Durham Light Infantry lost 12,500 men. The small borough of Tynemouth lost 1,700 men in the trenches and at sea between 1914 and 1918. The North East War Memorials' Project estimates that there are 60,000 names recorded on First World War memorials in Northumberland and Durham (albeit with some duplications), which suggests a death rate at least comparable to the Scottish figures which are often cited as the highest in Britain.[86] It is apt that the largest British cemetery on the Western Front is Tyne Cot, named for the Northumbrians who fought there who observed that the German redoubt looked like a Tyneside pit cottage; and that perhaps the most haunting piece of English pastoral music associated with the Great War, 'the Banks of Green Willow,' should have been composed by George Butterworth, the son of the Head of the North Eastern Railway, who was killed on the Somme as a subaltern in the Durham Light Infantry.

* * *

In the years that followed, it was economic exigencies that account for the full muster rolls of local regiments in the 1920s and '30s; but the martial DNA of the region was deeply implanted (and it was noted that even the men of Jarrow marched in step with military precision), and would reach something approaching an apotheosis in the Second World War. Again, the Tyne and the Wear would produce over half of the four million tons of shipping that was so decisive in the Battle of the Atlantic, and just like in the Napoleonic period the Northern Counties were the first in Britain to bring their territorial units up to wartime strength.[87] After Anthony Eden's appeal for local defence volunteers—men aged between 17 and 65 not in military service—was broadcast on the BBC at 9pm on 14 May 1940, one man had volunteered at Newcastle at four minutes past nine, and 464 had been enrolled before midnight in North Shields alone.[88] But then the North East coast was still as vulnerable to attack, even invasion, as it had been twenty-five years earlier, and the authorities' meticulous plans for a 'Tyne Stop Line' entailed the destruction of every one of the 100 bridges over the Tyne between Redesdale and Scotswood and the mining of major roads. The strategic importance of the bridges over the Tyne at Newcastle was such that they were to be defended to the last man, and if necessary ships would be sunk at the tidal bar at Tynemouth.

At least in the First World War the heavy burden of sacrifice was shared widely across the 'Poor Bloody Infantry'; but this was not the case in the

Second World War where only one in five British soldiers served as ordinary infantrymen—as compared to the long tail of engineers, artillery, logisticians and so on.[89] It is noteworthy that the 'most experienced battle fighting division in the British army,' as General Brian Horrocks called them, was the 50th Northumbrian, which comprised battalions of the two Durham and Northumberland regiments as well as those from the North and East Ridings of Yorkshire. In Sicily and north-west Europe, the 'Fifty Div' suffered 9,000 casualties, and over 12,000 more with the BEF and in North Africa, and no division in the British army won more than its four Victoria Crosses. It should be noted that only around a half of the soldiers who served in British infantry units during the Second World War had a close territorial connection to the county name displayed on their cap badge.[90] Nevertheless, the exploits of the 50th were a focus for local pride back home, and what was seen as their distinctively Northumbrian characteristics were much praised. Their rear-guard actions on the retreat to Dunkirk became legendary, where the 'marvellously gutful' tenacity of a handful of DLI territorial battalions at Arras—the only British or Allied infantry to turn to the offensive during the retreat—held off a much larger German force, and caused the SS *Totenkopf* Division to withdraw in panic, buying precious time to evacuate the BEF.[91] It was also during this retreat that a Lieutenant Richard Annand from South Shields (whose own father had been killed at Gallipoli leading the Collingwood Battalion of Northumbrian sailors) won the first army VC of the war, and, in an odd echo of Harry Hotspur, Lieutenant Alan Percy, the 9th Duke of Northumberland, was killed leading a bayonet charge by the Grenadier Guards near Dunkirk.

On the whole the British Army in World War Two did not enjoy an outstanding reputation, but some units like the DLI were highly thought of. 'There is no doubt,' said General Sir Giffard Le Quesne Martel, of their defence of the Arras salient, 'that those North Countrymen would have fought to the last man and this might have set a standard which we badly needed on one or two occasions later on in the war.'[92] Many of these Durham Light Infantrymen were miners (indeed the typically short and stocky men of the 9th Battalion prompted their nickname the 'Gateshead Gurkhas'), and their feats of trench-digging were much commented on by senior officers at the time; 'I have never seen any troops dig quite so fast as these small tough Durham miners.'[93] There is an account of some pitmatic light infantrymen from Chester-le-Street (who were already amused to discover that the BEF commander Lord Gort was a North Durham coal-owner) who found themselves fighting amid familiar pit heaps and skirmishing through the colliery yards of Northern France; one wit remarked 'Ah think we should get a few towkens on for this!'—meaning that a day's fighting around coalmines should entitle them to both pit pay and army pay.[94]

This business-like reputation meant that they were hand-picked for the most difficult operations. Churchill himself, stung by criticism that the British could only fight the Afrika Korps with 'colonial' troops, insisted that the 50th Division were sent to Egypt to stiffen British resistance. One officer in the Division, John McManners, the son of a Durham coal miner who went on to be Regius Professor of Ecclesiastical History at the University of Oxford, recalled that in the Desert the 'Australians regarded themselves as the best fighters in the world (and they were). The Northumberland Fusiliers got on well with them and were accepted as honorary Australians, not starchy Brits or stuck-up Poms.'[95] There is even a legend that Northumbrian troops were used there as 'code talkers' (much like the US Army used Navajo soldiers in the Pacific to communicate sensitive information), as North East dialects were indecipherable by the Germans. These men certainly burnished their hard-fighting reputation, from the Battle of Bir Hacheim and the Cauldron Corridors—where Churchill praised the stubbornness of the 50th—to the DLI patrols who took on the Germans near the 'Jarrow' gap in the 'Don' minefield, and the great battles of El Alamein and Wadi Akarit where the 50th led the line alongside the Indian Army and the 51st Highland Division.[96] Their workmanlike attitude to the business of fighting impressed those who saw them in action. Pitmen back in the North East were known to work in silence to conserve their energy, and one eyewitness observed that he had heard that 'the Durhams charged mute in the First World War' and in the desert the only thing he heard from them 'was a few grunts, curses and remarks of the "— you" kind.'[97]

This reliability meant that the 50th Division were barely rested at all, and this bred resentment. 'By their own reckoning they had more than 'done their bit' in this war.'[98] But despite fighting all the way through the North African campaign and into Sicily, Montgomery selected them yet again, this time for the planned assault on North West Europe. The top brass of the Division may have felt honoured by their commander's confidence in them, but it caused serious disorder in the ranks, with men of the 50th Division using grenades and 'Bangalore torpedoes' to blow holes in the fences of the sealed camps they were placed in on the South Coast. When Montgomery visited the division before D-Day, he was booed.[99] One private of the 6th Battalion DLI recalled how unhappy his comrades were about being chosen again: 'the only satisfaction we got was that Montgomery had asked for our division because he wanted experienced troops and at least we got some leave out of it.'[100]

So having been amongst the last off the beaches of France in 1940 the Northumbrian Division were in the first wave of troops to land back on the French coast in June 1944. Again, eye-witnesses recorded their respect for the determined way that they fought. 'The Durhams go like mad with the fixed bayonets into farm buildings,' wrote one officer who witnessed their exploits in Normandy, 'what magnificent troops these Durhams are. It was just sheer guts that got them into Verieres.'[101] The campaign in Normandy was relentlessly hard as the army struggled to break out from the D-Day bridgehead, and then up through the Low Countries. Monthly battle casualties between June and September 1944 were more than twice the average of the Western Front in the First World War, and there came a point where the Northumbrian Division became so exhausted and depleted that in November 1944 its remnants were sent home to England never to take the field again. But their contribution was remembered by Montgomery himself who wrote this effusive accolade to the Durham Light Infantry, vanguard of the elite 50th Division:

> Of all the infantry regiments in the British Army, the Durham Light Infantry was the one most closely associated with myself during the war. The DLI Brigade fought under my command from Alamein to Germany ... It is a magnificent regiment. Steady as a rock in battle and absolutely reliable on all occasions. The fighting men of Durham are splendid soldiers; they excel in the hard-fought battle and they always stick it out to the end; they have gained their objectives and held their positions even when all their officers have been killed and conditions were almost unendurable.[102]

The interdependence between the home front and battlefront was especially obvious in North East England, playing as it did such a vital role in the replacement of war material, in particular shipping and heavy weaponry. We can also see obvious compassion and fellow feeling between those in dangerous and demanding occupations and the fighting men overhead or overseas. The Durham pitman and author Sid Chaplin wrote of his sympathy with the RAF: 'They in the heights, we in the depths. They fighting in an element from which may sweep death at any moment; we, ant-like in the mother rock far from the surface'.[103] It was common for colliery output to increase when it was known that local regiments were heading into the firing line, or for shipyard workers to ramp up production when high profile ships were lost. Although the bombing of the North East was serious, and caused heavy casualties, the region was not as badly hit as other places—this was balanced by very high losses of merchant seamen.[104] The small South Shields-based 'Moor

Line' might be seen as typical: the company owned 17 tramp ships in 1939, but only four of those vessels were left afloat by 1945, and 257 of their seamen had been lost at sea.

The sense of a region united behind the war effort may account for the harshness of the Newcastle magistrates who turned down every single exemption from service appeal by conscientious objectors and Jehovah's Witnesses.[105] Although, it must be said, that the region was not slavishly united behind the war effort: strike action was just as commonplace, and drunkenness on Tyneside was over three times the national average, and always among the top five worst areas.[106] There was though, still, a sense of being overlooked and underestimated, with one author arguing that 'for such an important area ... Tyneside, and the people of Tyneside received scant recognition for the contribution they made.'[107] Not least the actions of a sixteen-year-old NAAFI assistant called Tommy Brown who, as his memorial in his native North Shields records, may have shortened the war by at least a year by rescuing an Enigma code book from a sinking U-boat in the Mediterranean.

As David Edgerton has written, after 1945 'Britons built not only a new Jerusalem, but a new Sparta' and by the 1950s Britain was militarised to an unprecedented degree, alongside a 'masculinisation of the public sphere.'[108] This British military-industrial complex suited the North East, which had overspecialised in armaments and military hardware, and, at a time when the armed forces were still a major employer as much as the first line of defence, it mopped up many of the unskilled young Northumbrians who were increasingly surplus to requirements as the old labour-intensive industries began to mechanise. Military service for North Easterners was unremarkable. Francis 'Geordie' Doran, one of the legends of the early SAS, started life as a Tyneside ship's caulker—'red hot, hard work which soon built muscle and toughened sinew'—and he recalled that life in the regiment in the 1960s was dominated by Geordies, Jocks, and Scousers.[109] Indeed, in 1972, the Newcastle *Evening Chronicle* noted that of the first 200 British casualties in Northern Ireland, twenty were from the North East—including the first British soldier killed in the Troubles—despite the region only having one twentieth of the UK population. The famous Northumbrian regiments were kept busy in the post-war years, with the Fusiliers seeing serious action in the Korean War, and in brutal colonial missions in Kenya and Aden, the DLI likewise in Borneo and Malaya, before they were both amalgamated in 1968, despite Montgomery's protestations in the Lords.

The Northumbrian martial tradition is one of the strongest markers of a cultural *longue durée* in North East England. I was vividly reminded of this when I saw, amid the homecoming parade of the Royal Regiment of Fusiliers through Morpeth, a bandsman in desert camouflage wearing the Northumberland plaid—the oldest tartan in the British Isles—and carrying a set of Northumbrian pipes. Outside the North East, these deep-seated martial traditions have crystallised into something of a popular stereotype—with television programmes like *Soldier, Soldier*, *the Likely Lads*, and *Alan Partridge*, as well as the movies *Dog Soldiers*, *War Horse* and *Kajaki* all including representations of the typically 'up for it' Northumbrian squaddie. Even W. E. Johns—who worked in the RAF recruiting office in interwar Newcastle—created Ginger Hebblethwaite, the working-class son of a Durham miner, as the sidekick to Flying Officer James 'Biggles' Bigglesworth.

Perhaps what best encapsulates the region's respect for its martial heritage are two monuments in the Haymarket area of Newcastle. The first of these is a rather Wagnerian depiction of Nike the Greek goddess of victory, a memorial to the 3,737 officers and men of the Northumbrian regiments who lost their lives in the Boer War. Nike is depicted as a ten-foot-tall winged angel with a sword in her left hand and a laurel crown in her outstretched right—reminiscent of the Siegessäule in Berlin that commemorate Bismarck's wars of German unification—while at the foot of her 68 feet tall obelisk a twice-life-sized, semi-naked figure of 'Northumbria' reaches up to receive Victory's tribute near the legend 'DULCE ET DECORUM EST PRO PATRIA MORI.' It was no doubt all very sincerely meant, but the melodrama of this composition gives way to an altogether more poignant structure at the other side of Barras Bridge.

Built in the romantic style of the 'Memorial to the Fifty-Fourth Massachusetts Regiment' on Boston Common, and unveiled by the Prince of Wales in 1923, Sir William Goscombe John's 'The Response, 1914' depicts a column of Northumberland Fusiliers leaving Newcastle for the front. It was conceived as a memorial to the three so-called 'commercial battalions' that were raised and equipped by the local chamber of commerce (at their own expense), but it has come to stand for much more than that. Under the gaze of Lord Armstrong—the man who did more than most to industrialise modern warfare—whose statue ponders the scene from the other side of the Great North Road—Goscombe John created an unforgettable tableau. Here is unashamed masculinity, as the drummer boys march alongside the old sweats; the natural transferability between dangerous industrial work and life under fire as men join the ranks still in their working clothes; and that dash of Northumbrian sentimentality as a young father says goodbye to his wife and bairns. It is without doubt the most vivid artistic synopsis of Northumbrian culture and history, and the martial traditions that have bound them together.

3

NORTHUMBRIAN ENLIGHTENMENT

Forst ther wes nowt
nowt and neewhere
God felt the empty
space wi his finga
Let's hev sum
light sez God
Ootbye and inbye
so the light happened.

U. A. Fanthorpe, 'Caedmon's Hymn'

The principles upon which a safety lamp might be constructed I stated to several
persons long before Sir Humphrey Davy came into this part of the country.

George Stephenson, Letter to the *Philosophical Magazine*, 13 March 1817

In 1838 J. M. W. Turner painted a picture of a bustling Tyne-built paddle-tug
beneath a setting sun. *Monarch* had been built at Edward Robson's shipyard at
South Shields in 1833, and Turner showed it towing an old three-masted man
o' war to be broken up for scrap. The painting is, of course, better known as
The Fighting Temeraire, and came to symbolise the eclipse of the age of sail
and the coming world of iron and steam. That such ingenuity should feature
so prominently in this famous picture and yet be unknown to posterity typifies how a once vibrant culture of Northumbrian innovation has been overlooked. The catalogue of world-changing inventions that sprang from a particular place and time are solid evidence of a Northumbrian Enlightenment
that had deep roots in the most literate part of provincial England. Unlike in
Scotland, where their Enlightenment gave the world new understandings of
economics and moral philosophy alongside great strides in practical science,

the Northumbrian Enlightenment dwelled more on the application of empirical thought to the challenges of geology, agriculture, engineering and architecture, but was nonetheless as far-reaching as its Scottish counterpart.

Some of the world's greatest scientific breakthroughs were made in the North East of England. A plaque adorns the former headquarters of the Newcastle upon Tyne Electric Supply Company dedicated to the Sunderland born physicist and chemist Sir Joseph Wilson Swan. It bears the inscription 'FIAT LUX' (let there be light) as a tribute to his invention of the incandescent lightbulb (his house in Gateshead was the first in the world to be lit by electricity). But the art and science of illumination has a much deeper history—from John Walker's invention of the safety match at Stockton-on-Tees in 1827, to the pioneering work of Humphrey Davy and George Stephenson on miners' lamps, and the twentieth-century manufacture on Tyneside of military searchlights and cathode ray tubes for the first television sets.[1] The search for enlightenment goes back even further if one considers that the first stained glass seen in England was made at Jarrow in the seventh century, and the medieval illuminated style itself—with the concomitant invention of the light-box and the array of knowledge of pigments that such work required—was born in Northumbria.

However, the radiance generated in Northumbria in the second millennium came chiefly from the mining and burning of coal. One of the earliest references to coal mining in Britain was found in the 'Boldon Buke,' a sort of Domesday book for the bishopric of Durham compiled in 1183—where 'a certain collier' ('carbonarius') is recorded at Escomb as being obliged to find coals. For three centuries the region became so synonymous with carboniferous capitalism that George Stephenson once urged the Lord Chancellor to get off his woolsack and sit on a sack of coals instead.[2] The shallowness and accessibility of the coal measures, and their proximity to navigable rivers and the sea, made the seams underneath Northumberland and Durham the oldest commercial coalfield in the world. By 1565, the Tyne was exporting 35,000 tons of coal annually, but by 1750, the North East was producing close to two million tons of coal every year. It has been calculated that if the heat provided by burning one ton of coal is equivalent to burning an acre's worth of woodland, then the miners of Northumberland and Durham were providing England with the equivalent of two million acres of woodland per year, a factor arguably as decisive in this island's history as the width of the English Channel.[3]

In 1649 the pioneering chorographer William Camden described Newcastle as 'Ocellus, the eye of the north, the harth [sic] that warmeth the south parts of this kingdome with fire.' John Cleveland added in 'News from Newcastle,'

Nay, what's the sun but, in a different name,
A coal-pit rampant, or a mine on flame!
Then let this truth reciprocally run,
The sun's heaven's coalery, and coal's our sun.

The natural advantages of the geology and topography of Northumberland and Durham were manifold, and these were fully exploited by several generations of intelligent Northumbrians who, by the early nineteenth century, had transformed the rivers Tyne and Wear into a veritable Silicon Valley of Georgian England. The advances in engineering required to extract and transport that most lucrative and plentiful of minerals—in excavation, pumping and shipping—were extraordinary. The steam locomotive and the railway originated here as well as 'so many other of the early mechanical inventions' that C. B. Fawcett, one of the founders of modern academic geography, thought that 'Tyneside may well be termed the "Florence" of the Industrial Renaissance.'[4] Such a comparison may seem fanciful, but, like Florence, the culture of North East England in its industrial Golden Age was both entrepreneurial and highly literate. By the nineteenth century Northumberland and Durham had probably the most literate population in provincial England. Through a study of how newlyweds in 1839–45 signed marriage registers, either with their name or a mark, only the far north—Cumberland, Northumberland, Westmorland, the East and North Ridings of Yorkshire—had fewer than 34 per cent making marks (Durham was between 35 and 39 per cent). This contrasts with the North West and Midlands where on average 58 per cent of spouses made marks—and it was even over 45 per cent in the Home Counties.[5]

The reasons for this were various, with roots in the deep past. Of all the Anglo-Saxon kingdoms, Northumbria in the age of Bede can reasonably claim 'a high place as the initiator of Anglo-Saxon literary endeavour at a time when vernacular literature was slow to develop on mainland Europe.'[6] And in Bede himself we have what the historian Sir Richard Southern called 'the first scientific intellect produced by the German peoples of Europe.'[7] We see some echoes of this intellectual culture in the Middle Ages through the lives of men like the poet St Godric of Durham; the philosopher John Duns Scotus who came from either Berwickshire just over the border, or Dunstan in Northumberland, and may have been educated at the Franciscan Friary at Newcastle before his studies at Oxford; or the Protestant reformers William

63

Tyndale and Nicholas Ridley (who 'learned his grammar with great dexterity in Newcastle') and who both had roots in Tynedale.[8]

One of the most extraordinarily learned Northumbrians of early modern England was the 9th Earl of Northumberland himself, Henry Percy. He was born in 1564 at Tynemouth Castle (and would later become governor of the same fortress), and while making a name for himself as a soldier fighting against the Spanish in the Low Countries and in the fleet sent against the Armada, he developed precocious literary tastes, devouring Guicciardini, Holinshed, and Machiavelli. Percy cultivated such an interest in astrology, medicine and alchemy that it earned him the sobriquet 'the Wizard Earl.' In a similar fashion to his contemporary Rudolf II in Prague, Percy gathered learned men around him at Alnwick Castle, and in the Tower of London after he was imprisoned on suspicion of involvement in the Gunpowder Plot. There he assembled a library and paid salaries to a trio of learned mathematicians to assist him in his experiments who were known as the 'earl's three Magi.'

For such a peripheral region, far from the seat of government and without a university until the nineteenth century, the history of Northumbria is marked by a predisposition towards learning and literacy. The first explanation for this was that as a legal and ecclesiastical centre, the County Palatine of Durham teemed with lawyers and clerics; it even had its own chancellor, chancery and courts. Defending the rights and privileges of the bishopric generated constant business for barristers and clerks, and this only accelerated with the discovery of coal seams on Palatinate land. Literate men were much in demand, and the supply of these were met by sending the brightest boys to Oxford and Cambridge. Several attempts were made to found a college at Durham—first under an enlightened local Bishop, Cuthbert Tunstall, a friend of Erasmus and Thomas More, and then again in the seventeenth century. This was repelled by Oxford and Cambridge, and Durham would not gain its own university until 1832. Nevertherless, the 310 marks left in his will by William of Durham, the Rector of Wearmouth when he died in 1249 led to the founding of University College, Oxford—the oldest college at England's oldest university. Likewise Durham College, Oxford, which was founded to educate the Benedictine monks of Durham, was home to the first lending library in England (it was originally dedicated to the Virgin Mary, St Cuthbert, and the Trinity—and at its reforming after the Reformation it took the name Trinity College). At Cambridge, statutes of St John's College, founded in 1511, provided for special favour to students from Northumberland, Cumberland and Westmorland.[9]

When it came to educating the masses, however, the proximity to Scotland had an enormous influence—after an Act of the Scottish Parliament in 1633, a locally funded and Church-supervised school was established in every parish in Scotland. When in 1842 the Poor Law Commissioners were taking evidence on the 'training of pauper children,' Edwin Chadwick asked the engineer William Fairbairn whether in the northern counties in England, 'from which the better educated mechanics come,' their better education arose from endowed schools or from the higher esteem in which education was held in the North, Fairbairn replied that

> The better education in the counties of Durham and Northumberland does not arise from endowed schools, but from schools conducted on the Scotch parochial principle, and supported by the fees paid by the scholars, as also from the amalgamation of that part of the English with the Scotch population on the borders, and a similarity of habit or impression respecting the advantages of education. The parents of children in those counties are very generally aware of the advantages of the Scotch system of education.[10]

Looking back on his childhood in 1760s Northumberland, Thomas Bewick recalled that nearly all the cottagers in the Tyne Valley could read their Bible as well as local histories and ballads, and some were so well-educated that it was common to discuss astronomy, history and politics with quite ordinary local people—such as Anthony Liddell, who they called 'the Village Hampden' after the Parliamentarian MP who resisted Charles I's demands for ship money. To Bewick, 'local labourers often seemed better informed than the farmers who were so preoccupied with managing their land that they never read a book.'[11] One study of late Georgian Alnwick concluded that at least two-thirds of the population could read and write, and Newcastle was well known for its lively tradition of ballad-selling and singing in the streets.[12] In 1624 the poet Abraham Holland seemed to mock the Northumbrian habit of sticking ballads and penny sheets on the walls:

> *North-villages, where every line*
> *Of Plumpton Parke is held a work divine.*
> *If o're the Chymney they some Ballad have*
> *Of Chevy-Chase ...*[13]

But this was typical of an increasingly literate population and their demand for printed material. In the eighteenth century, Newcastle had more printing presses than any town in England, after London, Oxford, and Cambridge and by 1790 the town boasted twenty printers, twelve booksellers and stationers, thirteen bookbinders and three engravers. The town had seven subscription libraries and three circulating libraries, plus the Thomlinson Library attached to St Nicholas's parish church with its 5,000 books—one of the oldest in England, and housed in Newcastle's first classical building.

The history of Northumbrian printing began around 1639 when Charles I came to Newcastle bringing with him his official printer Robert Barker who set up a press on the old Tyne Bridge. Under his aegis the first books ever printed in the town were a sermon by the Bishop of Durham, a book of instructions to the Royalist army, as well as a newspaper, probably the first printed outside of London, detailing the progress of the king's army in the north. The inventory of a thousand books left by one William Corbett, a seventeenth-century bookseller in Newcastle upon Tyne, give us a sense of what the Newcastle public were buying and reading. These titles included Henri Estienne's *An introduction to a treatise touching the conformitie of ancient and moderne wonders: or a preparative treatise to the Apologie for Herodotus*, and William Bourne's *A Regiment for the Sea, A mathematical guide to navigation* (which may have been the first technical manual written by an English person).[14]

Periodicals were very rare outside London, Dublin and Edinburgh, but Newcastle had ten during the eighteenth century. Even in the small town of Alnwick several magazines were printed in the nineteenth century—including *The Atheneum* [sic], the *Alnwick Quatro*, and the *Northumbrian Mirror*, 'the Young Student's Literary and Mathematical Companion.' Whereas most large towns in the eighteenth century had their own local newspaper, Newcastle had four, including *The Newcastle Gazette* (1710) and *The Newcastle Courant* (1711)—the first newspapers published in the north of England—and *The Chronicle*, founded in 1766 (and still being published to this day). Journalism continued to thrive into the nineteenth century where innovations helped local titles to reach a mass audience, including the Newcastle-based *Northern Daily Express*, established in 1855, the first *daily* newspaper to be published in the North of England (the other Newcastle titles soon followed suit); the *Northern Daily Express*, which was the first local newspaper in Britain to be sold for one penny; and the *Shields Gazette*, established in 1849, still the oldest provincial evening newspaper in the United Kingdom.

The trade in books and printed material was an important factor in the city's commercial success, and from the late seventeenth century onwards Newcastle published more children's books than any other town in England outside London.[15] Such material—primers and chapbooks—was designed to teach children in the home how to read, but the numbers of schools in North East England also increased in the early modern period. The Royal Grammar School was founded in 1525 and a century later the firebrand Leveller John

Lilburne was a pupil there. In his *Innocency and Truth Justified*, published in 1645, Lilburne recalled attending the 'best schools in the north—namely, at Auckland and Newcastle—in both which places I was not one of the drones-set [drone-like and lazy] schoolboys.' Or for bright but poor boys who couldn't get to grammar school, there were other routes to advancement—such as that of John Robinson (1650–1723), a labourer's son from Cleasby near Darlington whose master found him so addicted to book learning that he sent him to Oxford. This was a springboard to a career in holy orders which saw him become Bishop of London and the last ecclesiastic to represent Britain at a Peace Congress (Utrecht in 1712).

The reputation of Northumbrian learning was such that when George III wondered, after reading Cuthbert Collingwood's lucid despatches after the Battle of Trafalgar, where this sea captain had learned to write such splendid English, he quickly remembered that Lord Chancellor Eldon and his brother Lord Stowell, the great Admiralty Court judge, had been schoolfellows of Collingwood at Newcastle, and answered his own question: 'I forgot. He was one of Moises' boys.'[16] (Hugh Moises was the Headmaster of the Royal Grammar School for over thirty years.) The RGS was joined by three other schools set up by private endowment or by public subscription in Newcastle from the early 1700s, but many Northumbrian parents chose to send their children to one of the numerous private academies in the town, or the cut price boarding schools out in the country (the cruel character of Wackford Squeers in *Nicholas Nickleby* was based on William Shaw, the headmaster of Bowes Academy, near Barnard Castle which Dickens visited in the winter of 1837). Some of these more modest educational establishments had a good reputation for scholarship, despite their size. Robson's School at Benwell educated Charles Hutton, a coal miner's son who went on to be professor of mathematics at the artillery academy at Woolwich, and was the first man to calculate the density of the earth; and the Bruce Academy in Newcastle, which was run by the Roman Wall expert Dr John Collingwood Bruce from 1834 to 1859, had a number of distinguished old boys, including Robert Stephenson and the shipbuilding tycoon Charles Mark Palmer.

The growth of Sunday schools for the poor urchins who roamed the streets was notable too; the first in Newcastle was set up by the Rev William Turner to be 'a focus of light and learning' for the town, and these were soon educating thousands of children across the North East.[17] The increasing pre-occupation with respectability and good order—and a general desire to promote technical proficiency among the lower classes—was reflected in the objectives of the Newcastle's Sunday School Teachers' Association, who had their hands full dealing with the town's traditionally hedonistic pursuits: '[horse] races and their drinking, gambling, and unruliness; the Harvest Hire of reapers, most revolting scenes of tumult'; the drink question and 'the scenes of drunkenness which our streets exhibit on the Lord's Day.'[18]

That Newcastle was an important centre of learning and print culture may still surprise people. Stereotypes die hard, but the Tyne was no backwater; as an urban centre Newcastle was usually in the five biggest English towns since the 1300s (although its tightly drawn municipal boundaries—which did not include Gateshead or the urban areas along the riverbank, saw it drop down the population tables in comparison to unitary Birmingham or Manchester). 'Here I am on a spot within a hundred miles of which I never was before in my life,' noted a surprised sounding William Cobbett in Newcastle in 1832, who was nonetheless 'receiving the unsolicited applause of men amongst the most intelligent in the whole kingdom.'[19] The Tyne had always been an important transport hub on the route between London and Edinburgh (before the age of rail three coaches daily left from Newcastle to London), and as the coal trade up and down the east coast started to expand from the mid sixteenth century this only strengthened the links between the thriving River Tyne and the capital in a way that was not typical for other, usually landlocked, provincial towns. It's striking the number of places on the Tyne and Wear named after parts of the lower Thames where Northumbrian coal was unloaded, New Greenwich at Gateshead for example, Wapping near Wallsend, or the part of Sunderland known as Deptford.

Tyneside's transformation from provincial obscurity was much remarked upon, with Daniel Defoe describing it in 1724 as 'a spacious, extended, infinitely populous place,' and the native Tynesider William Hutchinson—who, after an extraordinary career at sea as a privateer, returned to England to invent parabolic reflectors for lighthouses—contrasted Northumberland in 1766 with its savage past:

> The ferocity of the inhabitants is [now] subdued; traffic, arts, sciences, manufactories and navigations, have taken the place of the brutal warfare, which is extinguished; Cultivation, with all the comeliness of Plenty, laughs in the valleys; streams are taught to labour in mechanic systems to aid the manufacturer; every Creek and Bay is thronged with Ships ... Desert plains stained with Slaughter and track'd with the progress of Rapine and Violence, formerly spread forth an extensive scene of desolation, where now rising woods, inclosed [sic] farms, villages and hamlets are disposed under the smiles of Prosperity.[20]

The intellectual and social climate was certainly propitious—eight hundred books were printed in Newcastle upon Tyne in the course of the eighteenth century[21]—and manifest in the birth of learned and polite institutions there like the Barber Surgeons Hall with its statues of Aesculapius, Hippocrates, Galen and Paracelsus, the infirmary of 1752 (one of the oldest in the country), the Palladian Assembly Rooms of 1776 and the Literary and Philosophical Society of 1793. It seems fitting too that eighteenth-century Tyneside was the greatest glass-producer in the world, and specialised in articles of great delicacy such as the famous Newcastle Light Balusters, seven-inch tall glass chalices, claimed by some antique dealers to be 'the pinnacle of elegance in Georgian drinking glasses,' with 'a propensity to be brighter than other English lead metal drinking glasses of the same period.'[22]

But what of the thought that this culture germinated? In 1757 the Rothbury-born cleric John Brown (who had distinguished himself as a soldier in the defence of Carlisle against the Jacobites in 1745), and who would become vicar of St Nicholas's in Newcastle, published his *Estimate of the Manners and Principles of the Times* (1757–8)—a satire on what he perceived to be the sybaritic laxity of his day.

> It was a shrewd observation of a good old writer 'How can he get Wisdom, whose Talk is of Bullocks?' But Rusticity is not more an Enemy of Knowledge than Effeminacy: With the same Propriety therefore it may now be asked, 'how can he get Wisdom, whose talk is of Dress and Wagers, Cards and Borough-jobbing, Horses, Women, and Dice?' The Man of Fashion is indeed cut off from the very Means of solid Instruction. His late Hours occasion a late rising; and thus the Morning, which should be devoted to the Acquisition of Knowledge, is devoted to Sleep, to Dress, and Ignorance.[23]

This sort of sober diligence even found fans among the intellectual elite of France (Maximilien Robespierre called his dog 'Brown' in tribute) and it was no doubt familiar to the French revolutionary Jean Paul Marat, who practised as a vet—and occasional doctor—in Newcastle in the early 1770s. Marat may have taken Brown's advice as he wrote and published his first overtly political work, *Chains of Slavery*, in Newcastle in 1774—completing the sixty-five chapters in three months, living on black coffee and (he claimed) sleeping only two hours a night.

Writing from Newcastle in 1739 the poet and physician Mark Akenside submitted 'A Hymn to Science' to *The Gentleman's Magazine*:

> *Science! thou fair effusive ray*
> *From the great source of mental Day,*
> *Free, generous, and refin'd!*
> *Descend with all thy treasures fraught,*

Illumine each bewilder'd thought,
And bless my lab'ring mind....

The pursuit of that effusive ray seemed to preoccupy an impressive cohort of Northumbrian enlighteners in the eighteenth century. Men like the County Durham savants William Emerson, the Weardale mathematician who wrote the *The Arithmetic of Infinites and The Elements of Optics*, or John Bird from Bishop Auckland (1709–76), one of the most famed mathematical instrument-makers in eighteenth-century Europe, who made dividing rods to measure the standard yard and the huge quadrant for the Royal Observatory at Greenwich, and the Byers Green astronomer Thomas Wright (1711–86), a former instrument-maker educated at a free school in Gateshead who was the first to describe the shape of the Milky Way and to speculate that faint nebulae were distant galaxies. (It was also during this time that the mathematical prodigy George Coughran (1752–74), the son of a farmer from rural Northumberland, was appointed Calculator to the Astronomer Royal—a sort of human computer.) Nor should we overlook another County Durham man, the astronomer and surveyor Jeremiah Dixon (1733–79), who by drawing the Mason-Dixon line between Pennsylvania and Maryland gave us 'Dixie' and inspired one of the weirdest rhyming couplets in popular song when Mark Knopfler crooned about Dixon and his confrere Charles Mason—'A Geordie and a baker's boy/in the forests of the Iroquois.'

What is perhaps more remarkable in this period are the erudite Northumbrian women who emerged to take a prominent place in Enlightenment discourse. We should begin here with Mary Astell (1666–1731), the daughter of a Tyneside coal merchant and possibly Britain's earliest feminist thinker. She was educated by her uncle on the Newcastle Quayside in Latin, French, logic, mathematics and natural philosophy, and one hundred years before Mary Wollstonecraft wrote *A Vindication of the Rights of Woman*. She then took the bold step of moving to London to try to make a living as a writer. In 1694 she wrote a book entitled *A Serious Proposal to the Ladies* arguing for greater female agency, and the right to what we might now think of as a career, rather than the stultification of early marriage. This appealed to her friend, Elizabeth Elstob, another Newcastle woman who was a serious scholar of Anglo-Saxon history and in her *Rudiments of Grammar for the English-Saxon Tongue* (1715), the first such work written in English, wrote a preface entitled 'An Apology for the Study of Northern Antiquities.'

This independence of mind was emulated by yet another Tyneside woman: Jane Gomeldon, nee Middleton (1720–79), who, after travelling in Europe disguised as a man (and attempting to elope with a French nun) returned to

Newcastle where she wrote 'Maxims'—a sort of English haiku—and in 1766, to raise money for the city's lying-in hospital, a book of thirty-one essays entitled *The Medley*, in which Jane assumes a male persona to discuss, *inter alia*, Milton and Homer. Of course, these women were by no means entirely typical, and nor was Elizabeth Montagu (1720–1800) the 'queen of literary London' who regularly visited her family's manor house at East Denton Hall to supervise her husband's lucrative collieries (Horace Walpole wrote to George Montagu to declare that 'our best sun is Newcastle coal') and host literary salons in Newcastle. Nevertheless, it is interesting that it was a Newcastle schoolmistress, Ann Fisher (1719–78), whose *A New Grammar: Being the Most Easy Guide to Speaking and Writing the English Language Properly and Correctly* of 1745 made her the earliest female author to publish on the subject and that her book ran to thirty-three editions.

'I would like the girls to be taught mathematics and geometry', wrote Vice-Admiral Cuthbert Collingwood to his wife in 1805 from a man o' war in the Atlantic.

> Of all sciences in the world these are the most entertaining. Also astronomy to give them an idea of the beauty and wonder of creation so they may have a fixed idea of the nature of that Being who could be the author of such a world. Whenever they have that, nothing on this side of the moon will give them uneasiness of mind.[24]

Whether this was an unusually enlightened attitude towards female education is unclear but we do see examples of female participation in learned institutions, as at the Alnwick Literary Society, where, in 1820, Annabel Carr, the daughter of a Newcastle banker and author of *Conversations on Chemistry* (1807), lectured on 'mechanics and hydrostatics.'[25] It was in this same milieu of Northumbrian intellectualism that Anne Milbank, the daughter of the High Sheriff of Durham, received an ambitious education at Elemore Hall near Pittington, in classics, maths and science. Her daughter Ada, Countess of Lovelace is now widely regarded as the world's first computer programmer for her work with Charles Babbage and others on analytical engines, but Anne herself had such a formidable intellect that her husband (and Ada's father) Lord Byron dubbed her his 'Princess of Parallelograms.'

Perhaps the most luminous example of a Northumbrian bluestocking was the social reform campaigner Josephine Butler, nee Grey (1828–1906). She was born near Wooler, where her high-minded abolitionist father was a cousin of the Northumberland-born Prime Minister Charles, Earl Grey. She too was thoroughly educated at home in arts and sciences, and then at a Ladies'

Seminary in Newcastle, whose headmistress Catherine Tidy, Josephine recalled, 'had a large heart and ready sympathy.'[26] It was the misery she saw in the slums of mid-Victorian Liverpool that possessed her with what she described as 'an irresistible urge to go forth and find some pain keener than my own, to meet with people more unhappy than myself.'[27] This drove her vocation to combat what she saw as the exploitation inherent in prostitution, with signal courage and determination (and in partnership with the Tynesider W. T. Stead, editor of the *Pall Mall Gazette*) and all this while serving as first President of the 'North of England Council for Promoting the Higher Education of Women' and writing biographies of Catherine of Siena and the Protestant pastor Jean Frederic Oberlin. Few places in Victorian Britain were more rigidly patriarchal than North East England. It is ironic then that a Northumbrian woman like Butler, albeit a middle-class one, was perhaps the most effective campaigner for women's rights of her time—from ending coverture in English law to the criminalisation of child prostitution and human trafficking. She was joined in this movement by her close contemporary Emily Davies (1830–1921), the daughter of the Rector of Gateshead and editor of the *English Woman's Journal* and founder of the all-female Girton College Cambridge; but to the leading Suffragist Millicent Fawcett, Butler was simply 'the most distinguished Englishwoman of the nineteenth century.'

There is a sense in Northumbrian history that its most celebrated women have had to outdo the men in 'manly' feats of courage and daring (Butler was in physical danger on many occasions). One could point here to Grace Darling, the lighthouse-keeper's daughter from Bamburgh who rowed a 21-foot coble out to rescue the drowning passengers from the sinking wreck of a paddle-steamer. Portraits show her as a tall, raw-boned lass, and the Northumbrian poet Algernon Swinburne penned her this effusive, if rather overwrought tribute:

> Not our mother, not Northumberland, brought ever forth,
> Though no southern shore may match the sons that kiss her mouth,
> Children worthier all the birthright given of the ardent north
> Where the fire of hearts outburns the suns that fire the south.

We might also note the suicidal bravery of Emily Wilding Davison (1872–1913)—'Deeds Not Words' is the inscription on her grave in Morpeth—when she died intercepting the king's horse at the 1913 Derby (and this after her hunger-strike in Strangeways prison). But none had a greater geo-political impact than Gertrude Bell (1868–1926). Born in Washington Old Hall in County Durham, she was the granddaughter of the wealthy Tyneside ironmaster Sir Lowthian Bell. After achieving an unprecedented First in Modern History at Oxford, Bell then lived an extraordinary life travelling and mountaineering independently across the Middle East, writing *The Desert and the Sown* (1907) and translating the poetry of Hafiz from the original Persian. She even found the time to campaign *against* women's suffrage. Her unparalleled expertise meant she was recruited in the First World War—with the title of 'Major Miss Bell'—as the first woman officer in the history of British military intelligence. She played a decisive role in the defeat of the Ottoman Empire, the preservation of Mesopotamian archaeological treasures, and the creation of the modern state of Iraq. 'By Allah!' an Arab is supposed to have said, 'What must their men be like?'[28]

* * *

In his essay 'On the geographical distribution of British intellect,' Arthur Conan Doyle once attempted an appraisal of the characteristics of British and Irish counties. He thought the proportion of celebrities to the total population was low in the five Northern counties and noted that 'Northumberland produces men of practical turn [and] there are no poets and few authors in her records.'[29] *Mens agitat molem* ('mind moves matter') was the motto of Armstrong College (which would become Newcastle University in the 1960s), and practicality was perhaps the key underpinning of a sort of Northumbrian heuristic that emerged through the Industrial Revolution. This was the defining feature of the generations of tinkering engineers that followed in the wake of George Stephenson and William Armstrong, and the Northumbrians of the industrial age looked for and found deeper roots for their practical outlook.

In 1854, the pre-Raphaelite artist William Bell Scott, whose murals at Wallington Hall saw Northumbria's ancient past as the source of its Victorian greatness, wrote 'Bede in the Nineteenth Century,' a poem depicting the saint being shocked by what he sees on returning to his native Tynesde: 'A wilderness of smiths ... Of reeking furnaces, and cells made bright/By magic flames.' But Bede himself was an industrious man of practical bent, who took his cues from his warden the Abbot Ceolfrith, the sort of 'man who worked hard at everything' ('*industrius per omnia vir*'), who doubled the size of the library at Wearmouth-Jarrow—then the largest, and perhaps only library in England. (One of the Bibles made at that time by the hardworking monks of Ceolfrid's monastery—the door-stopping *Codex Amiatinus*—is the earliest surviving complete manuscript of the Latin Vulgate bible.).

73

Bede was obsessed by the measurement of time, so as to construct reliable calendars that could set the correct date for Easter. A religious object, but one deduced from the most rigorously scientific study, challenging old theories with new and better data, processing those mathematically and then drawing rigorous conclusions. From Augustine to Galileo, observers of the almost tide-less Mediterranean had missed what Bede had noticed of the Northumbrian seaboard: 'more marvellous than anything is the great fellow-ship that exists between the ocean and the course of the Moon.'[30] When Isaac Newton wrote that 'If I have seen further it is by standing on the shoulders of Giants,' Bede was certainly among that number—not just for the correct conclusions he drew, but for his meticulous approach to problem solving that we can still discern thirteen centuries later in his methodical reasoning.

> For in the course of 29 days, the Moon lights up the confines of the Earth 28 times, and in the twelve hours which are added on to make up the fullness of the natural month, it circles half the globe of the Earth, so that, for example, the new Moon which emerged last month above the Earth at noon, will this month meet up with the Sun to be kindled at midnight beneath the Earth. Through this length of time, the tides will come twice as often, and 57 times the high seas swell breaking their barriers and once again retreat unto themselves.[31]

The study of nature was long a wellspring for inquisitive Northumbrians. William Turner (1508–68), the 'Father of English Botany,' was the son of a tanner from Morpeth, who published *A New Herball* in 1551, the first system-atic survey of the 'uses and vertues' [sic] of British plants, and the first such work written in English. Two centuries later, Lancelot 'Capability' Brown (1716–83), a robust country-boy from nearby Kirkharle, would show the world how to gain mastery over nature. Brown had roamed the fells of Redesdale with his brothers from an early age, an experience that gave him 'the ability to smell the landscape, looking to the skies for the coming squall, sensing the dangers of a sucking bog, the way to hide in and escape from a gorse thicket, skills once practised in bloody earnest, which were now boys' adventures and games.' Some have claimed that Brown's intelligence came from the Redesdale shepherds from whom he was descended who had 'the manners and bearing of gentlemen and a store of knowledge far beyond farm-ing matters'; from their long winter evenings reading, the shepherds tended to sturdy independence in their opinions, not aping their landlords and 'cer-tainly not cowed by marquess or duke.'[32] Brown's topographical and horticul-tural acumen were unsurpassed—itself remarkable for a humble son of a land agent and a chambermaid—and his own insouciance in describing how he moulded the landscape to suit his purposes is almost Promethean:

> there I make a comma, and there, where a more decided turn is proper, I make
> a colon; at another part, where an interruption is desirable to break the view,
> a parenthesis; now a full stop, and then I begin another subject.

A preoccupation with nature was characteristic of the Northumbrian Enlighteners of the eighteenth century. Brown himself just missed the great period of agricultural enclosure in the North East, when between 1760 and 1810 over a quarter of a million acres were enclosed and then 'improved' in the two counties of Northumberland and Durham. The eighteenth and nineteenth centuries would also see great advances in animal husbandry, with the Colling brothers of Ketton, near Darlington, whose world-famous production line of shorthorn cattle culminated in the birth of a giant steer known as the Durham Ox, which at the age of five years weighed almost two tons. Even the breeding of intelligence was possible. In 1893 Adam Telfer, a Northumberland shepherd, bred a sheepdog called 'Old Hemp' at West Woodburn, not far from where Capability Brown grew up. The monument in the village to Telfer describes his dog as 'the father of the modern border collie ... a natural herder who could move and control sheep with a mere look.'

One of the greatest Northumbrian enthusiasts for the natural world was, of course, Thomas Bewick. He had engraved a Northumberland shepherd's dog for his 1790 bestseller *A General History of Quadrupeds*, and his 'Chillingham Bull' of 1789 has been described by Simon Schama as 'an image of massive power, perhaps the greatest icon of British natural history.'[33] Bewick would often play truant as a child simply to roam the Tyne Valley and observe its flora and fauna, which would have a major influence on his work as an artist. For Bewick, nature prompted profound questions. It was much discussed in Newcastle when perfect mussels were found two hundred feet below ground, embedded in ironstone at a colliery at Mickley Bank, and it was the Rector of Bishopwearmouth, the Reverend William Paley, who in his *Natural Theology* of 1802 drew the famous analogy between the universe and a clock, and that the marvels of the natural world reveal God's intelligent design of the cosmos. In the 1780s Bewick and his friends formed their own small 'lunar society,' when the full moon lit the dark streets of the town, to discuss erudite subjects. But Bewick was much struck by the maxim of Socrates 'that the summit of our knowledge is only to perceive our own ignorance,' and his biographer Jenny Uglow notes that he used to quote this often 'with great emphasis and solemnity, and often added some such remark as "Why sir, it would take a man a lifetime to write the history of a spider."[34]

Of all the inventors of the nineteenth century it was Sir William Armstrong who most effectively practised a Northumbrian empiricism rooted in nature. As a child he was absorbed by the study of electricity, chemistry and mechanics, and his biographer has written of 'his desire in general to commune with the natural world,' which had an 'intensely practical side: a fascination with channelling elemental power to useful ends.' As befits a man of Reiver pedigree, and his later career as an armourer, he used the vocabulary of conquest to describe his own philosophy as one which sought 'the subjugation of nature.'[35] This subjugation—in everything from hydraulics to hydroelectricity—made Armstrong one of the richest men in the world, and he was the first scientist ever raised to the peerage (in 1887). Armstrong's whole outlook was in fact shaped by the example of George Stephenson, who he praised for his practicality: 'unaided by theoretical knowledge, he rightly saw that coal was the embodiment of power originally derived from the sun.' Stephenson's genius, he explained in 1861 to the Society of Mechanical Engineers, was in the iterative application of scientific ideas, not in original inventions themselves but in 'the subsequent elaboration, and in the successful struggle with difficulties, unknown to the mere theorist, and often requiring years of labour, blended with disappointment, for their removal.'[36]

Note here Armstrong's scorn for 'theoretical knowledge' and 'mere theorists.' This empiricism found many adherents among the generations of problem-solving Northumbrian engineers: intensely practical men such as the Tyneside engineer William Coulson who was commissioned by the Prussian government to solve the problem of how to access the deep coal seams underneath the Ruhr Valley, or Sir Charles Hartley from Hedworth who first made the mouth of the Danube navigable, and Sir George Elliot, a former colliery labourer from Gateshead, who worked himself from the coal-face via night classes to the ownership of the company that manufactured the first trans-Atlantic cables. And it was Arthur Holmes, the son of a cabinet maker from Hebburn, who had worked as a demonstrator at Imperial College, and then as a geologist for an oil company in Burma, before achieving professorships at Durham and Edinburgh, who first accurately calculated the age of planet Earth (he set it at 4.5 billion years).

This intellectual atmosphere would not have been possible without the associational culture that has long been characteristic of North East England. Writing in the 1770s, the radical political thinker Thomas Spence, who began his working life making fishing nets on the Tyneside quays, asked who is most likely to attain

> a distinct knowledge of any intricate subject, he who searches into it by contemplation and the help of books only, or he who attends a well-regulated society, where the subject is freely debated as a question on both sides, or demonstrated by the joint endeavours of the members?[37]

Spence was also an agitator and controversialist. When in 1775 he presented a lecture to the Newcastle Philosophical Society on the people's right to property (there were moves afoot to enclose the Town Moor), the members voted his expulsion at their next meeting, and he ended up getting punched by Thomas Bewick after a heated debate in a Bigg Market pub. There was a growing demand for more reasoned conversation, and in 1793 the Newcastle Literary and Philosophical Society was founded. Perhaps wisely, the original statutes of the 'Lit & Phil'—still Britain's largest private membership library outside London—expressly forbade any discussion of religion or politics, and their cool neo-classical building on Westgate Road, which they moved into in 1825, was to be a temple of rational scientific discussion. In its heyday the Lit & Phil was a cross between a gentlemen's club and MIT, and within its rooms Humphrey Davy and George Stephenson demonstrated the efficacy of their new safety lamps, William Armstrong showed how water pressure could move machinery, and the Cumbrian metallurgist Hugh Lee Pattinson described how to separate silver from lead by crystallisation. The Lit & Phil even received the country's first specimens of the wombat and the duck-billed platypus seen in England from John Hunter, Governor of New South Wales and an honorary member of the Society.

John Wigham Richardson, one of the founders of Swan Hunter shipbuilders, recalled seeing William Armstrong deliver a lecture at the Lit & Phil:

> One dark night in the Christmas holidays, our father took us four elder children to see Lord Armstrong (then Mr William Armstrong, solicitor) exhibit his electrical machine... It was a weird scene; the sparks or flashes of electricity from the machine were, I should say, from four to five feet long and the figure of Armstrong in a frock coat (since then so familiar) looked almost demoniacal.[38]

Although many other learned societies were founded in the town—including the Society of Antiquaries of 1813 (the oldest in Britain), the Northumberland Institution for the Promotion of Fine Arts in 1822, the Mechanics Institution in 1824, the Natural History Society in 1829 (one of its founding members, Albany Hancock, enjoyed a long correspondence with

Charles Darwin on their mutual enthusiasm for the burrowing barnacle), the College of Medicine in 1834, and the North of England Institute of Mining Engineers (the first of its kind in the world) in 1852. Such intellectual endeavours were not confined to Newcastle. There were equivalent 'Lit & Phils' at North Shields and Seaham, and at Sunderland a grand 'Athenaeum' was built between 1839 and 1841 as the home of the town's own Literary & Philosophical Society, founded in 1810 by the local abolitionist James Field Stanfield. It was here in 1847 that the inquiring mind of a young Joseph Swan was first stimulated by a lecture on incandescent lamps, and where Lewis Carroll saw—among its collection of zoological specimens—the stuffed walrus that would appear in his *Adventures of Alice in Wonderland*.

Such institutions were housed in fine new buildings, and as we'll see in Chapter 4 much of the redevelopment of North East towns can be seen as part of an enlightened impulse to rationalise and sanitise. In Newcastle, John Dobson's panopticon gaol at Carliol Square and Richard Grainger's hygienic new covered market (the biggest in Europe at the time) were perfect examples of this. Indeed when the market opened in 1835 the 2,000 or so guests who sat down to dinner in its precincts were illuminated by gaslight, moving one visitor to exclaim that 'nothing has been seen like it, since the days of Belshazzar.'[39] One gets a strong sense of nineteenth-century Tyneside, with its vast mineral wealth and pioneering architecture and technology, being a sort of Dallas or Dubai, and the place would welcome some of the great intellectuals, from Oscar Wilde and the physicist Lord Kelvin who lectured at the Town Hall, to George Bernard Shaw (who made his last stage appearance at the end of the People's Theatre performance of his play *Candida* in 1936), to Ludwig Wittgenstein who lived and worked in Newcastle during the Second World War.

The magnetism of Tyneside enticed potentates and plenipotentiaries from across the world. In 1816 the future Tsar Nicholas I came to Northumberland to see Davy's new lamp and George Stephenson's engines at Killingworth Colliery (although he refused the offer to descend the shaft at Wallsend Colliery, exclaiming, in French, 'My God, it's the mouth of hell. None but a madman would venture into it'), and in the latter half of the century Tyneside and Wearside were visited by a string of presidents and potentates all eager to browse the latest military and industrial hardware. These included President Ulysses S. Grant (who opened the new Sunderland Library in 1877), Emir Abdur Rahman Khan of Afghanistan, King Rama V of Siam, also known as Chulalongkorn (his son, the future King Rama VI, was later made Colonel in Chief of the Durham Light Infantry, the regiment he served with after

'Keelmen Heaving in Coals by Moonlight', J.M.W. Turner, 1835. Widener Collection, National Gallery of Art, Washington, DC.

In the Coal Exchange, City of London, c 1903, artist unknown.

'Barge Day', 1891 (oil on canvas), Ralph Hedley (1848–1913). The annual Ascension Day procession of boats along the Tyne was also known as 'Barge Day'. The event was held to assert the right of the City of Newcastle to hold authority over the Tyne from Hedwin Streams, near Newburn, to the mouth of the river.

Belsay Hall, built between 1810–1817 to a design by the owner Sir Charles Monck.

A view on board the Japanese Imperial Navy's battleship *Yashima*—launched by Armstrong, Whitworth & Co at Elswick on Tyne in 1897—as she passes Jarrow.

The Crown Posada public house, Side, Newcastle, with original stained-glass windows from 1880. Posada derives from the Portuguese word for inn, and reflects the historic trading links between the Tyne and the Tagus.

'Going Home', 1888 (oil on canvas), Ralph Hedley (1848–1913), Laing Art Gallery, Newcastle-upon-Tyne.

'Fawcett Street, Sunderland', c. 1895 (oil on canvas), Daniel Whiteley Marshall.

View of Sunderland and Rowland Burdon's Iron Bridge looking eastwards, 1833. Artist unknown.

A coastal outcrop of the 'Bottom Hutton' coal seam, near St Mary's Island on the Northumberland coast.

'The Women' (1910) by John Charlton (1849-1917), depicting the launch of the Cullercoats lifeboat in 1861.

'Sunderland v Aston Villa, A Corner Kick' (1895) by Thomas Marie Madawaska Hemy (1852–1937).

Northumberland and Durham Miners Permanent Relief Fund.

Bow view of HMS Opal, torpedo boat destroyer, ready for launch at the shipyard of William Doxford & Sons Ltd, Sunderland, September 1915.

'Out of Work or Nothing Doing' (1888), by Ralph Hedley (1848–1913).

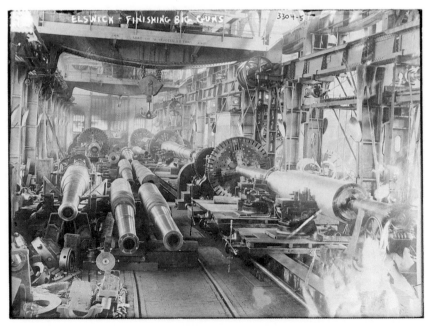

'Finishing big guns', Armstrong-Vickers factory, Elswick, Newcastle upon Tyne, 1911.

Sandhurst), and Naser al-Din, the Shah of Persia, who processed through Newcastle in 1889 escorted by a squadron of Northumberland Hussars.

* * *

What did this propitious environment mean for industrial development in North East England? In his official history of the Newcastle Lit & Phil, Robert Spence Watson—a solicitor, social reformer and lifelong member of the Society—described how the scientific experiments and debates that took place there had 'an immediate and important influence upon the entire district, and upon the social and intellectual advancement of Newcastle.'[40] The Society's list of past presidents is an embarrassment of riches—Robert Stephenson, William Armstrong, Joseph Swan, and Charles Parsons, the inventor of the compound steam turbine all made a huge impact on the wider world as much as they did on Tyneside. We might add here lesser-known Northumbrian innovators, such as Mawson, Swan and Morgan, at one time the largest suppliers of photographic dry plates in the world (George Eastman of the Kodak company spent time in Newcastle studying their processes); mechanical tinkerers such as Arthur George of the Newcastle Aero Club, whose 'triplicate control' was the forerunner of every aircraft and games console joystick; Sunderland's William Mills, whose 'bomb' was the most lethal hand-grenade of the First World War or J.A. Joblings, who started making Pyrex glass on Wearside in 1922; and Gladstone Adams, the Whitley Bay photographer who invented the windscreen-wiper after a snowy drive back up north after watching Newcastle United lose the 1908 FA Cup Final. Nor should we overlook the gaggle of local chemists that conceived both Fairy Soap and Domestos on Tyneside, as well as those effervescent remedies for debilitating crapulence: Andrews Liver Salts, Eno's Fruit Salts and Lucozade.

The Northumbria of the nineteenth century throbbed with industrial activity. It may only have had 5.1% of Britain's population, but it mined 19.6% of the coal, made 36.5% of the coke, mined 37.5% of the iron ore, produced 37.7% of the pig iron, and built 51% of the merchant ships in Britain.[41] The motto of the County Borough of Gateshead—'*Caput Inter Nubila Condit*'—was a quote from Virgil's *Aeneid* meaning 'its head is in the clouds,' chosen by the town clerk as a witty reference to the smoke of industry that wreathed the town. The Tyne itself rapidly transformed into one giant industrial complex where 'the whole distance betwixt Blaydon and the sea, on both sides of the river, forms one huge manufacturing town, so thickly are the factories strewed overall the district.'[42] The catalyst for this development was the growing industrial demand for fuel, which drove the expansion of the coal mines, which in turn required more efficient modes of transport. There had been 'railways' in the North East since 1606 when Huntingdon Beaumont constructed a horse-drawn waggonway near Bedlington, and in the eighteenth century these wooden, and later iron, highways linking the outlying collieries to the Tyne came to be known in England as 'Newcastle roads.'

The life of George Stephenson—who followed his father down the pit at Newburn as a 'penitent' (an occupation sometimes known as a 'fireman': the miner who, swathed in damp sacking, undertook the lethally dangerous task of igniting pockets of flammable gas)—spans the transition from the pre-industrial era of coalmining to the mechanical age of the railways. The resumption of war with France after 1808 led to a shortage of horses, and this spurred on innovations in locomotion. Indeed, while Napoleon was on the Retreat from Moscow, locomotives were being used on the Kenton-Coxlodge wagonway, William Hedley had designed the first of several engines used to pull wagons from Wylam Colliery to Lemington Staithes, and in 1814, George Stephenson designed 'Blucher,' a locomotive for Killingworth colliery named after the Prussian Field Marshal. Stephenson—who had been illiterate until the age of eighteen—built a reputation as an engine 'doctor,' able to fix engines and keep them running longer and more cheaply. From 1814 to 1826 he was practically the only engineer in the world building and developing new locomotive engines. From these early stirrings in the grimy colliery yards of Northumberland grew a transport system that was as decisive for the expansion of commerce as the invention of the three-masted ship in the sixteenth and seventeenth centuries. Railways subdued 'time and space' and compressed 'the march of twenty centuries … into a few prolific years.'[43]

It was Stephenson's engines that were used on the world's first passenger railway, the Stockton & Darlington, and it was his famous 'Rocket' that achieved a world record speed of 36 miles per hour at the Rainhill Trials in 1829. It was fitting that the vital spark that lit the firebox of the Locomotion came from a Darlington navvy, Robert Metcalf, who used his pipe-glass, a little magnifying lens with which he could light his pipe using the rays of the sun; 'so it was that the first locomotive to be fired on the world's most celebrated railway was lit with celestial flame stolen by Prometheus and given to man so that he might liberate himself.'[44] This was a flame passed on to George's son Robert, who despite a modest education in local schools, went on to have an astonishing career as a locomotive designer, and builder of bridges and tunnels from Egypt to Colombia. Indeed, the Kilsby Tunnel alone—vital in connecting London to Birmingham—was widely seen at the time as the greatest feat of civil engineering since the building of the Great Pyramids. After Stephenson senior died a statue was erected in 1862 near the grand terminus of Newcastle Central Station. The sculptor, John Lough—himself a self-taught Northumbrian from a modest background—modelled the composition on Pietro Tacca's gruesome monument to Ferdinando de Medici in Livorno with its four chained slaves writhing in agony. Instead of slaves, Stephenson (resplendent in a Northumbrian plaid worn like a Roman toga) is supported by four muscular figures representing the key industries that he helped to transform on Tyneside: a pitman, a smith, a railway plate-layer and an engineer modelled on George's son Robert.

The advances made in mining engineering by the Stephensons and others were as decisive as their innovations in locomotion. This was especially true after the breakthrough at Hetton Colliery in 1820 where the seemingly impermeable layer of magnesian limestone was penetrated to reach the rich seams of coal a quarter of a mile underground. This was part of the general movement of coal mining towards deeper pits at the coast, where mines would go out under the sea (in *Twenty Thousand Leagues under the Sea* Captain Nemo's crew obtain coal from subterranean seams 'like the mines of Newcastle.') The geological risks of sinking pits like these required huge capital outlay: Monkwearmouth was won in 1834 at a cost of £100,000; Murton in 1843 at a cost of £250,000—much larger sums than were spent in other coalfields, or indeed in the cotton mills or engineering works elsewhere. But the global distribution of those black diamonds, from the Baltic to Bombay, was as much down to innovations in shipbuilding as it was to the railways. By 1900 four out of every five ships in the world were built in the United Kingdom, and two out of those five were built in the shipyards of the North East coast of England. The specialties of the Tyne were, inevitably, colliers to carry coal (and latterly the first oil tankers built in Britain) and, after the rolling of armour plate was developed by Palmer's of Jarrow, the manufacture of ships for the navies of the world. It was said of yards like Armstrong's and Palmer's that iron ore went in one end and battleships came out the other.

In shipbuilding terms, Northumbria was like renaissance Venice, to the extent that the Lord Mayors of Newcastle would exert their dominion over the whole River Tyne on Ascension Day in an aquatic ceremony reminiscent of the Venetian Doges 'marrying' the Adriatic in the *Sposalizio del Mare*. The output of Sunderland alone was astonishing, and by 1850 it was considered the biggest shipbuilding town in the world. In 1905 the Wearside firm of William Doxford & Co. built twenty ships averaging 4,332 tons, and in the following year the yard launched an average of one ship per fortnight. Despite the efficiency of this output, ships were typically bespoke to the purchaser's requirements, and often objects of great beauty and precision. The clipper *Torrens*, built by J. Laing & Co in Sunderland in 1875, was a good example. In 1891 Joseph Conrad was her first mate during her voyages to Australia, and he wrote of her that this was a vessel

> of brilliant qualities—the way the ship had of letting big seas slip under her did one's heart good to watch. It resembled so much an exhibition of intelligent grace and unerring skill that it could fascinate even the least seamanlike of our passengers.[45]

Such was the last generation of sailing vessels, but Northumbrian innovations helped to conceive the next generation of great ships. In 1897 Charles Parsons shocked the world with his Wallsend-built steamship *Turbinia*, then the fastest thing on the seven seas thanks to Parsons' invention of the compound steam-turbine, and it skipped along past the Grand Fleet anchored at Spithead for the Diamond Jubilee in 1897 at an unprecedented 32 knots (38 miles per hour). The *New Marine Motor* described it as

> like a living creature endowed with intelligence, the staunch little vessel seemed palpitating with a resolve to show what she could do. The deck openings were fastened down, the air, driven by a fan, roared through the fires and into the chimney, steam was pressed into the motors, and the vessel leaped forwards as a greyhound darts from the leash.[46]

The first of the Royal Navy's Dreadnoughts were all fitted with Parsons' engines, as was the famous *Mauretania*, launched in 1906 by Swan Hunter and Wigham Richardson at the Neptune Yard in Wallsend. Kipling called her a 'monstrous nine-decked city' and her 70,000 horsepower steam turbines made the *Mauretania* the biggest and fastest liner in the world (she held the Blue Riband for the fastest Atlantic crossing from 1907 to 1929). Such innovations were matched by the building of mighty warships on the Tyne, from the Edwardian capital ships *Hercules*, *Canada* and *Malaya* that fought at Jutland, to HMS *King George V* which caught the *Bismarck* in the Denmark Strait in 1941. Even the landing craft used on D-Day were designed by Susan Auld from Tynemouth (1915–2002), the first woman to graduate as a naval architect from Armstrong College in Newcastle.

The insatiable local demand for sources of power led to the birth of the electricity industry on Tyneside. Armstrong and Swan had been the pioneers, and North East England saw the first house in the world lit by electricity (Swan's home at Underhill, Gateshead), and the first street to be so illuminated (Mosley Street in Newcastle), but there were others who conceived world-changing inventions. It was a Quaker from Newcastle, John Henry Holmes, who invented the modern 'quick break' electrical switch in 1884 at his factory in Shieldfield. The use of Charles Parsons' turbines on ships is still their best-known application but their role in the development of power generation was just as decisive. In 1902, two Parsons 1500-kilowatt steam turbine driven turbo-alternators, then the largest in the world, were used at Neptune Bank on the Tyne, the first real central power station with integrated control in Great Britain, and the only British power station to provide electricity for industrial purposes (rather than for domestic use or street lighting).

The driving force behind this were Theodore and Charles Merz, father and son industrialists and innovators from Newcastle. Merz senior, a chemist and intellectual of German origins—who somehow found the time to write a four-volume *History of European Thought in the Nineteenth Century*—had founded what would become the North Eastern Electric Supply Company (NESCo) in 1888. His son, the electrical engineer Charles Hesterman Merz (1874–1940)—dubbed the 'British Edison'—with his partner, the Scotsman William McLellan, used this company as a platform to pioneer power distribution using standard voltages and frequencies across the North East, and in so doing create Britain's first large scale network of power distribution—the forerunner of the modern National Grid.[47] NESCo had a global order book and exported cutting-edge turbine machinery that lit up cities in Germany, Australia, and the USA (the city of Chicago had two major power stations equipped with hardware made in Newcastle).[48] This generated further industrial growth on Tyneside, with Reyrolles of Hebburn specialising in heavy electrical equipment and switching gear, and led directly to the creation, in 1904, of the first electrified railway outside London: 'the Tyneside electrics' which in its first year issued 42,800,000 tickets on its network. Its eventual successor, the Tyne and Wear Metro, was still transporting over 40 million passengers over a century later.[49]

* * *

To a remarkable extent the industrialists of nineteenth-century Northumbria were learned men. We have one account of a pit-sinking at Percy Main in the 1820s where, after beef and plum pudding, strong beer and punch were served, and 'The Keel Row' was sung, the master sinker quoted Virgil in his opening speech.[50] These were more than just entrepreneurs looking for the next business deal—although they were certainly ruthless capitalists—they were men who kept abreast of the latest technologies and scientific research. When the British Association chose Newcastle for its annual meeting in 1838—with some of the greatest boffins of the time in attendance: Babbage, Herschel and Whewell—they would have been among like-minds. These were the sort of men who published papers in the *Transactions of the Newcastle Chemical Society*, attended lectures at the College of Science (endowed by Armstrong), or like those of a more literary bent, such as the shipbuilder John Wigham Richardson, held regular Virgil evenings at home for the movers and shakers in industry, commerce and local government. 'When the main works of that poet had been covered, Horace came next, though a proposal to move on to Lucretius 'frightened some of our members."[51] Even the chairman of Armstrong Whitworth—then one of the largest arms manufacturers in the world—John Meade Falkner, moonlighted as an antiquarian and highly successful novelist, authoring *Moonfleet* and *The Lost Stradivarius*. But the Northumbrian Enlightenment was not solely an elite project. The innovation and productivity that characterised North East England relied on the keen intelligence of upper and middle management as well as the men literally at the coal-face of industry.

The intelligence of the ordinary working man was hymned by the former miner turned writer Sid Chaplin, who wrote that the great achievements of Northumbrian industry were only made possible by a 'brilliant generation of colliery managers and pit engineers'; and for all of the great names—Palmer, Swan Hunter, Merz et al.—each of these had their 'legions of workmen who included incomparable engineering craftsmen.'[52] But their keen practical intelligence was matched by a deep curiosity and surprising intellectualism. In Robert Colls' classic history, *The Pitmen of the Northern Coalfield*, he described how 'a secular trinity of Reason, Knowledge, and Labour Value beamed upon those pitmen who could spell words, read books, and perform intellectual arguments.'[53] For autodidacts like Thomas Burt, a Northumberland miner and trade union official, who became Britain's first working class MP, or Peter Lee (1864–1935), a Durham miner, Methodist preacher and leader of Britain's first Labour-controlled County Council, intelligence and commitment to self-improvement was a route to high office. This, and their high wages, contributed to the miners' sense of themselves as a 'Labour Aristocracy,' a concept that gained a bad name in Marxist circles, where miners in particular were seen as capitalism's 'fifth column.' Lenin himself, upon studying the British working class, criticised the 'the petty bourgeois craft spirit which prevails among this aristocracy of labour' and their 'insular, aristocratic, and philistine' trades unions. But on that last point at least Lenin was wrong: these were the least philistine proletarians in the world.

To begin with, coalmining was not just about brute strength: it required a workforce that understood maths, physics and chemistry just as much as one with tenacity and muscle power. They may have been patronised by W. H. Auden as 'lurcher loving colliers, black as night' but their keen practical intelligence made for curious minds, and the autodidact from a humble background is a common trope in Northumbrian history. In his hugely influential 1859 book, *Self-Help*, Samuel Smiles's argued that it was a man's duty to educate himself, and when the Tyneside-born philosopher John Gray remarked on BBC Radio 4 in 2018 that 'I'm prouder of what I've read than of what I've written', he was expressing a view that was once common in the coalfields and shipyards. These were home to bibliophiles such as the Gateshead miner Joseph Hopper, the founder of the Durham Aged Mine-Workers' Homes Association, a staunch Primitive Methodist who preached his first sermon at fifteen and who read avidly in political economy, history and biography (with Macaulay and J.S. Mill among his favourite authors)[54]. Or the Sunderland-born Thomas Dixon (1831–80), who—when he wasn't cutting cork in the shipyards of the Wear—would spend his evenings in the Sunderland Mechanics' Institute, which was inaugurated in 1825 to 'educate the illiterate, to direct the studious, and to afford everything necessary to the intelligent and ingenious'. Dixon carried on a long correspondence with some of the leading artistic and literary figures of the day, most notably John Ruskin who saw Dixon as 'the highest type of working man.' (Ruskin published his side of the correspondence, with extracts from Dixon's letters as an appendix, in *Time and Tide by Weare and Tyne: 25 letters to a Working Man of Sunderland on the Laws of Work*.)

But as well as the studious there were ordinary men who wore their learning lightly and amusingly, such as the pitman who worked with the South Shields miner Tommy Turnbull—known as 'Two Williams' because he would recite William Blake or William Wordsworth at the coalface. As Turnbull recalled:

At times maybe something had happened and the machines had stopped running, or you were somewhere away from the main part of the pit and somebody had said something that had made everybody go quiet. Then all of a sudden you'd hear this big deep voice of Two Williams:

Ti-ger, ti-ger, bur-ning bri-ght
In the for-ests of the ni-ght.

What im-mortal hand or eye,
Could weave thy fear-ful sym-me-try.[55]

The archetype here is the Durham miner, Jack Lawson, who ended his career in the House of Lords (via Ruskin College) after serving as Attlee's Secretary of State for War. Lawson's marvelous autobiography *A Man's Life* describes how, from his early teens, this ordinary pitman from Boldon Colliery immersed himself in great literature and philosophy. In wonderfully lucid prose Lawson paints magical vignettes of pitmen discussing the finer points of Nietzsche and Thomas à Kempis at the coalface, or Lawson himself reading Milton to his new wife in their tiny pit cottage. For Lawson, book-learning and exposure to the best of art and culture was a simple matter of justice:

> I had actually arrived at the conclusion that if there were any good life, and freedom from insecurity, and beauty and knowledge, or leisure, then the men who did the world's dirty, sweaty, toilsome, risky work, and the women who shared the life with them, ought to be the first entitled to these things ... I held that no man needs knowledge more than he who is subject to those who have. That if there is one man in the world who needs knowledge, it is he who does the world's most needful work.[56]

Much of the groundwork for this pursuit of knowledge was laid by the Methodists, whose love of scripture and hymn-singing cascaded literacy across rural and urban Northumbria. In 1842 the cleric William Gilly wrote of an encounter in North Northumberland with the family of 'a fine tall man of about forty-five—a fair specimen of the frank, sensible, well-spoken, well-informed Northumbrian peasantry' where it was noted that 'as to the food for our peasant's mind ... it is the Bible ... and the Prayer Book, some few other books of devotions, of history, or of useful knowledge, are ranged side by side of the Bible; and they all show that they have been frequently read.'[57] This was the same culture that produced the first Protestant missionary to China: a former shoe-maker from Morpeth called Robert Morrison (1782–1834), who translated the Bible into Chinese and compiled the first major Chinese-English dictionary. Indeed, it has been said that the spread of Non-Conformist Christianity in the coalfields led to a sort of cultural revolution where colliers were encouraged to turn away from drinking and gambling towards the Wesleyan light of order and respectability.[58]

The effects of Methodist preaching and Bible classes could be remarkable: at Killingworth Colliery in 1818 it was noted that, since the introduction of a Sunday school in the village, even at the coalface 'where blasphemies of every description used to be heard, one of the lads is to be seen reading the Bible to those sitting around him in the most profound silence.'[59] Methodist Chapels and Workingmen's Institutes came to fulfil the same role for the Northumbrian working classes as Yeshivas did for the Jews of Eastern Europe. Nor should we forget the remarkable degree of religious literacy among the Irish Catholic working classes in Britain in the era of the 'penny catechism.' This culture was reinforced by their employers too who invested in foundations like the Elswick Mechanics' Institute, with its well-equipped laboratories, 500-seat lecture theatre and ambitious scientific curriculum. 'It is by means of books that working men can bring themselves into communion with highly gifted cultivated minds,' declared the institute's funder and patron Lord Armstrong, and it is from this that they will 'derive instruction, refinement and amusement from doing so ... it will increase his happiness and exalt his nature.'[60]

In the winter of 1883, over 1,000 miners lost wages and paid fines for missed shifts to attend workers' lectures in Newcastle on science, history and political economy, and the North East became an early hotbed of the Workers' Education movement where 'the only qualification was an enquiring mind.' In Sting's Broadway production of the self-penned *The Last Ship*, a show based on his hometown of Wallsend, he plays the character of shipyard foreman Jackie White, whose surprisingly broad literary references—Homer, Pliny, Tacitus—epitomise a certain type of auto-didact that once flourished in the North East, and may have been inspired by the work of the real-life shipyard poet Jack Davitt, a welder at Swan Hunter's, whose *nom de plume* 'Ripyard Cuddling' and heroic verses on industrial and historic themes were a sardonic allusion to the work of Kipling and others.

We should be careful not to exaggerate how commonplace was such a love of learning; the race track and beer house always retained their charms (as we shall see in Chapter 5). At Seaton Delaval Colliery in the 1850s it was admitted that only a self-taught elite had joined the library—33 out of 850 colliers. Much of the high-minded attempts to steer working men towards self-improvement were driven by the sense that if they were reading, they were reading the wrong things. The antiquarian Eneas Mackenzie asserted in 1827 that the Newcastle Religious Tract Society was intended 'to drive foolish ballads, tales, and stories out of circulation.' Some of these objections were political, as in the case of the Sunderland informer William Coxton who wrote to Robert Peel in 1828 complaining about a publican whose shop opposite Bishopwearmouth church was 'covered with infidel placards; songs calculated to bring sacred subjects into contempt; and books of a similar

tendency.' Such Chartist material was undoubtedly popular. In 1851 the largest vendor of periodicals and papers in Newcastle sold 3,976 copies of such
matter, to only 888 classified as 'Religious and Moral. Containing useful
information.'[71] Even into the twentieth century the North Shields-born
writer Tom Hadaway recalled the common admonition for bookworms like
him that 'you cannot catch a fish with a pen nib,' while the playwright Lee
Hall wrote that as a child he had 'no idea what a play was, or how you wrote
them,' and 'when I grew up the notion of reading books didn't make you a
swot, but a poof.'[62]

And yet, there was a steady stream of supremely talented working-class
writers who made their mark. Catherine Cookson, whose tales of family life
on industrial Tyneside would make her the most borrowed author from
Britain libraries, first had her love of words kindled by finding a copy of Lord
Chesterfield's *Letters to His Son* in South Shields library. She was working as a
laundress in the local workhouse at the time, but Chesterfield's advice that 'if
you improve and grow learned everyone will be fond of you' spoke directly
to the young Catherine who recalled falling asleep reading his letters and
waking 'round three o'clock in the morning deep in the fascination of this
new world ... where the brilliance of words made your heart beat faster.'[63]
The novelist Jack Common, future friend and correspondent of George
Orwell, was similarly smitten with *belles-lettres* growing up in a Tyneside flat
near the railway sheds in Heaton. A love of great literature sharpened the pen
of this 'Geordie Proust' who was moved by 'the birds at dawn, as well as the
babble of the lounge bar,' yet as Common himself admitted in later life, the
life of a working-class writer was not an easy one: 'There's no talking to the
lightning-struck, the fatally illuminated are always alone.'[64]

Nevertheless, the light-from-darkness possibilities of coal-mining in particular has provided a rich seam for writers and dramatists, starting perhaps
with Michael Redgrave attempting a Tyneside accent in *The Stars Look Down*
(1940), and continuing with Alan Plater and Alex Glasgow's *Close the Coalhouse
Door* (1968) and Lee Hall's modern classics, *Billy Elliot* (which no
Northumbrian can watch with dry eyes), and *The Pitmen Painters*, those
Ashington miners that represented what was probably the high-water mark
of the North East working class's culture of self-improvement and intellectual
curiosity. (The permanent collection of their work was the first exhibition of
Western art held in China after Mao Tse-tung's Cultural Revolution, as
Chinese officials were much taken with the idea of workers' art.)[65] Leaning
on his own mining experiences, few could describe the coalface as evocatively
as the former Durham miner Sid Chaplin:

They take a little and go into the belly of Leviathan. They take a lamp into the most terrifying darkness and they are not afraid. They take a little light because underground they know their poverty. Without light their arms are useless. In the strata they meet a darkness like a velvet pad pressed against the open eye, and this darkness, without a little light, is impenetrable and eager. At 200 fathoms the sun takes no levy nor gives of his majesty ... All is without form and void.[66]

Self-expression through the plastic arts has not always been associated with North East England. John Martin's apocalyptic canvasses were utterly unique, and Northumbrian painting over the last three centuries has seldom achieved real distinction. One author has written that it's 'piss artists [that] are the group most commonly associated with Newcastle.'[67] But there were occasional shafts of artistic light amid the darkness. The career of the sculptor John Lough is illuminating. Born in 1798 near Shotley Bridge, the son of a blacksmith whose dog-eared copies of Homer and Gibbon inspired him and his brother to make thousands of clay models of Greeks and Gladiators, Lough was thought by many to 'rank with Bewick and Stephenson, whose humble origins he shared, as the third great Northumbrian of the age.'[68] One of his first jobs was as a stonemason building Newcastle's Literary & Philosophical Society, but Lough had a passion for the heroic and dramatic, and we have a touching account of him hitching a lift to London on a North Sea collier to see the Elgin marbles.[69] After his death, his technically brilliant but rather pompous compositions fell quickly out of fashion, but the ambition of his works and their classical allusion—from his 'Fall of Phaeton' that graced the porch of 10 Carlton House Terrace in St James's to his massive clay model of the Olympic wrestling champion Milo of Croton that required him to break a hole in the ceiling of his London lodgings—well-illustrate the heights of erudition that were within the reach of ordinary Northumbrians, but which was often met with incomprehension. 'I'm sick of being looked at like some sort of zoo animal or specimen,' observed the Durham pitman turned artist Norman Cornish in an interview; 'out of the depths comes this bloke and paints his pictures. It assumes that a man who works in a mine is not up to writing or painting or playing music. But it simply isn't true.'[70]

This erudition was communicated in a language that was sometimes hard for outsiders to understand but was a euphonious instrument in the hands of experts. In 1884 the *Newcastle Daily Chronicle* serialised a novel by their proprietor. In *A Sea Queen* one of the protagonists remarks that

In the mouths of the lower orders, Newcastle English is ... a very rugged and grotesque tongue, as unintelligible to the stranger as Dutch ... On the other hand, there is nothing sweeter than the pronunciation of the educated

Tynesider. There is something fascinating to listen to in the silken rippling of a Newcastle lady's speech, and the burr and an unconscious sprinkling of expressive local words will make the veriest commonplace attractive in a cultivated male speaker.[71]

We can hear this characteristic combination of musicality and terminological exactitude in a record of Thomas Bewick telling an anecdote of fighting off a mastiff dog, which he caught by the hind legs and gave 'such a hell o' a thwacker owre the lumbar vertebrae, that sent him howling into a hovel.'[72] The modern children's writer David Almond has talked of the richness of North-East dialect and his desire to 'illustrate the artistic richness of the North-East voice, and its aptness for engaging with intellectually demanding subject matter.'[73] The word for this industrial dialect was 'pitmatic,' and its similarity with mathematics and mathematical was meant to convey something of the practical craft of mining. Richard Heslop in the 1880s listed 'pitmatics—the technicalities of colliery-working' in his dictionary of Northumberland words. This private language of pitmen soon pervaded the speech of Northumbrians across the coalfields, blending older dialect with modern technical terms.

Consider the analysis offered by a Parliamentary Commissioner in the 1840s when faced with the task of interviewing North East pitmen:

> The barriers to our intercourse were formidable. In fact, their numerous mining technicalities, northern provincialisms, peculiar intonation and accents, and rapid and indistinct utterance, rendered it essential for me... to devote myself to the study of these peculiarities ere I could translate and write the evidence.[74]

The third main theory as to the origins of Geordie (along with supposed allegiance to the Hanoverians, and the local preference for 'Geordie' Stephenson's miner's lamp over Sir Humphrey Davy's rival design) comes from the evidence that George Stephenson had to give to Parliamentary enquiries into railway building in the 1840s. The great engineer's accent and dialect caused the mostly Southern and upper-class parliamentarians no little difficulty, and 'Geordie' Stephenson's accent was mocked and mimicked. But his forthright style did earn him everlasting fame when he responded to one questioner who suggested that would it not be very serious and awkward if any obstructions—a cow, for instance—got upon the railway in front of the engine? 'Yes,' he replied, 'varry aakward—for the coo.'[75]

Despite such accusations of incomprehensibility, the language was—and still is—considered an attractive one, and in his book *The Pronology of a South*

Durham Dialect the distinguished surveyor of English dialects Professor Harold Orton described the inhabitants of the colliery village of Byers Green as being characterised by an

> alertness of mind and independence ... [the villagers] tend to express their opinions with an outspoken blunt candour. Their everyday speech—Pitmatic, they call it—is free from all traces of mumbling and drawling. It is in fact an extremely vigorous dialect.[76]

The Lee Hall play *The Pitmen Painters* (about an unlikely art class of Ashington miners) makes great use of the richness of this language, and the comedic potential for misunderstanding—ye dee dee *art* divvunt ye? ('you do do art don't you?') always brings the house down when performed in the North East—but for workingmen to have an intellectual hinterland was as surprising to modern theatregoers as it was to baffled art professors and mass observers in the 1930s. One review criticised Hall for dabbling the otherwise solidly working-class vocabularies of his characters with 'randomly refined verbs and adjectives,' thinking it unlikely that miners would use a word like 'gallivanting.'[77] Yet my own grandparents' speech was exactly like this: unalloyed 'pitmatic' Geordie, with frequent Dickensian flourishes, like gallivanting (a word they used all the time). Their everyday conversation was littered with words such as vexed, reconnoitre, transpire, and my grandmother's favourite: impertinent (pronounced 'impittent').

Alongside the deep roots of Northumbrian literacy there had always been a highly developed oral culture in Northumbria, where chapbooks, printed songs and broadsides sold in huge numbers.[78] The nineteenth-century headmaster and historian John Collingwood Bruce was obsessed by preserving the 'great wealth of history and tradition, legend and story, poetry and song ... which abound in the ancient kingdom of Northumbria ... no district is richer.' The growth of popular works of local history—such as the *Monthly Chronicle of North Country Lore and Legend*, published in Newcastle—was an ideal prop for story-telling.[79] This fed a culture where the 'the crack' (whose Hibernicisation into 'the craic' is a modern development) was vital, and wit was celebrated. Once while watching Newcastle United struggle as usual from the bar of New Hartley Workingmen's Club I was much amused by the deadpan literary rejoinder to one fan's plaintive cry that the Toon 'need an impact sub here, man!' 'Aye', came the response, 'like the f***ing Nautilus.' But badinage like this is commonplace: think of the Sunderland comic Bobby Thompson's witty monologues, the surprisingly erudite humour in *Viz* ('in the 1930s RAF boffins discovered that their 'Gaydar' technology could also detect enemy aircraft'), or how Sid Waddell, the Ashington miner's son who went to Cambridge, peppered his unsurpassed darts commentary with surreal classical allusions: 'When Alexander of Macedonia was 33, he cried salt tears because there were no more worlds to conquer ... but Eric Bristow's only 27!'

But where did such eloquence come from? Walter Scott believed that the wilder the society the more violent the impulse received from poetry and music, and this had led to a uniquely vibrant culture of song and poetry on both sides of the Anglo-Scottish border.[80] The lives of the industrial working classes could be similarly dangerous and unpredictable and caused a flourishing of poetry and popular song—especially 'disaster ballads'—in the coalfields. One native poet, Joseph Skipsey (1832–1903), a self-taught miner from Percy Main who'd worked underground from the age of seven (whose father, Cuthbert Skipsey was shot dead by police in the industrial disturbances of the 1830s) was the first example of a group of 'pitman poets' among whose number we could mention the Durham miners Tommy Armstrong and Jock Purdon who gained a large following in the twentieth century. In 1866 Skipsey published *Carols from the Coalfields*, drawing praise from Rossetti and Oscar Wilde, who likened the poems to those of William Blake, and, in an eclectic career that included stints as a librarian at the Lit & Phil and the custodian of Shakespeare's birthplace in Stratford upon Avon, Skipsey returned to mining as the pay was better.

Joseph Robson's *Blossoms of Poesy*, published in Newcastle in 1831, can be considered typical of a dialect oeuvre that was widely popular. Robson was even invited to translate the 'Song of Solomon' into the 'dialect of the colliers of Northumberland':

> Fine raws o' jools hing doon thaw cheeks;
> Thaw neck's wiv goold-cheyns fet;
> But gooldin borders thoo mun ha'e,
> Wiv filler buttons, pet![81]

The traditional Northumbrian appreciation for the dramatic arts shared similar roots (although only a fragment remains of the fourteenth-century Newcastle Mystery Play cycle, where, on the Feast of Corpus Christi, the Shipwrights' Guild performed the biblical story of Noah's Ark). Venues like the Sunderland Empire and Newcastle Theatre Royal have long been nationally important—the latter gained its royal license in 1788—and the North East was one of the last areas in England to retain a strong music hall scene, where good humour and verbal dexterity were highly prized. Such venues helped to launch the careers of men like Geordie Ridley (composer of the

Blaydon Races), Ned Corvan and Joe Wilson, whose work was compiled in the best-selling *Allan's Tyneside Songs and Drolleries*.

In J. B. Priestley's *English Journey* he seemed to have forgotten how much he had enjoyed Newcastle theatres while stationed there as a soldier in 1915, and was astonished to find a group from the *People's Theatre* (a socialist theatre company co-founded by Colin Veitch, the intelligent captain of Newcastle United's great Edwardian team) rehearsing Euripides' *Trojan Women* in a pub by the castle (the Bridge Hotel). Successive Royal Shakespeare Company directors have referred to 'Newcastle's discerning and intelligent theatre-going audiences,'[82] but this extended into the coalfields too, where actors of national renown performed at the Everyman Theatre in Spennymoor under an outreach scheme led by the Old Vic. Here miners and their wives in the Drama Group spent their evenings discussing Stanislavski's 'Method,' and Peggy Ashcroft once announced to an audience at the Globe Theatre that 'the most educated and the most responsive audience she had ever found was a group of miners at their community theatre in Spennymoor!'[83] Max Roberts, the long-standing creative director of the Live Theatre on the Newcastle Quayside once told me that when he first joined the company in the 1980s he toured quite high-brow shows around community venues—including the Miners' Rehabilitation Centre near Bedlington, where the audiences were never less than tough, yet 'it was always a canny gig though but.'

* * *

Can we say with confidence that the North East of England is still as thickly spread with intelligence and ingenuity? One recent study concluded, depressingly, that the North of England in recent years has been 'poorer, less healthy, less educated and slower growing than the south,' and this was largely explained by 'selective outmigration of the educated and talented' to more promising areas of the country.[84] The precipitate decline of hegemonic heavy industry pulled the rug from under the local economy, and hard data on GCSE results tells us that in 2018 64.5% of entries in the region were at least a grade C (or a 4 under the numerical system now used for the majority of reformed exams), up from 63.4% in 2017 but still behind the UK pass rate of 66.9%. And yet much was made in 2014 of the fact that the North East was the only region of the UK with a positive balance of trade in exports. Part of this was down to the resilience of manufacturing, as any drive past the industrial sheds on the A19 will attest, but also in new and innovative industries—especially in hi-tech sectors. It is little known that Britain's first online purchase was made in 1984 by a Gateshead pensioner called Jane Snowball (via a home-shopping scheme run by the local council), and the chief design officer of Apple, Sir Jony Ive, designer of the iMac and iPod, is a graduate of Newcastle Polytechnic (now Northumbria University). And the Centre for Life in Newcastle—a collaboration between the city's University and NHS Foundation Trust under the direction of the pioneering clinical geneticist Professor Sir John Burn (who was born and raised in the old Durham pit village of West Auckland)—was the first institution in Europe to be licensed to carry out stem cell research and clone human embryos.

Perhaps, then, the Northumbrian Enlightenment has not yet run its course, and remains a motive force in North East England. 'Invest North East England' claims that the region has the highest proportion of students studying STEM subjects in the UK,[85] and there was much satisfaction in the North East when the powerful teraelectron beams of the Large Hadron Collider in Geneva confirmed the reality of an elementary particle known as 'the Higgs Boson' after the Newcastle-born physicist who first predicted its existence, Professor Peter Higgs. In the tech sector the North East now has over 28,000 people employed in Digital and IT—leading the Minister for Digital, Culture, Media and Sport to describe the North East in 2017 as the fastest growing tech hub outside of London (prompting 'Tech on the Tyne' headlines in *The Times*).[86] It is significant though that even in this dynamic, entrepreneurial sector that Northumbrian inclination towards a certain corporatism, and the guiding hand of the state, has manifested itself in an 'Innovation SuperNetwork,' which we are told is the first network of its kind in the UK' using its 'unique position and overview of the region to ignite innovation and new collaborations.'[87] Moreover, despite the surface gloss, these industries are just as male-dominated as heavy engineering ever was, full of obsessive men tinkering with code where once they'd have been fiddling with gears and sprockets. The local tech sector may be growing fast, noted the *Evening Chronicle*, but it's 'still a boys club' with 'some of the lowest proportions of female workers in the country.'[88] Sunderland now pitches itself as 'Software City' and Newcastle is home to accounting software specialists Sage Group (now the UK's second largest technology company) and Ubisoft, the world's third largest producer of video games. Even Greggs the Bakers, which grew from a single shop on Gosforth High Street in 1951 to 1,968 branches nationwide by 2019, is one of the leading companies in Britain to effectively utilise 'the internet of things,' using technology to connect their tills and ovens to 'forecast and replenish' and better respond to the ever-growing customer demand for their stottie-cakes and sausage rolls.

* * *

Visitors to the Gateshead Quays in 2018 would have seen a touching evocation of the enduring pursuit of illumination in North East England. 'To Give Light (Northern Aspirational Charms)' by the artist Ryan Gander comprised ten black concrete sculptures, each representing light-emitting Northern inventions, the 'Geordie lamp' of 1815, the friction match of 1827, and the incandescent light bulb of 1875. What made this composition especially potent was that each of these sculptures featured a light-emitting ring of 'Nitecrete'—a patented type of photo-luminescent aggregate made by a firm from the former coal-mining town of Prudhoe. But this impulse towards illumination can be as much emotional as practical. When Sunderland AFC demolished their old football ground at Roker Park in 1997 they built a new stadium on the site of the old Wearmouth Colliery, and gave it a name that—although much-mocked by Newcastle fans for its rhyming potential—was a moving evocation of what the old industries did to illuminate the people and places of North East England:

> For many years, miners at Wearmouth Colliery carried with them a Davy Lamp as part of their everyday working lives. Reflecting this tradition, the name allows the image of this light to shine forever. The Sunderland Stadium of Light reflects the desire of the Club and its supporters to be in the limelight, and like a torch signifies and illuminates the way forward. The name—like the Stadium—will radiate like a beacon to the football world.

This theme of *chiaroscuro* recurs in Wearside history: from the dazzling light of Wearmouth-Jarrow in the Dark Ages and William Reid Clanny's invention of the very first practical miners' lamp in 1812, to Joseph Swan's experiments with incandescent materials in the 1850s. Sunderland even launched a festival of light amid the gloomy depths of post-war Britain when the annual 'Sunderland Illuminations' were inaugurated on the Roker seafront in 1949. This drew four million visitors in its first year and has been a fixture ever since, but Sunderland now has competition from its neighbours on Wearside. 'Lumiere' in Durham has become the UK's largest light festival, and takes over the old city for three days in November with fantastical displays—an elephant on Elvet Bridge and a whale in the Wear! But the festival's most spectacular *coup de theatre* is the projection onto the very walls of the cathedral of some of Northumbria's first, dazzling attempts at illumination: the stained glass of Durham itself and the pages of the Lindisfarne Gospels.

Fiat Lux!

4

THE SPARTA OF THE NORTH

Here was an architecture for storm and driving cloud, for sombre ships and battering sea.

Niklaus Pevsner, *Northumberland*, 1954

Tramlines and slagheaps, pieces of machinery,
That was, and still is, my ideal scenery.

W.H. Auden, 'Letter to Lord Byron,' 1937

Northumbria in the age of Cuthbert and Bede was the Tibet of the British Isles. In windswept monasteries on rocky headlands, muddy riverbanks and tidal islands, bands of shivering monks would offer up Latin incantations for a good harvest or protection from sea-borne danger. When the Danes invaded in 793 the monks of Lindisfarne departed their island for good, hoisting St Cuthbert's incorrupt body onto a bier and beginning an epic peregrination through Northumbria in search of a new home. After years of wandering this caravan of monks settled first in Chester-le-Street, but when they again became vulnerable they were guided by providence to Dun Holm (meaning the 'hill-island'): a steep and wooded rock on a peninsula in the River Wear. There they planted a church, which would grow into the great cathedral of Durham.

Cuthbert's asceticism—he only seemed to eat raw onions and the eggs of seabirds, and would stand on the shore for hours knee-deep in prayer and freezing sea-water—seemed to match the landscape of the places he inhabited, in life and in death. That monastic tradition has helped to shape much of what is still a recognisable Northumbrian aesthetic: unfussy, unadorned, even Spartan. This is especially true of the vernacular architecture of North East England, but in public art too. The starkness of Fenwick Lawson's sculpture in Durham City, 'The Journey,' of six hooded monks carrying St Cuthbert's coffin (which the artist carved out of rough blocks of wood with a chainsaw), is illustrative. It captures a sense of the severity of that world, and the grit of the people who lived in it. The same too could be said of other recent public art in Northumbria, which looks back to a harsh and gruelling past. The Sisyphean 'Steel Men' spring to mind here, those stick-like figures at Sunderland bent double pushing great boulders of coal up the banks of the Wear; or the sky-scraping 'Angel of the North,' Gateshead's response in all its uncompromising virility to the priapic giant of the South at Cerne Abbot.

'Northumberland is a rough county; that is its great attraction,' wrote Nikolaus Pevsner in his introduction to the Northumberland volume of his *Buildings of England* series:

> Rough are the winds, rough the moors, rough the miners, rough are the castles, rough the dolerite cliffs by the Roman wall and on the coast, rough is the stone of the walls which take the place of hedges, if you compare it with the walling of the Cotswolds, and rough seems even the smoother and more precisely worked stone under the black soot of Newcastle.[1]

Northumbrian landscapes have gripped the imagination for centuries. Thomas Bewick wrote of his time spent in London that he was 'determined to return home to the scenery of Tyneside, which seemed altogether to form a paradise for me & I longed to see it again.'[2] The 2012 posters for the first of Peter Jackson's 'The Lord of the Rings' trilogy used the view from Corby Crag, above Alnwick, looking west towards Edlingham Castle and the Simonside Hills to depict Middle Earth. Even the more picturesque stretches are more often described as austere, the north Pennines in particular, above all the barren stretches North of the Wall up towards the border, broken only by blocks of solid woodland like manoeuvring columns of Roman infantry. As the Scottish journalist Alex Massie once wrote of a particularly scenic part of Northumberland: 'Redesdale is so stern and wildly beautiful it should be in Scotland.'[3]

In the eighteenth century Montesquieu argued that 'the physical aspect of the country' ('*physique du pays*'), the terrain, location and extent, alongside the climate are decisive in shaping the 'the way of life of the peoples ... their inclinations, their wealth, their number, their commerce, their mores, and their manners.'[4] That French concept of *terroir* in describing both the human use of landscape and how this has had a fundamental role in shaping patterns of behaviour, is useful here. For it is hard to avoid a similar conclusion about the North East of England, especially when the relationship between people and landscape was so symbiotic. 'Canada's a bare land / For the north wind

and the snow. / Northumberland's a bare land / For men have made it so'—
as Basil Bunting put it in *Briggflatts*. The landscape here grabs your attention,
as the terrain which slopes down from the Pennines in the south—the
Romans called them the *dorsum Britanniae* as if England were a great whale—
to the Cheviots in the north is divided by rivers and burns that flow generally
west to east through a distinctive rolling landform of sequential ridges, valleys
and denes.

Such scenery has coloured how the rest of the country views the inhabitants. 'The miners and fishermen of Devon, Cornwall and Northumberland
were as far away from London as the English could get' wrote Robert Colls
'and were usually described in the same terms as their environment: hard,
simple, natural.'[5] It was the extractive industries in particular that drove a
fascination with the land and the natural world, in every strata of society.
There were the gentleman geologists of Newcastle who made fortunes
from coal and ironstone (the city had a natural history museum decades
before it had an art gallery), but there were also the obsessive allotment
gardeners, leek-growers and pigeon-fanciers of the pit villages. That unusual
emulsion of rural and industrial life that was such a feature of the mining
country of eastern Durham and south east Northumberland made the
people who lived there literally and figuratively down to earth, and peculiarly well-matched to a countryside that was if not always beautiful then
certainly visually arresting.

For several years in the early part of this century North East tourism was
marketed with the slogan 'Passionate People, Passionate Places.' At the time
this didn't make sense to me (how can places be passionate?), but I now think
it articulated a truth about place and people—and explains so much about the
Northumbrian imagination. This feeling was shaped as much by the Methodist
revivals of the nineteenth century—'the theology was battle raising, the
hymns were martial, the preaching was led by men who saw the world as a
fight'—but that they first got under way in the wild open air of Weardale and
Teesdale must have swelled a sense of divine communion.[6] Indeed, the sub-
lime backdrop of his native Allendale was a major influence on that extraordinary painter of Old Testament devastation, John Martin. His great celestial
masterpiece *The Plains of Heaven*, is thought to be based on his native valley.
Martin started out as a Newcastle coach painter but works like *Sadak in Search
of the Waters of Oblivion*, or *the Destruction of Sodom and Gomorrah*, with their
signature flourishes of tiny figures in vast, vertiginous, blood-tinged landscapes, confirmed him as the greatest set-designer of his age, and firmly
placed in the company of Shelley, Byron, and Delacroix.[7]

It is not only the natural landscapes of Northumbria that have impressed and inspired. 'Who says there is no beauty nor poetry in coal and grime and smoke, in huddled tenements, high chimneys, and such things?' wrote the novelist William Clark Russell after visiting the Tyne in the 1880s. 'Viewed from the rushing, broken, tossing river,' there were 'screw-ships with volumes of steam blowing from their sides…tugs rapidly darting to and fro or toiling along with a string of barges in their wake,' steamships looming 'tall, gaunt and bare' and 'colliers…lifting their ill-stayed spars into the whirling gloom.' Iron foundries, shipyards, chemical and cement factories lined the river on either side, along with 'timber yards, warehouses, wharves—leagues of them stretching in one long unbroken chain,' signifying, for Russell, 'the breadth of its interests, the wealth of its industries, the amazing spirit of progress' that animated the locality.[8]

What has been built in this landscape has only compounded this sense of scenic drama. These begin with the mighty strongholds that punctuate the terrain from Norham in the north to Barnard Castle in the south, and the great churches that speak of the deep Christian past of Northumbria—from the Abbey of Hexham in the West to the Priory of Tynemouth in the East. Indeed, the Tyne valley has the highest concentration of Anglo-Saxon churches in England. These solid, often gloomy, military and ecclesiastical buildings have done much to shape our understanding of what is quintessentially Northumbrian architecture. This sense was heightened still further in the industrial age through the science of bridge-building. Rowland Burdon's stupendous bridge of 1796 over the Wear was the first show-stopper—the widest single span in the world, and at 240 feet twice the width (and only three quarters of the weight) of Abraham Darby's iron bridge at Coalbrookdale. Northumbria also boasts the huge Victoria Aqueduct over the Wear at Penshaw (an 1838 design based on Trajan's Alcantara bridge over the Tagus) which Pevsner described as 'a glimpse of arcadia amid the colliery strewn landscapes of County Durham,'[9] and the awe-inspiring concentration of bridges over the Tyne, dominated by the art deco towers and Teesside-forged arch of the 1928 Tyne Bridge—Tyneside's *Arc de Triomphe*.

When Kenneth Clark explained the thought behind his epic TV series *Civilisation*, he cited, with approval, John Ruskin's dictum that 'Great nations write their autobiographies in three manuscripts, the book of their deeds, the book of their words and the book of their art,' and of these three 'the only trustworthy one is the last.' This is axiomatic, but historians of Northumbria have seldom applied this insight to really understand the people who lived here—their way of life, their passions, even their identity. For architecture is in some ways the most visceral art form. Buildings are not purely functional, they can also express—and elicit—feeling and emotion. Take Ronnie Lambert's popular 1981 football anthem 'Home Newcastle' and its verse

It's cold up there in Summer
It's like sitting inside a fridge,
But ah wish ah was on the Quayside,
Looking at the auld Tyne Bridge.

Or Sam Slatcher's 2018 political ballad 'City of Sanctuary' that evokes the ancient rights of asylum—first confirmed by King Guthred of Northumbria in the ninth century—that were granted to anyone who rapped the great knocker on the door of Durham Cathedral:

In these ancient streets, there's a heartbeat of sanctuary
All are pilgrims of a kind
In these stones you're not alone, there's a place to be
In the city of sanctuary.

Walking through these streets, the market place, the library
The bridges and the railways and the university
The scholars and the buskers, the pilgrims on the road
The city's arms are wide, where all can find a home.

Johann von Goethe once wrote that architecture is best thought of as 'frozen music' in the way it can influence the temperament of those who live in the shadow of great buildings. The singer Bryan Ferry grew up near Penshaw Hill, infamous lair of the Lambton Worm but also the site of a grand folly dedicated to the 1st Earl of Durham. Built in 1844 by the Northumbrian architects John and Benjamin Green, Penshaw Monument was modelled on the Theseion, the Temple of Hephaestus in Athens. It is a building of great gravitas, and its austere Doric silhouette dominates the landscape for miles around. It also had a profound and edifying effect on those that lived near it, as Ferry admitted to his biographer:

Years later, when I showed this place to [the fashion designer] Antony Price, he said, "Now I know why you're so interested in visual things: it's because of that monument." And it seemed to me like a symbol—representing art, and another life, away from the coalfields and the hard north-eastern environment; it seemed to represent something from another civilisation, that was much finer.[10]

Given the proximity of the nearby Victoria Aqueduct there must be few places in the world where one can stand beneath a Roman aqueduct and a Greek temple. This fusion of dramatic landscape and distinctive built environment has given the region such a cinematic quality—from Ridley Scott basing his Bladerunner aesthetic on the industrial Teesside he knew from his youth, to Mike Hodges setting his classic 1971 movie *Get Carter* on the Gotham-like streets of Tyneside (despite the novel originally being set in Yorkshire), with Carter's denouement on the coal-black and almost lunar coastline of East Durham. While everywhere else had abandoned crenallation, Newcastle retained its medieval walls and towers well into the eighteenth century.[11] This was a style adopted with relish by the Percy Dukes of Northumberland at both Alnwick Castle and Syon House in London, embodying a regional identity rooted in their perceived role as defenders of the North against Scottish incursions—a style that was copied at places such as Castle Eden, Heaton Hall and Stella Hall, where castellated exteriors and classical interiors blended Roman and medieval allusions. The local taste for Palladianism was certainly conservative but the façades of Northumbrian country houses were almost always plain and 'astylar' (meaning without columns) in contrast to the more elaborate fashions espoused by Robert Adam and James Wyatt.

One thesis has proposed that the Roman heritage of the North was highly influential in the adoption of classical architecture by an eighteenth-century regional élite who already saw themselves as the heirs to a Roman civilisation that held at bay the 'barbarians' to the north (a sense that was only intensified by the threat of Jacobitism in 1715 and 1745).[12] Indeed there was a local belief that the medieval church of All Saints in Newcastle—rebuilt in classical style in the 1780s—was on the site of a Roman pantheon, hence the original name Pampedon for the area of the town in which it stood (this had mutated to Pandon by the eighteenth century). The north-east élite also liked to see themselves as heirs to Rome in their industrial endeavours. Thus the Durham coal tycoon George Bowes built a classical column to 'British Liberty' in the grounds of his estate at Gibside and made a feature of the colliery wagonways that made his fortune, which he compared to the Via Appia in Rome.

Architectural styles expressed something about the cultural identities of the region. The Greek revival retained its vitality much later than elsewhere in England—one thinks here of the dourly Greek entrance to Jesmond Old Cemetery; William Stokoe's forbidding Moot Hall by the Castle Keep, described by the Newcastle historian Aeneas MacKenzie as 'among the finest and purest specimens of ancient architecture ever attempted in this kingdom,' and perhaps the first Grecian public building in the whole country; or the entirely *sui generis* Belsay Hall, almost brutalist in its geometrical severity, built by the Hellenist Sir Charles Monck, because he had become enamoured with Periclean Athens and wanted a Parthenon to live in.[13] The taste for Greek architecture was not only visual; it also reflected a political and philosophical outlook which saw Greece as the birthplace of democracy and civilization, and therefore its architecture represented justice, democracy and liberty. The taste for Greek Doric in particular—the simplest of the classical orders—is revealing too for in England it was a term that came to mean 'rustic' from its roots in Sparta, and was applied to the language of Northumbria and Lowland Scotland from the 1720s after Allan Ramsay's dialect play *The Good Shepherd*.[14] These democratic principles certainly appealed to the confident citizens of burgeoning Northumbrian towns, and downtown Sunderland, for example, provides a handsome example, with John, Frederick and Foyle Streets laid out in fine neo-classical style. But the example par excellence of this Northumbrian confidence is Newcastle itself.

If Edinburgh is the Athens of the North, then Newcastle is the North's Corinth, or better still its Sparta. William Cobbett described the place as 'this fine, opulent, solid, beautiful and important town,' and Pevsner concluded that it is 'the best designed Victorian town in England and indeed the best designed large city in England altogether.'[15] On seeing Christopher Wren's Royal Hospital Chelsea for the first time, Thomas Carlyle decided that this was obviously 'the work of a gentleman,' and one gets a similar impression from walking the streets of Grainger Town of the refinement and intelligence of the people that built the city in the 1820s and 1830s. On a visit to Newcastle in 1862, William Gladstone called Grey Street 'our best modern street,' and in 2010 Radio 4 listeners voted it as 'Best street in the UK.' Sir John Betjeman, that great connoisseur of Victorian streetscapes wrote of his first encounter with Newcastle's most famous thoroughfare:

> As for the curve of Grey Street, I shall never forget seeing it to perfection, traffic-less on a misty Sunday morning. Not even Regent Street, even old Regent Street London, can compare with that descending subtle curve.[16]

Again, the visual splendour is heightened by the topography of the place. 'It's a magnificent city for sheer excitement' wrote Ian Nairn in an essay on 'Superlative Newcastle,' 'the view that stops you dead half-way along a street, or the flight of steps that sucks you in like a vortex ... walking around it is an ennobling experience.'[17] He described the local architectural style as 'loosely Adam, but with Adam's effeminateness discarded and replaced by a tense, crisp virility,' adding that Thomas Oliver's colossal quadrangular block of Leazes Terrace in beautiful honey-coloured sandstone is like a 'latter-day

Northumbrian keep.'[18] These same themes were picked up by another architectural writer, Adrian Jones, who summed up the place as

> the most dramatic of the big northern cities with all this topography and engineering bravado, but it is also a city of restrained, masculine elegance. It has a confidence and pride rooted in exceptionalism, its character, like its accent, so very different from commercial Leeds or Manchester, or maritime Liverpool or Hull. Looking more like Edinburgh or Glasgow, it has a strong whiff of the Baltic too.[19]

When Richard Grainger redeveloped the old medieval town in the 1820s he was inspired by the classicism of the Scottish capital, but Grainger eschewed the neat right-angles of Edinburgh New Town and instead repeated the existing street pattern to create a more picturesque effect. He was fortunate that there was a cohort of talented local architects at his disposal, such as the father and son John and Benjamin Green, and the great John Dobson, who, in using the hard and durable local stone developed a Northumbrian classicism that possessed a 'distinctive heaviness and strength'—he even renovated Henry II's grim keep of the New Castle itself, giving it pristine new battlements in the style of the Durham-born architect Anthony Salvin's restoration of castles such as Brancepeth, Alnwick and Warkworth, or Eugène Viollet-le-Duc's work at Valenciennes and Carcassone.[20] This quality of construction may have developed from older building traditions: wood was never much used as it was elsewhere—'both the climate and the constant menace of the Scots pointed to something more robust, whenever it could be afforded'—and for a time 'a Northumbrian mason [was] considered the best that could be found.'[21] These traditions had other important legacies: that fundamentally important modern building material reinforced concrete was perfected by a Newcastle man, William Wilkinson, in 1854, and alongside George Stephenson's 4 ft $8^1/_2$ inch 'standard gauge' becoming the worldwide standard, the neat neo-Tudor 'lineside style' first developed on the Newcastle and Carlisle Railway in the 1830s by the local architect Benjamin Green was imitated throughout the world.[22]

The survival of Newcastle's 'city of palaces' was a narrow squeak: the Council Leader in the 1960s, T. Dan Smith, failed in his attempt to demolish the old Georgian streets and replace them with an ill-conceived plan for a 'Brasilia of the North.'[23] It was ironic that the architect of the actual Brasilia, Lucio Costa, was an old boy of the Newcastle Royal Grammar School (whereas Terry Farrell, whose MI6 building on the Thames has the air of an Art Deco Mayan Temple, was a former pupil of St Cuthbert's, the city's

Catholic grammar). The Northumbrian taste for the grand and monumental still flourished in the twentieth century with buildings like the Art Deco Wills Cigarette Factory on the Coast Road, the stupendous Parthenon of a bus depot in Jesmond, and the Gotham City-style Northumberland County Hall overlooking the Tyne Bridges.

Newcastle's 1960s Civic Centre, modelled on the Stockholm *Stadhus* by the city architect George Kenyon and opened by King Olav V of Norway, was a nod to the history of the Baltic trade (coal went out from the Tyne and timber came back in vast quantities to be used for pit props and railway sleepers). With its twelve-storey tower, elliptical drum-shaped council chamber, fortress-like banqueting hall and copper-capped lantern 250 feet above the ground, the Civic must be one of the few buildings from that era to stand the test of time—not least because the city fathers didn't scrimp on building materials, as the yards of Portland stone and Portuguese marble still testify. But even the not so well-loved Northumbrian brutalism of the 1960s could still grab you by the lapels; think of Frederick Gibberd's sci-fi water-tower in Kielder Water (he promised the Northumberland County Council Planning Committee that his austere landscaping scheme would keep the lake free of 'music, coke and bikinis'); and Owen Luder's colossal Trinity Square multi-storey carpark in Gateshead, site of Cliff Brumby's demise in *Get Carter*, and described as a 'counterpoint to Newcastle's outrageous, brilliant medieval cathedral' by Owen Hatherley, who enthused that it is simply one 'one of the most visceral architectural experiences available in Britain, in terms of sheer physical power, architecture that both hits in the gut and sends shivers down the spine.'[24] It was demolished in 2011 and replaced by a bland shopping centre.

The medieval counterpoint to the grandeur of Georgian Newcastle is the City of Durham. Pevsner thought the primeval power of its Norman Cathedral derived from its dramatic setting and consummate mastery of scale and proportion, and perfectly represented King William's dominion over Northumbria following his bloody campaigns in the North.[25] Pevsner just rhapsodised about the place:

> Durham is one of the great experiences of Europe to the eyes of those who appreciate architecture, and to the minds of those who understand architecture. The group of cathedral, castle, and monastery on the rock can only be compared to Avignon and Prague.

This seat of the Prince Bishops and shrine of Saint Cuthbert is like a vision of Tolkien or George R. R. Martin, an architectural fantasy floating above the tree-tops and perched on a sort of isthmus like those other great Benedictine houses at Monte Cassino, Mont St Michel or the Abbey of Melk on the Danube. 'If Venice is reckoned to be a mandatory component of a topographical syllabus,' observed Jonathan Meades, 'then surely Durham should be included.'[26] The view from the west across the Wear to the Cathedral has been compared to a 'nineteenth-century imagination of a clerical ideal city,' and the 1924 woodblock print of that scene by the Japanese artist Urushibara Yoshijirô, aka 'Mokuchu,' perhaps captures best its dream-like quality.[27] John Ruskin described Durham as the 'eighth wonder of the world,' and the heart-stopping silhouette of the castle and cathedral from the train as it pulls into Durham Station ranks only with the Tyne Bridges for emotional impact, and tells the weary Northumbrian traveller that they are home.

* * *

Where else should we look for evidence of continuities in architecture and patterns of living? Again, we must start from the fundamental point, namely that for a longer time than most Northumbria was a dangerous place to live. In a pungent sketch Hugh Trevor-Roper (himself descended from an old Northumbrian line) described the position of the Newcastle merchants:

> alone in a barbarous country among illiterate and boorish squireens, constituted a single element of civilisation … separating them from their elder brothers who bit their fingernails in draughty castellated farmhouses and murdered each other over the biting of a greyhound or even less important matters of dispute.'[28]

As we saw in Chapter 2, the hazardous nature of life in Northumbria was a simple fact, and, in shaping the building styles that were needed to deal with that danger, it shaped the people too—not least their predilection for security over aestheticism—from the Middle Ages into the industrial period. To this we must also add the tradition of planned settlement building—from the planting of medieval villages after the Conquest to the building of industrial settlements and then the 'New Jerusalem' with its acres of council housing after 1945. The evidence we have of pre-historic building patterns and into the Roman period shows a society that appears to have been extremely conservative (for at least 1,500 years there was no departure from the traditional circular ground-plan), and the 'camps' in which these dwellings were gathered were bolstered by defensible earthworks from the time that the Romans left, and many of these were still inhabited into the Elizabethan period.[29] The repeated forays of Border lords meant that villages and monasteries were ravaged and burnt time and again, an insecurity that prompted continued construction of new strongholds long after castle building had died elsewhere in England. The distinctive innovation in Northumbrian castle-building was the tower house or 'pele' (pronounced 'peel'—and derived from the Latin word *pilum*, meaning a stake or palisade). These varied in size from large keep-like buildings to small blockhouses. These were typically thickly-walled and three or four stories high: the windowless ground floor was used to corral livestock away from raiders, and above that was a hall for living, a bower for sleeping and a deck for fighting. William Camden wrote of the Northumbrians that 'there is not a man amongst them of the better sort that hath not his little tower or pele.'[30] By Henry VIII's time there were 120 of these in Northumberland alone, but they were still being built into the nineteenth century (such as the one at Crooks Altar in Weardale, dating from 1811), as much out of habit as a need for security.

Did these traditions influence later dwelling patterns in the industrial age? Before the building boom of the later Victorian period began to address the growing demand, Karl Marx in *Das Kapital* described 'infernal' housing conditions in Newcastle and cited a doctor who described the town as containing 'a sample of the finest tribe of our countrymen, often sunk by external circumstances of house and street into an almost savage degradation.'[31] Slum housing was usually the handmaid of infectious disease, and there were major cholera outbreaks in the North East in 1831 (where a young doctor called John Snow had his first experience of dealing with an epidemic). Even as late as 1869 a Newcastle council report listed 9,639 families living in single rooms and nearly 14,000 people without 'water closet or privy accommodation of any sort.'[32] In neighbouring Sunderland Murray's *Handbook for Travellers* of 1864 was uncompromising about the misery of coaly Wearside:

> The whole town is black and gloomy in the extreme, and the atmosphere is so filled with smoke that blue sky is seldom seen, especially in the lower part of the town, which consists for the most part of a maze of small dingy houses crowded together, intersected by lanes rather than streets; dirt is the distinctive feature; earth air and water are alike black and filthy.[33]

Much of Northumbria's economic life was tightly concentrated in the shipyard and fishing towns on the rivers Blyth, Tyne, Wear and Tees—placing a premium on housing that was as close as possible to these riverfronts. These peculiarities led to exceptionally dense styles of accommodation, notably 'Tyneside Flats' (pairs of single-storey flats within a two-storey terrace), and the unique single-storey Wearside equivalent: the bijou Sunderland Cottage.

In England and Wales in 1911, 2.9% of the population lived in flats whereas the level in Northumberland was 25.4% and in County Durham 14.6%—and within that 44.5% in Newcastle and 62.5% in Gateshead.[34] In Leicester in 1911 only 6.2 % of houses had three rooms or fewer, but it was 62% in Sunderland. These were closer to Scottish living patterns where tenements were the norm, and it meant that the top five boroughs for overcrowding in England in 1907 were Gateshead, South Shields, Tynemouth (essentially North Shields), Newcastle and Sunderland.[35]

Writing in the 1920s the social reformer Henry Mess blamed these poor housing conditions on the 'backwardness which has its roots deep in the conditions of life of past centuries ... where life and property were insecure and the standard of comfort was very low' (as was also seen to be the case in Scotland), and noted that with Northumbrian towns being so isolated 'from the other great industrial districts of England ... for good and for evil their inhabitants are very tenacious of habit and custom.'[36] In North Shields, where about a quarter of all babies were born in one-roomed homes in 1920, the saying 'aaltigether like the folks o' Shields' was as much a comment on the living conditions amid the teeming rookeries above the Fish Quay as it was about local people's instinctive solidarity.[37] Studies of Sunderland noted that in its industrial heyday between around 1840 and 1910—the town felt like a 'vigorous Australian or 'Yankee' frontier settlement.'[38] This was a confidence built on the possession of the world's deepest mine, longest single-span bridge and its most productive shipyards. Local housing styles manifested this confidence too: those Sunderland cottages were built for well-paid shipyard artisans, and so had unusually high ceilings and separate access to each room; they may have been small, but that made them unsuitable for sub-letting, guaranteeing both 'territoriality and privacy.' In 1970 the influential Oxford sociologist A.H. Halsey described Sunderland as a town with a distinct character:

> It is geographically set off by its position on the river and coast. Centred visibly and closely on its productive work, it is the antithesis of suburbia; housing is an annexe to the workplace and the community is a working community. It is, in a double sense, a working-class town.[39]

Taking the long view, we can see the origins of the way of life of Northumbrian industrial communities—where communal or high-density living was commonplace, and tied housing was usually in the control of powerful entities like coal companies—in the patterns of land-ownership and tenancy that began in the Medieval period. The power of the great magnates to lead the region in war made them almost omnipotent, and after the Normans laid waste to the North this provided opportunities to landlords to reorganise and re-plan whole villages, particularly in the south and east of Durham, where the land was good for growing corn and fattening cattle.[40] Similarly, a charac- teristic feature of farming in Northumberland by the nineteenth century was the large farmstead, more like a hamlet than anything seen in the south of England. These were like the agricultural prototypes of the pit villages which would become such a feature of the Northumbrian countryside, and Ilderton, in the Cheviot foothills near Wooler, has been described as 'perhaps the best survival in Northumberland of a self-contained mediaeval farm settlement rebuilt in the eighteenth and nineteenth centuries: a village which is virtually one farm.'[41] With its paucity of common farmland, and the dominance of major landowners, the landowners had a free hand to industrialise agricultural production on their estates. Northumberland was the earliest English county to be affected by the switch from the flail to the threshing machine (indeed the reaping machine was invented by John Common, a Northumbrian mill- wright), and we can see the evidence for this in these large farmsteads, with their adjoining 'hind houses' (farm labourers' terraces).

Much of the worst conditions within mining communities in the mid-to- early nineteenth century occurred in older towns like Bedlington, Spennymoor, and Houghton-le-Spring, where older dwellings had become tenemented by poorer families, usually Irish migrants to the coalfields. But some of the new model mining villages erected later that century, such as Cambois (pronounced 'Cammus') in Northumberland and Esh Winning in Durham, had much better housing and sanitation.[42] They were certainly utilitarian in design—'dreary (O so dreary),' commented William Morris about a Northumberland colliery vil- lage, 'an endless back-yard.'[43] The working class novelist Harold Heslop described New Hunwick, the small mining village where he grew up, as a place where men had so 'rarely essayed so mean and contemptible a habitation of souls,' which looked like a 'festering wound' on the Durham landscape.[44] The utilitarian atmosphere of these places was heightened by the penchant for giving the streets Manhattan-style numbers (my own grandfather grew up on Eleventh Avenue in Blyth), but more evocative street-names were not unknown. There was a Voltage Terrace and an Electric Crescent in Philadelphia (Co. Durham), an Industrial Street and Provident Street in West Pelton, and, famously, the terraced streets in Stanley named after Lenin and Karl Marx (although Scrogg Road in Byker remains my favourite).

These traditions of settlement building provided fertile ground for the massive programme of post-war house-building. The new town movement saw many of the old Tyneside and Wearside slums cleared and families re-housed in the more salubrious precincts of Cramlington, Killingworth, Washington and Peterlee. The architect of the welfare state himself, Sir William Beveridge, was the chairman of the Development Corporation in Newton Aycliffe, County Durham—and even lived in one of the council houses there for a while (at the top of Pease Way). To many of the people who lived in these pristine new estates, with unimagined luxuries such as running water and indoor toilets, they were the culmination of decades of struggle and the hoped-for fruit of a Labour government. But to appreciate how the landscape and built environment of Northumbria interact so distinctively, best to go and see. Rather than heading for the tourist honeypots we should instead take the less-beaten track and consider the unfashionable bottom-right hand corner of historic Northumberland, running along the industrial north bank of the Tyne and then up the jolly coastal strip towards coal country.

Deepest Tyneside

The town of North Shields contains all the quintessential features of urban Tyneside: knots of russet-coloured brick terraces within sight of the river, intermingled with grander stone-built streets of surprising refinement. But even the terraces in the working-class areas usually have modest neo-classical details: with Doric pilasters and architrave lintels above windows and doors. These were a nod to the traditions of Northumbrian classicism, and embody something of the craft and dignity of the artisans whose toil built the 'Shielings' (huts) around a small wind-battered harbour into a Victorian boom-town.

North Shields is not much known outside the North East. Neil Tennant was born here, Stan Laurel grew up in Shields, and the sea-shanty 'Dance to Your Daddy' was probably written in the town. The clever motto of the old Borough of Tynemouth was 'Messis ab Altis' ('our harvest is from the deep', in other words: fish and coal), and, in its heyday, Shields was a hub of heavy industry and maritime trades like chandlery, ropeworks and ship-repair. The Tyne has literally marinated this town in history, and the fact that this place has witnessed everything from the splash of Hadrian's galleys in AD122 to the full-steam of the liner *Mauretania* in 1907 has given the streets of Shields a tremendous historical depth and emotional power. This really is Tyneside *profonde*.

But this tough little town was badly battered in the twentieth century: a disproportionately high number of men from the borough were killed in the

Warkworth Castle, c 1798, by Thomas Girtin (1775–1802).

Wood engraving by Thomas Bewick of a Chillingham Bull, executed for Marmaduke Tunstall of Wycliffe, Yorkshire, in 1789.

Vice Admiral Cuthbert Collingwood, Baron Collingwood (1748–1810), by Henry Howard.

Statue of the 3rd Marquess of Londonderry by Raffaele Monti, unveiled in the market-place, Durham, in 1861.

Durham Cathedral from the southeast, in 1865.

'Iron and Coal' (1855–60), William Bell Scott (1811–1890) part of series of frescoes depicting scenes in Northumbrian history at Wallington Hall in Northumberland.

'The Destruction of Sodom and Gomorrah' (1852) by John Martin (1789–1854) in the Laing Art Gallery, Newcastle-upon-Tyne.

'The Response, 1914' (detail), memorial to the Northumberland Fusiliers, at Barras Bridge, Newcastle by William Goscombe John and unveiled in 1923 by the Prince of Wales.

The re-built Wearmouth Bridge (1929). Sunderland has used 'Nil Desperandum Auspice Deo', a line from the Odes of Horace, as its motto since 1849.

Hirst Industrial Working men's Club, Ashington, Northumberland.

'Fisherfolk on the Beach at Cullercoats' (1881) by Winslow Homer (1836–1910).

Wives, daughters, relatives and friends of the victims of the Easington Colliery disaster, in which miners were killed in 1951, meet Lord Hyndley, chairman of the National Coal Board.

Great War, even for the North East, and it suffered the second biggest single civilian loss of life in the Second World War after a direct hit on an air raid shelter in 1941. Slow industrial decline followed the war, and North Shields gained a certain notoriety after the 'Meadowell' riots of 1990. These were arguably the direct result of crude town planning, when the gritty families who lived in the rookeries above the Fish Quay were thoughtlessly scooped up and dropped into new council estates, dissipating the familial networks that had always made the place tick. A good deal is still shabby, particularly the main shopping drag around Bedford Street and its southern and western fringes, but the well-built streets and handsome public buildings of its northern and eastern parts are worth exploring and give North Shields a dignity that deserves our attention.

The best way to approach the town is to begin uphill, near the broad acres of Preston Cemetery whose funerary urns and weeping angels give a good sense of nineteenth-century prosperity and the rapid expansion of the town northward and away from the Tyne. Head south first down the proudly-pruned 1930s suburbia of Walton Avenue, towards the ebullient Tynemouth College (1909). Originally the borough's grammar school, its 'massing' could make this a gloomy building were it not for the rhubarb and custard colour scheme and playful Art-Nouveau details: note, for example, the curlicues on the BOYS and GIRLS entrances and the quirky janitor's house fit for a hobbit. From the College, head east to see one of the most distinctive urban vistas in the North East. Were it not for the kink at the junction with Preston Road, Queen Alexandra Road and Trevor Terrace would present a relentless terraced kilometre bristling with two-storey bay windows. These are the distinctive signature of the better sort of Tyneside flats, small but dignified homes fit for clerks or foremen (indeed 'bay-window' became something of a deprecation, suggestive of social-climbing and la-di-dah airs and graces). The North East shares much in common with its northern neighbour, but where the Scots built tenements to save space when land was expensive, the Northumbrians preferred the dominion of their own front door.

North from here are the leafy terraces of Preston Avenue and Sandringham Gardens, the severe former vicarage, like Wagner's *Wahnfried*, and the solemn villas of Preston Park. For this is the North Shields that John Betjeman might appreciate—'under cedar-shaded palings, low laburnum-leaned-on railings'—from the quiet Georgian serenity of Camp Terrace to the Edwardian affluence of Cleveland Road. Here again are the ubiquitous bay windows, but grander still with heavy Downing Street-style wooden front doors, fanlights, basements and smartly striped cornices. Alma Place is worth a stroll too

(Dr Hastings Banda, later the dictator of Malawi, lived here in the 1940s while practising as a doctor in the town); it's spacious and comfortable with distinctive creamy brickwork, and those heavy stone lintels which are a feature of almost all the residential buildings put up in Shields between c. 1850 and 1910.

Emerging from Alma Place—and passing Keel Row Books (the finest bookshop in North East England)—we are confronted by the sooty basilica of Christ Church. This replaced the ruined medieval Priory Church on Tynemouth headland and was built in stages from 1668 to 1789. Seven miles north of here Ian Nairn wrote of the 'dour Northumberland grandeur that Vanburgh captured so perfectly at Seaton Delaval Hall'[45] and Robert Trollope pulled off something similar in Shields: huge stone slabs, gloomy battlemented tower, little ornament. (It has an almost matching pair over the water in South Shields: St Hilda's of 1675, also by Trollope.). Christ Church sits on the ridge that formed the natural route of the Newcastle turnpike and once commanded views of the Tyne and the sea. From here the town gradually, and then steeply, falls away to the river.

Eighteenth-century North Shields now takes shape, notably in the form of Northumberland Square—one of three such squares, and the focus of John Wright's 'New Town.' As in Edinburgh, Shields New Town was built on virgin ground and provided a refined Georgian oasis above and away from the stink and squalor of the teeming 'bankside' slums. Pevsner thought the square too wide for the scale of its graceful two-storey ashlar houses, but it is undoubtedly an elegant space. This part of town provides much interest for the church-spotter.

The centrepiece of Northumberland Square is St Columba's of 1853 (formerly English Presbyterian, now URC), a typically crisp neo-classical essay by the great John Dobson, a native of North Shields. But most styles are catered for: further east along Albion Road is the Gothic Wesleyan church of 1889 (now a dreaded 'soft play' centre), with its peculiar tower like a rocket idling at Cape Canaveral, and south of the square the broad and handsome Howard Street reveals three more Victorian churches. Two of these are by Dobson again, including his 'Scotch Presbyterian' church of 1811. It reveals that even at the age of twenty-four he had mastered the tricky Greek Doric vocabulary of friezes, triglyphs, attic floors and all the rest. Yet Dobson could converse in several architectural languages, and on the opposite corner he demonstrates his stylistic dexterity yet again. His Elizabethan Town Hall of 1844 is actually a precinct of buildings, atypically domestic and not at all grandiose like its municipal contemporaries. Its scale and stonework are reminiscent of an Oxford college: Mansfield perhaps, or University College, but rather more compact. Tynemouth Corporation was notoriously penny-pinching which may explain its modest dimensions—the large, mullioned south-facing oriel window describes the width of the poky council chamber—but this makes the building all the more humane, and its well-pointed stone compliments the sturdy residential architecture nearby.

The Italianate Free Library of 1857 picks up the rhythm of Howard Street south of the junction with Saville Street, and introduces a nice stretch of well-mannered former banks done up like palazzi, as was the fashion. The street culminates with a little piazza offering thrilling cliff-edge views over the river to South Shields, west to Jarrow Slake ('Jarra Slack') and east to Tynemouth. Perched next to this is the charming North Shields Literary and Philosophical Society of 1806, now North Tyneside Register Office. The pedimented Tuscan doorcase and gorgeous big Venetian window wouldn't look out of place on a Georgian rectory, but is entirely typical of classical Tyneside.

In his essay on Newcastle, Ian Nairn described how the Tyne gorge's steep sides provide a sort of 'topographical ecstasy as you go up and down perpetually seeing the same objects in different ways.'[46] You get this in Shields too: from the pleasing way Grey Street slouches down to the Pow Burn (a tributary of the Tyne, now Northumberland Park—the Jesmond Dene of North Shields) to the view, from the otherwise cheerless Charlotte Street, of Knott's Flats which loom, like Prague Castle, over the Black Middens, the infamous ship-wrecking reef in the Tyne estuary. But Tyne Street offers the most invigorating vistas of all. It's built on an escarpment parallel to the Tyne, and a fantastic riparian panorama unfolds beneath you like a sort of Northumbrian Lilliput. From here you pass the site of Dockwray Square, the grandest of the town's eighteenth-century squares, and the childhood home of Stan Laurel (sadly, his cartoonish statue is hideous). The literal focal point here is the most Heathcliffian building in Shields: the impossibly romantic 'High Light' of 1808 which clings to a windswept eyrie above the Quay. It was used as a rudimentary, but effective, navigational aid to enter the Tyne (skippers would line up the high and low lights to find a safe channel) but now I wouldn't be surprised if a romantic poet spent his days here musing on the seascape.

* * *

Now we must descend to the Fish Quay. This was once a moral, as well as a physical, descent into a seedy land of sex and violence. The Northumberland Arms (known locally as 'The Jungle') at the western end of the Quay was built as the grandly be-columned townhouse of the eponymous Duke, but became one of the most notorious sailors' pubs in the world. Alas, 'the Jungle' is no longer trading—now remodelled into pricey apartments—and the whole stretch from the former Smiths Dock to the river mouth is a rewarding place to stroll around.

The authenticity of the place is still striking. This is a working fishing port after all, and although the forces of gentrification have made inroads, the heart of the place remains 'The Gut' and the salty tang of surrounding fish shops and processing units. The cyclopean Low Light (companion to the High Light) dominates the scene. A square white pylon, seven stories high with whittled corners like an unfinished chair leg, it is a striking sight (and was sketched by J.M.W. Turner in 1818), but delve further and from amidst the clutter of the Fish Quay emerges the Vaubanesque ramparts of Clifford's Fort. This comes as a surprise amid the fish crates and forklift trucks but then Northumberland is the most fortified English county, and North Shields is a kind of counterscarp at its most southeasterly tip. Built by the Swedish engineer Martin Beckman in 1672 (on the orders of Lord Clifford 'of Cabal') to prevent the Dutch doing to the Tyne what they did to the Thames, its twenty-nine gun embrasures now stare blankly out to sea. Within the bailey of the fort is yet another 'light,' in this case the seventeenth-century Old Low Light (now an excellent heritage centre). An illuminated third floor window on the narrow sea facing side served as a beacon until the new Low Light came along.

Ascending Tanner's Bank we then dip under Hawks, Crawshay and Sons' sturdy iron bridge, built for the North Eastern Railway in 1863, to reach Correction House Bank. As the name suggests justice was once meted out here, and the borough's bridewell—an intriguing pale stone shed of 1792—still stands, forming a striking contrast to the caramel tiles and red brick of the Tynemouth Lodge Hotel next door. The 'Bier Garten' of the Lodge overlooks Northumberland Park, a nineteenth-century pleasure ground hemmed in by the tight streets of Shields. In New York, Frederick Olmsted had wanted Central Park to be a place of 'silence, peace and repose away from the ills and agues of the city.' The dene of the Pow Burn is certainly a blissfully arcadian *rus in urbe*, but given the park's proximity to the quay, it's unclear how well the burghers of North Shields ever escaped the agues and bad airs of the fish industry. North Tyneside Council has now restored it to its former Victorian glory.

Further along Tynemouth Road you find two wonderful examples of 'social housing' built exactly a century apart. First, the cheerfully Jacobean Master-Mariners' Homes, put up in 1837 by John and Benjamin Green (major con-

tributors to Grainger's rebuilding of Newcastle) as a sort of retirement complex for grizzled matelots. 'Northumberland knows no prince but a Percy,'
and the family are still the major landowners in these parts. As such the
Mariners' Homes are arranged obsequiously around a rather rum-looking
statue of its benefactor, the 4th Duke of Northumberland—but it's a great
treat to observe that, on closer inspection, beneath his Garter mantle, His
Grace is wearing what can only be described as frilly hot-pants.

The final stop on our tour is a stupendous sight. Knott's Flats is six storeys
tall and zigzags almost 900 feet from west to east. This colossal block was
built in the 1930s, thanks to funds left by Sir James Knott, to house families
displaced by slum clearance around the Fish Quay. Knott had been born in
humble circumstances in Howdon, near North Shields, but his 'Prince' shipping line made him one of the richest men in Britain. Losing two of his sons
in the Great War inspired him to great heights of philanthropy which has left
a great architectural, as well as charitable, legacy. The Arts & Crafts SS James
and Basil in Newcastle (named for his two fallen sons), the strikingly Art
Deco YMCA on Church Way in North Shields, and even St George's Memorial
Church in Ypres, are all buildings of great quality and originality. Knott's Flats
is similarly unusual. Built on a vast scale by Charles Holden (famous for 55
Broadway and Senate House in London), it was completed in 1938 and constructed, tellingly, out of fire-resistant materials with integrated air-raid
shelters. An urban myth persists that the Luftwaffe—or was it the Gestapo?—
had it lined up as their prospective Northern HQ post-*Sea Lion*, its vertiginous balconies perfect for defenestration. Knott's Flats is actually a more
humane building than that, reminiscent of noble *Gemeindebau* like the Karl
Marx Hof in Vienna, with comfortable living space and, in this case, incredible
views of the sea. This places the building firmly within the architectural traditions of Tyneside: well built but not flashy, vigorous but not unfriendly. Rather
like the people who live here in fact.

Geordie Shore

To the coast! And an abrupt change of mood as riverside North Shields
turns 90 degrees north to seaside, business turns to pleasure, and production to consumption. Just as the Victorians invented industrial life, and the
discipline of the factory hooter and dockyard clock, so too did they conceive of leisure as a commodity that was consumed at certain times and in
certain demarcated zones. By 1911 Britain had over a hundred substantial
seaside resorts, from the big boys of Blackpool and Brighton to lower

league Largs and Llandudno. The Northumbrian Riviera fits somewhere in between these poles, more akin to the maritime resort suburbs of Penarth or Southsea; but like all of them it was a place of beaches, bathing and boarding houses—with a big slug of hedonism.

Here the twelve miles of metal-bashing Tyneside—from Newcastle to the sea—transforms sharply into the coastal playground of the Northumbrian middle and working classes. While the Tyne was clogged, grimy and hard work, this Geordie Shore was a Mecca of relaxation, amusement and lung-fuls of fresh air. Consider the working-class novelist Jack Common in *Kiddar's Luck*, sallying forth eastwards—on foot—from industrial Heaton to the glories of the Riviera:

> From North Shields on the air was full of the sea glow, a salt radiance bright-ened all the long Tynemouth streets. And at the end of them, the land fell off at the cliff-edge into a great shining nothingness immense all ways over the lazy crimping of seas on their level floor.

But earlier visitors were also struck by its luminescence; the writer and social theorist Harriet Martineau, recuperating in Tynemouth in the 1830s, wrote in *The Three Ages of Political Economy* of looking out across the Tyne estuary to where

> The myrtle-green sea tumbles… and the air comes in through my open upper sash, but sun-warmed. The robins twitter and hop in my flower-boxes… and at night, what a heaven! What an expanse of stars above, appearing more stead-fast, the more the Northern Lights dart and quiver.

Charles Dickens too had walked to the coast from Newcastle on one of his frequent visits to the city:

> We escaped to Tynemouth for a two hour sea walk. There was a high wind blowing and a magnificent sea running. Large vessels were being towed in and out over the stormy bar with prodigious waves breaking on it, and spanning the restless uproar of the waves was a quiet rainbow of transcendental beauty. The scene was quite wonderful.

The tide may have gone out on this coastline as a holiday destination, but it still remains a distinctive place, with a seductive rhythm of beaches, cliffs and promenades, punctuated by some of the most iconic buildings in the Northumbrian imagination.

The coast was long a dreamland and a resting-place for some, but for others it was always an edgy, liminal quarter where drink was taken, trousers were unbuttoned (for various reasons) and steam was let off. Respectability and debauchery were held in tension as True-Blue Tory Tynemouth—the constituency of the very grand Conservative MPs Dame Irene Ward and then Sir Neville Trotter—with its stockbrokers' Tudor, Masonic lodges and gin-drinking golf clubs, chafed alongside the fleshpots, arcades and Wurlitzers of Whitley Bay's South Parade and Spanish City. The saddest legacy of this uneasy occupation by genteel middle-class tipplers and teenage revellers—sad for me anyway as a resident—has been a dearth of decent pubs in Tynemouth, Cullercoats or Whitley Bay (although a craft beer explosion is happily now changing all this). This is certainly in contrast to the solid, characterful boozers of North Shields, of which the Tynemouth Lodge is the final outpost, and it is here that we begin our tour.

Northumberland Park, now magnificently restored, has long acted as a *cordon sanitaire* separating proletarian NE29 from patrician NE30. Some estate agents market properties in eastern North Shields as 'West Tynemouth,' but the change in affluence is palpable as we stroll east towards Tynemouth Metro. Frank Hornby himself could not have conceived of a more perfect collection of toy railway stations than the coastal stops of Tynemouth, Cullercoats, Whitley Bay and Monkseaton; each one is a gem—but Tynemouth (1881) is the grandest. A graceful exterior in polite Victorian gothic opens up to a vast platform covered by a full acre of glass roof and frilly ironwork. This usually quiet station is thronged at weekends by visitors to the Flea Market that takes up the whole concourse; prime mooching territory, and the regular Book Fair is always worth penciling in.

If we dart back across the road and down Oxford Street we reach a path high above the Black Middens and towards the 'Spanish Battery' (so named for the Iberian mercenaries quartered there by Henry VIII) for the stunning views over the river mouth and the fascinating Cape Cod style clapboard Watch House of the world's oldest Volunteer Life Brigade. When looking from the south, the drama of Lord Collingwood's statue is an effective curtain raiser to the castle and priory on the headland behind. If the Statue of Liberty bears a message of welcome and humanist principle, Collingwood the sentinel—with its inscription from Nelson, 'see how that noble fellow takes his ship into action'—says to the incomer 'take note: we are a martial race,' and reminds its much press-ganged native sons of their traditional role when England needed men for fighting.

As the Tyne (with the Wear) was the most important industrial and population centre on Britain's east coast, it was always strongly defended. The castle was in continuous military use from the seventh century until the 1950s, making the current site a palimpsest of monastic cloisters, medieval battlements and twentieth-century military architecture. Three Kings were buried on the magnesian slab of Pen Bal Crag: the Northumbrian warlords Oswin and Osred, and Malcolm III of Scotland (look out too for the gravestone of Alexander Rollo, the man who held the lantern at the burial of Sir John Moore at Corunna). Forget the chocolate box of Dunstanburgh and Warkworth, it's the ramparts of Tynemouth where the 'Lordly Strand of Northumberland' really begins. Here is a set-piece of serious voltage: tense, Wagnerian and easily on a par with Dover Castle, Montjuic in Barcelona or even Dubrovnik. The gesticulating shell of the Priory must be one of the most prominent ruins in the country, but for all that its skeleton retains a tremendous energy, its ruined barbican presenting an unnecessarily snaggle-toothed face to the town (the ruins only date from the 1940s, when the army left and took down their barracks). So never mind John Ruskin, this really does need the full Viollet-le-Duc treatment. Repair those crenellations!

As Ian Nairn put it, the broad high streets of Stockton and Darlington were a 'great northern breath of fresh air,' and Tynemouth Front Street is similarly expansive: narrowing gradually from a tranquil green in front of the Kings School—with its fine bronze of the Queen Empress (of the eight statues on Tyneside of real women—rather than female archetypes—five are of Victoria)—and up to the castle gates. The domestic and commercial architecture here presents an embarrassment of riches: late Georgian red brick and Parisian wrought iron balconies (and in the Northumberland Terrace group overlooking the estuary a rival to Thomas Oliver's 1829 masterpiece at Leazes Terrace in Newcastle), the exotic ogee arches of the Cumberland Arms, a jewellery-box of an RC chapel, and more besides. Among the drinking classes Tynemouth has a rather poncey reputation, a place where pretentious hipster cafes charging £12 for an 'artisan' breakfast jostle with distinctly arriviste bars like *Lola Jeans* and the unspeakably named *Hugo's at the Coast*.

North East of Front Street we find the noble lawns of Percy Gardens, a lavish crescent of 1880 with a rippling drumroll of bay windows broken only by the sympathetically Brutalist (is that possible?) post-war bomb-site infill at Priory House. Hidden furtively around the street's northern corner is an extraordinary lookout tower, built by the Royal Navy in the First World War but now strictly in domestic use, its slit window peering across the North Sea to Heligoland and the mouth of the Elbe.

The sands of the Northumbrian littoral unfurl northwards from this point, overlooked first by the stout and matronly Grand Hotel (built as a summer residence for a Duchess of Northumberland, it was found to be too accessible to the Tyneside *hoi-poloi* for Her Grace's taste). Longsands is the Bondi of the

North East; its proportions, even its municipal street furniture, are remarkably similar to the *plage* at Sydney, and the surf is up here all year round. There's also the soggy shell of a 1930s open-air salt water Lido which hosted the impossibly glamorous 'Miss Tyne Tees TV' competition in the 1970s, but whose future still hangs in the balance.

The Frenchified Grand finds a trim Art Deco foil in the Park Hotel (this could be Tyneside's answer to the Midland Hotel in Morecambe, but it's been depressingly shabby for years). What's missing here is the stupendous Tynemouth Plaza, tragically destroyed in a suspicious fire in the early 1990s. One of England's great lost buildings, in detail and giganticism reminiscent of Cuthbert Brodrick's Grand Hotel at Scarborough, it was a huge and stately pleasure-dome whose terraces billowed down from the dunes onto the beach below. In Victorian photographs its cetacean bulk reminds me of nothing so much as the beached Star Destroyer in the opening frames of *Star Wars VII*. Indeed, dominion over earth and water was an important theme in Northumbrian history; we could dredge it, tunnel under it, launch things into it, mine it and bend it to our will. The natural drama of the sea edge here was and is heightened by the buildings on the shore, not least engineering feats like the 900m-long harbour-mouth pier itself, fifty odd years in the building, and the prodigious galleries, promenades and sea-defences from the headland to South Parade, a concrete mantle as forbidding as Hitler's own *Atlantikwall*.

Longsands is bookended by Tynemouth and Cullercoats, and the next great landmark on the coast is the emphatically vertical extrusion of St George's (1884) whose stiletto-sharp steeple erupts from the Beaconsfield above the beach. Pevsner admired its antiquarian exactitude, but thought it a little cold-blooded. Here promenading is taken as seriously on the Northumbrian Riviera as the Cote d'Azur, but this is no catwalk; whatever the weather you'll find a great caravan of wind-cheatered Geordie pedestrians, not so much to 'be seen' as to participate in the sort of bracing communal act that the locals have always enjoyed. And what a backdrop! Beverley Terrace on the sea-front is a real blockbuster, lofty Edwardian villas of real bounce and vim; a Fishermen's Lookout of 1879 shrouded by an immense pitched roof like the shell of a nautilus, and the mysterious Cliff House (1768), a shuttered and white-washed evocation of *Moonfleet* and *Jamaica Inn*. The only fly in the ointment is the Dove Marine Laboratory, a clumsy building of 1908, with an even clumsier 1960s extension, that squats on the sands ruining the view. Cullercoats was an 'artists' colony' for a while, the home of Winslow Homer amongst others; and whilst these painters undeniably romanticised the hard

119

and precarious lives of fishing villagers, they also commemorated the informal matriarchy that predominated in the North East while men were away at
sea, working underground or in the pub.

Longsands and Cullercoats Bay have developed something of a Newquay
vibe, with surf shops and bike hire places but, typically, no decent pub (apart
from the Crescent CIU Club with its stunning views and biennial literary
festival). It's worth descending the stairs to Brown's Bay, north of the Marconi
station, to read an extraordinary interpretation board, put up by the council
to describe 'Table Rocks' tidal bathing pool:

> Formed in 1910 the Whitley and Monkseaton Bathing Club made good use of
> the pool. They had a winkle motif adorning their red and black swimming
> costumes. It is believed that later in the club's history each member was given
> a gold-plated winkle shell and that the custom of ladies and gentlemen show-
> ing each other their winkles came from this.

Whitley Bay

The ying and yang of refinement and raffishness, primness and vulgarity recurs
both within and *between* British seaside towns: think of neighbouring Lytham
and Blackpool, Hove and Brighton, even Portstewart and Portrush. The dilapi-
dation of downtown Whitley Bay is of a piece with this: its residential zones are
rich and abundant—especially the Hampstead-like Marine Avenue and
Queen's Road axis—but the area of boarding houses and happy-hour drinking
joints off South Parade and the Esplanade is dismal, peeling and radiates the
seamier side of kiss-me-quick seaside culture. The stag and hen parties may be
long gone—I can vividly recall, in the 1990s, seeing a naked man being cling-
filmed to the promenade clock at three o'clock in the afternoon—and Whitley
Bay Bank holidays were always a grisly bacchanal of fighting and fornication.
By the time I first started coming to the place as a child in the 1980s the sea-
front in particular was a forlorn stretch of artless municipal flowerbeds, indif-
ferent hotels (including the Rex, where a young Shirley Williams worked as a
waitress), and aggressive Geordie seagulls. Yet it had been a serious resort—
'the Blackpool of the North East'—whose attractions were primped and pack-
aged by great commercial artists like Fred Taylor and Tom Purvis for LNER,
each of whose technicolour posters are a masterpiece.

The architecture of Whitley (the 'Bay' was added in 1903 to stop it being
confused with Whitby) presents a mixed bag: the churches in the town centre
are generally boring (although St Paul's has an exquisite lych-gate), the
Jacobean town hall was sadly demolished, and the miles of commercial prem-

ises from Park View to Whitley Road speak of the town's prosperity (they were obviously built in large stretches, on spec, to meet local demand). What is most exciting are those buildings devoted to pleasure from the town's Edwardian heyday, all, tellingly, in the neo-Baroque style: the cheerful station of 1910 with its swagged and garlanded clock tower and Paris Metro style canopy, the main destination for Tyneside day-trippers and vacationing Glaswegians; the classical 'Coliseum' picture house (1919), and the Belvedere Building on the corner of Park Avenue, a creamy brick confection whose elevations undulate like Boromini's church of *San Carlino* in Rome.

This taste for voluptuous neo-baroque was partly an Edwardian reaction to the severity of Victorian Gothic, and, as Jonathan Meades has pointed out, 'mammarian' domes were neo-baroque's signature tune. When the famous Spanish City was built in 1910—following the success of a visiting Toreador act *from Hebburn*—only St Paul's Cathedral had a larger unsupported dome in Britain, and its silhouette is as distinctive as the Qubbat al-Sakhrah in Jerusalem. It was influenced by and contemporaneous with the development of Atlantic City in New Jersey, especially the Marlborough-Blenheim Hotel there of 1906, and both places specialized in the architecture of pleasure, of lubricity in place of temperance, of sybaritic escapism. Tynesiders had much to escape from; that they chose a 'Spanish' building that exudes the Moorish sensuality of *El Andalus*, or the dazzlingly white Mediterranean sunlight of a Sorolla painting—decades before the final victory of Torremolinos over the British seaside—speaks to a yearning romanticism in the Northumbrian soul, and stays with you (just as 'Rock away, rock away; Cullercoats and Whitley Bay' obviously stayed with local boy Mark Knopfler in his 1981 hit *Tunnel of Love*). This is why the Spanish City's igloo-dome is the town's cynosure, its visual shorthand, and I'm delighted that it's finally, *finally*, been restored. Could there be wider signs of life? Better standards of restaurant are popping up, and the superb Di Meo's is leading an ice-cream led regeneration pro-gramme of its own; South Parade has lost most of its sticky-carpet bars, including Pier 39 (a teenage haunt of mine, which, in what I can only read as a heavy-handed metaphor directed at me personally, is being turned into a care home); and Park View was named as one of the coolest places to shop in the world by *The Guardian* in 2018.[47]

From the Spanish City the 1950s concrete promenade and close-clipped green baize of the links sweep northwards towards St Mary's Lighthouse, sepa-rating the coal-streaked Bay of Whitley from the somnolent *Walmington-on-Sea* streetscape of the town's northern suburbs (look out for a fine example of Miami-style *seaside moderne* at the end of Links Road). The image of this

Lighthouse has been massively reproduced, but deservedly so as it's a fine spectacle: a tapering white Tuscan column of 1898 perching on a tidal island (in design similar to Souter Lighthouse in South Shields, and its twin in Gibraltar), and surrounded by a picturesque group of cottages, rockpools and the lapping waters of Tyne, Dogger and German Bight. On the northern horizon you can see the Cheviot Hills on the Scottish border, while to the South the sands of Whitley curve towards the Spanish City with the North Sea shimmering like the Bay of Naples. This is a place that arouses great affection.

The northern edge of the town is actually delineated by Whitley Bay Cemetery, a chilly granite necropolis that seems to declare in stone that the party's over. The chapel there has a very fine Arts and Crafts interior of 1913, with angels rendered in icing-sugar plasterwork wielding motivational quotes from scripture: 'The Lord Giveth—The Lord Taketh,' 'Watch For Ye Know Not The Hour.' This is a fitting change of mood, and a good introduction to the next leg of our journey up the coast to the burned over country of pitmatic south-east Northumberland, a terrain of 'Ranter' chapels, industrial tragedy and that brooding, unsettling hulk of English baroque virtuosity: Sir John Vanbrugh's Seaton Delaval Hall.

'Oh, Delaval is a Terrible Place'

The county of Northumberland contains some of the most savage countryside in the whole of England. By this I do not just mean the barren borderland of wind-blasted Cheviot, or the shivering milecastles strung out along the Whin Sill. The part that is usually hurried through on the way to somewhere else and hardly known at all, is what Pevsner demeaned as the 'tawdry sub-countryside that makes up much of the south east of the county.' This coastal plain was hacked and scraped, tunnelled and poisoned for centuries in the pursuit of the coal that made other people and other places rich; a typical 'edgeland,' where urban collides with rural. Such untidy, liminal zones were once defined by Victor Hugo as 'bastard countryside'; but where some see illegitimacy, this landscape—more chthonic than bucolic—was once a great stage of world history, an engine of national progress, and a place that still conceals great riches.

In the sixteen centuries between Publius Aelius Hadrianus and Charles Edward Stuart, the energy of the Northumbrians was absorbed in skirmishing in the county's border fastnesses, or defending its coastline from the Norsemen. Following the Hanoverian peace, the coalfield triangle of Riding Mill to Tynemouth and up to Amble became the cockpit of the county. Whilst the 'Middle March' had always been the quietest sector of the Anglo-Scottish battlefront, it now seethed and crackled with industry, drawing in, amongst others, James Watt and Humphrey Davy, and giving birth to the Stephensons, father and son. To the unobservant this is merely an unpretty landscape of dismal dormitory towns and industrial units, bisected by arterial roads and marching pylons. The untidy overspill of Greater Newcastle. But look closer at the terrain, at the now-wooded heaps of spoil like the worm-casts of the coal industry, at the constellation of pit-ponds that tell of the subsidence on the unstable surface of this vast carboniferous wormery, and the web of lonnens and waggonways along which trundled the coal down to the Tyne, and then out to flare in hearths and fireboxes across the world.

Our domain here is the land that straddles the ninety-fathom fault—the 'ugly colliery districts' as Nancy Mitford called them, bounded by the North Sea to the east, Tynemouthshire Moor to the south, and west as far as Killingworth. Its northern limit is the river and town of Blyth and the edge of Bedlingtonshire (once an odd exclave of the County Palatine of Durham) and the first of the straggly line of ancient towns that lead up from Newcastle to the hilly Scottish border that frames the horizon. This was the dominion of the Delaval family, the most junior ranking of the armigerous houses that infest this part of the county, but—in contrast to the parvenu Smithson dukes and Ridley viscounts—residents here for almost a thousand years.

Northumberland is mainly north of 55 degrees, at the same latitude as Hudson's Bay and the Baring Sea. There are few topographic barriers between here and the Russian steppe, and westerly isotherms make this the coldest part of England. The historic sparseness of the population and absence of intensive farming has left us with big windswept fields, sporadic hedgerows, and severely geometrical blocks of coniferous woodland that adumbrate the sites of long-gone collieries. This gives the landscape a pitiless character, with abrupt field edges yielding to the fringes of bland housing estates, built from the 1970s onwards (including 'Agincourt' in Killingworth, the street of semis that Bob and Thelma upgraded to in *The Likely Lads*). Broadleaved foliage is confined to the steep valley sides that incise this landscape, of the river Blyth and the lesser known Seaton Burn which 'with mazy error under pendant shades' of oak and alder, ash and willow, drain the fields and seep into the sea via salt marsh and mud flats.

The railway lines here are some of the very oldest in the world, built mostly for coal-hauling purposes, but there were ancient passenger lines too that were laid down as early as the 1840s. In their desuetude there is a whisper of Edward Thomas's Adlestrop around the disused stations and abandoned bridges. These ancient waggonways and lonnens have scattered ruderals like ragwort, toadflax, and foxtail barley, alongside more respectable species like speedwell, gorse, prickly heath and Danish scurvygrass. In the spring and summer the colour palette is dirty green streaked with Papal yellow and white, with dayglo rapeseed field and gorse blossom, matched by that frothy hawthorn that when in flower reeks of putrefaction.

The flatness of the topography is broken by the pit heaps, once Fuji-esque pyramids of black combustible slurry, but now landscaped into something more verdant and Uluru-esque. At the coast the looming wind turbines and bauxite hoppers at Blyth, like Kentish oasthouses, dominate the horizon. The abstract painter Sean Scully, now one of the richest artists in the world, came to the beaches here in the late 1960s while studying at Newcastle University and living with his grandfather, a Durham pitman. Scully was greatly influenced by the stark lines of old industrial Tyneside, its bridges and the cranes, but also as he has put it 'the long spectacular beaches of Northumberland, that nobody wanted to visit ... their majestic loneliness was permanently uncompromised.' Scully's style is known for its striking horizontal stripes which now adorn galleries around the world, but he first found his muse here under the tutelage of Ian Stephenson, an artist from Blyth with whom he would visit the beaches at Seaton Sluice and Druridge Bay.

> The North East coast of England, where the horizon line is a blurred strip for half the year, and every colour is fluctuating between definition. The light of the North East is clear and bright and closer to Scandinavia than Cornwall and the weather is thunderous and unstable.[48]

A few miles inland from the coast there's a line of old villages on the higher ground at Hartley, Holywell and Earsdon, then Backworth, Burradon and Killingworth. The cores of all of these places have a stone-built Cotswoldian charm, that always contrasted sharply with the industrial detritus and urban overspill that almost engulfs them. Earsdon in particular is illustrative here, and one of the oldest villages in Northumberland. John and Benjamin Green's St Alban's church is sited on iron-age hill-top foundations (Tynemouth Priory was a daughter house of the Benedictines at St Albans). Pentecostal winds swirl around its churchyard and clock tower and provide panoptical views across the coalfields and coastal plain. From here a spine of pit heaps extends northwards at least as far as Ashington (I recommend 'bagging' them, much as Scotsmen do with Munros, reaching the summit and then breathing in the coal gas). Earsdon's setting from the north and east looks almost more North Umbrian than Northumbrian, and from the south a column of Edwardian terraces emerges from a favela of allotment buildings and advances up the hill like a Roman *testudo*.

Earsdon Front Street introduces us to a distinctively Northumbrian architectural vernacular: that of restrained, but still imposing classicism. Buildings as grave as Belsay Hall are the *sine qua non* of this style and may owe something not only to the Grecian tastes of Northumbrian elites of the early nineteenth century, but also the heritage of defendable peles and bastles that defined the border style—of which there were several in this vicinity. Consider Earsdon Manor House of 1780: barrack-like in its no frills stolidity, but with refined Tuscan lintel and pilasters framing the doorway. The soot-black Bleakhope House across the street is similarly austere, as is the former vicarage of St Alban's, and dozens of other halls, farmhouses and colliery managers' villas in this neighbourhood. This sense is echoed in the workers' dwellings of the industrial age: generally well-built, but usually following the most utilitarian design possible—in contrast to other parts of Northern England where modest ornamental brickwork on terraced housing was not uncommon. Northumbrians in the pit villages had no time for such trifles. These terraces follow no particular pattern, and can appear in random, isolated spots—usually near a pithead and chapel, the textbook arrangement that announces another identikit workers' colony. Most of these old colliery buildings are slowly detriting, or they've been cannibalised by light industry; but some, like Church Pit at Earsdon, are intact and whitewashed like an old Spanish mission, or in the case of the Fenwick Pit at Backworth, they present us with a silhouette as graceful as the Maison Carrée.

Coalminers were undoubtedly the elite vanguard of the working class. Few other industries rewarded muscularity and stamina as much as pit work, and where workers' dwellings in much of the urban north were often little better than hovels, the terraced pit cottages of the Northern Coalfield were well-built and designed to maximise their output. For even in the domestic realm coal still dominated, with easily accessible 'oot-hooses' (outdoor coal-bunkers) into which the fuel was poured, which the pitman's wife would then use to fire the range, cook heavily calorific meals (artery-hardening Northumbrian cuisine was never known for its sophistication), and boil the water for washing him and his 'claes' when he returned from the pit.[49] This was almost a form of stabling, where miners' horsepower was carefully nurtured by wives who played a vital groom-like role in servicing this proletarian bloodstock. Coalfield wives and daughters were almost as much pit employees as the miners themselves, and it was said that collieries produced coal 'as much by the pounding of the pit wife's' 'poss' [the long-handled implement that mashed the laundry] as by the nicking of the pitman's pick.'[50] For all the bland utility of these miners' homes they were typically kept spotless by women whose work ethic was every bit as furious as miners at the coalface, and in the 1920s Henry Mess noticed that 'very low standards of house-room and of comfort go together with a good deal of house-pride.'[51]

The pit cottages themselves, once trim terraces of red firebrick, are now more typically caked in various shades of grubby pebbledash and uvpc—as in the thrillingly dismal Astley Road in Seaton Delaval where I would catch the school bus. The single-storey variants speak of a time when old age was a major cause of poverty, and the Mining Unions responded by building 'Aged Miners Homes,' comfortable, well-built, complete with neat gardens and dedicatory plaques. David Hockney once described coal as 'solid sunlight, the stored memory of millions of uninhabited summers,' so it's ironic that many of these old cottages are now festooned with solar panels, annihilating at once the 359 million years it had previously taken to mature the sun's rays into rich seams of underground energy.

Mines were not expected to last forever. Collieries typically had a life expectancy of 50 to 100 years before new pits needed to be sunk elsewhere (usually closer to the sea). This meant that the pit villages themselves were originally little more than work camps, a temporary home for the thousands of workers who arrived in the coalfields from across Northumberland and Durham, and from all over the British Isles—Ireland (inevitably) but also Cornwall after its tin mines began to close. Living nomadically had deep roots in the Borders of course, where the Reivers developed a sort of guerrilla way of life based around livestock rustling and living off what meat they could drive in front of them: 'they could build a house in a few hours and have no qualms about abandoning it; they could travel great distances at speed and rely on their skill and cunning to restock supplies by raiding.'[52] What turned something transitory into permanence were the institutions that these miners built.

First of these was religion. The Northern Coalfield was like the 'Burned Over Districts' of the USA in its zeal for hard-core Christianity. Methodism—in all its flavours, from Primitive to Wesleyan—was the preferred confession, but as well as the 'Ranters' there was room for Baptists, Congregationalists, Spiritualists (known locally as 'the Spuggies,' the dialect word for sparrow)—and even Catholics. Anglicanism on the other hand was often literally peripheral, with its churches and vicarages on the fringes of pit villages. (Maybe those who worked with death close at hand preferred the black and white certainty of Wesley or the salve of Roman dogma?) The group of six old chapels on Double Row and Foreman's Row at Seaton Delaval illustrate the strength, and sharp decline, of Nonconformity in the coalfields. Only the Spuggies are still trading; the rest are now engineering workshops of various kinds. But the confidence of the architecture is striking, from the ogee arched doorway of the former Presbyterian church, to the big galleried Primitive Methodist chapel of 1886. Even the Catholics of *Hagulstadiensis et Novocastriensis*—as the foundation stone of Our Lady & St Joseph's in New Hartley declares—had the prolific local architectural firm of Dunn & Hansom ('Dunn saw that it was handsome, and Hansom saw that it was done') churning out imposing churches like St John's Annitsford (modelled on Ghent Cathedral) or St Wilfrid's Blyth—each with a grand Craggy Island-style presbytery for priests, curates and housekeepers.

George Orwell wrote in *The Lion and the Unicorn* that English culture centres round things 'which even when they are communal are not official—the pub, the football match, the back garden, the fireside and the 'nice cup of tea'. The liberty of the individual is still believed in.' But the emphasis on the communal was much stronger in the Great Northern Coalfield, perhaps best exemplified by its other two great participatory institutions: the social clubs and the Co-operative Societies. The first ever Co-op Store may have opened in Rochdale, but Blaydon was home to the second, and every pit-village and mining town had a least one branch, and their architectural output was prodigious and impressive—from their *grand magasin* at Ashington, to modest corner stores. Their grandeur always makes them easy to spot even when hidden behind ugly modern signage.

But aside from religion and shopping, the other great distraction was beer. Coal miners were almost permanently thirsty, and while pubs were popular, their favourite place to drink was in clubs. Many of these are miserably windowless and flat-roofed post-war structures, now with knots of wheezing smokers gathered around their battered front doors. Yet some social clubs are ambitious, creative buildings, expressive of pit-men's aspiration for social progress and sociability. Only the façade now remains of Seaton Terrace CIU's Edwardian splendour, but this was the MGM Grand of social clubs, festooned with heavy mullions, turrets, gables and dormers like a Northumbrian Neuschwanstein, the best example I know of pitmen's confidence. Although 'the Terrace Club' was the place where I bought my first ever pint (of McEwan's horrible 'Best Scotch'), they weren't always simply beer shops. These were not-for-profit institutions that kept down the cost of beer and provided a range of opportunities for leisure and education. These were temples to hard work—where toil was rewarded with subsidised beer, and which were able to pull in huge stars as the Saturday night 'turn.' My parents still talk of Shirley Bassey appearing at High Pit CIU in Cramlington, Lulu at Shiremoor, and Tony Henderson of the *Newcastle Journal* once told me the tale of a befuddled club secretary shuffling up to the microphone at Elmfield Social Club in Hebburn and announcing 'put your hands together for ... I-Ock!' (reader, it was 10cc ...).

It was no wonder that entertainment was taken seriously, as these were tough, hardscrabble places, totally dedicated to industry. No wonder the local football team is called Blyth *Spartans*. Growing up in New Hartley I would count the thirty-six cars on the coal train trundling down the Blyth and Tyne railway, and was even encouraged by my parents to wave 'night night [to Blyth] power station' at bedtime—as if I were a child in a Soviet propaganda film, and this was Seaton Valley Oblast. But I was aware of the dangers that lurked here and had claimed the lives of so many. Just read the gravestones at Seaton or Earsdon: 'lost his life in the pit,' 'killed by a fall of stone,' 'died in an explosion at Backworth colliery.' The Labour MP Jack Lawson wrote in his classic autobiography that whether the pits 'are deep and hot, or drifted into the hillside, pits are pits, and they are tigers, clawing and rending men and boys every day the wheels go round.'[53] Every child in New Hartley learns about the tragedy of the Hester Pit in 1862 when the engine beam snapped and crashed down the shaft, trapping 204 men and boys underground where they would die slowly of asphyxiation, 'little boys in the arms of their fathers, and brothers sleeping dead in the arms of brothers.'[54] A note of 'et in arcadia ego,' is struck by the monument that marks their mass grave amid the ancient foliage of Earsdon churchyard with its unspeakably mournful list of those who met their end underground—'Ts Wanless, aged 19; Jn Sharp, aged 13; Wm Liddle, aged 10'—and its doleful inscription 'In the Midst of Life We Are in Death.'

If death was often in the air of south-east Northumberland then Seaton Delaval Hall was its temple of the dead. 'When Vanbrugh and Hawksmoor worked together they produced great art—Blenheim, Castle Howard, the City churches,' wrote Jonathan Meades. 'Seaton Delaval, just north of Newcastle, is an exemplar of the architecture of fear.'[55] It was built on the instruction of Admiral George Delaval, a naval officer who'd made a fortune through privateering and diplomacy and wanted to rebuild the mouldering family pile where the Delavals had lived since the eleventh century. He called in Sir John Vanbrugh, a libertine and playwright who also dabbled in architecture, and construction began in 1718 on what would be his masterpiece.

THE SPARTA OF THE NORTH

The Vanbrughian style was ideally suited to the north, which Vanbrugh preferred to what he called the 'tame and sneaking south.' For although Seaton Delaval is considered a Baroque building, its essential strength and bulk are redolent of a Northumbrian fortress when compared with the architect's more conventionally palatial Blenheim and Castle Howard. As a younger man Vanbrugh had been imprisoned in the Bastille on charges of espionage by Louis XIV, and the central block of Seaton Delaval—festooned with pirate trophies and obscure escutcheons—has a similar silhouette to that great Parisian fortress, or even border strongholds like the Hermitage in Liddesdale or the keep at Warkworth. Meades saw the beginnings of 1960s Brutalism in Vanbrugh's 'extremely butch, aggressive, sullen [design]. Think Oliver Reed after about eight bottles of whisky.'[56]

It seems fitting that even the statuary at Delaval Hall is GBH-themed, with a spritely David viciously smiting Goliath in the courtyard and Cain smashing Abel's head in by the lily pond. But Vanbrugh's patron didn't live to see the completion of this threnody in stone: he fell from his mount, and with one foot stuck in the stirrup of his galloping horse, the admiral was stotted to death along the byways of the Delaval estate. Another accidental death in a landscape that came to know them all too well.

5

HARD WORK AND HEDONISM

He seldom thinks, that sits at ease,
I' warm an' cheery room,
While at his feet the big coals blaze,
O' Geordy's dreary doom

Alexander Barras, *The Pitman's Social Neet*, 1897

Ah me lads, ye shud of seen us gannin',
We pass'd the foaks upon the road just as they wor stannin';
Thor wes lots o' lads an' lasses there, all wi' smiling faces,
Gannin alang the Scotswood Road, to see the Blaydon Races.

Geordie Ridley, 'The Blaydon Races,' 1862

Northumbrian 'rapper' is the acceptable face of English folk dancing. There is
no danger here of men in bells and feathers mincing around a maypole; rapper is fast, complex and vigorous, danced by men in mining gear—a long-
sleeved vest, knee-length 'pit hoggers,' long stockings and clogs. The rappers'
'swords' (basically metal strips with a handle at each end) were once used to
scrape the sweat and coal dust off the backs of pit ponies, and in the dance's
intricate finale they are woven together into a five-pointed star which is then
brandished in panting exultation. This style of dancing—which to see in the
flesh is utterly exhilarating—is like a cross between a whirling Jewish *mitzvah*
tantz and an Irish slip jig and melded older traditions of medieval long-sword
dancing with industrial themes. When the famous compiler of English folk
dance and song Cecil Sharp saw the Rappers of Winlaton go through their
paces he wrote that

> it would be difficult to exaggerate the force and energy with which it was
> executed when I saw it … the great difficulty is to catch its barbaric spirit, to

131

reproduce the breathless speed, the sureness and economy of movement, the vigour and abandonment of the 'stepping.'[1]

The earliest record of this kind of sword dancing in England dates back to the Tyne Valley in 1715 and flourished within the growing number of mining communities in Northumberland and Durham. The vigorous steps themselves seem to embody so many of those typically Northumbrian traits that those places were known for—especially an intense solidarity with the marras (workmates) you laboured with in dangerous conditions, and the lust for life that was so often made manifest above ground.

This Northumbrian dance tradition is little known, but after all it was Nan Liscombe, the daughter of a Tyneside clog dancer and publican, who taught Gene Kelly how to tap, while David Bowie and Kate Bush learned how to dance under the tutelage of Lindsay Kemp from South Shields. A preference for vigorous styles of dancing is still manifest in the North East and exemplified by the music and dance of 'makina' (the stress is on the second syllable). This is a form of high energy Spanish techno characterised by hard trance music, which has created 'a genuine youth culture phenomenon in the North East in general, much like grime has been in London, or bassline in Sheffield.'[2] The dance steps of makina, also known as 'New Monkey' after a Sunderland nightclub where it first flourished, can appear like a frantic sailor's hornpipe accompanied by turbocharged 178 beats-per-minute synth and amusing, bawdy lyrics delivered with swaggering rapid fire eloquence. One writer has described the makina scene 'as one of the most deep-rooted and self-contained I've ever come across,' made by young men who scorn the lightweight music of other cities (apart from Glaswegian hardcore), and have created a sort of 'cross-generational folk music' where the MCs' technique, 'a constant on-the-beat flow' born out of tough council estates and army tours of Afghanistan (several of the best known makina performers are ex-military), 'is as brutally efficient as the music.'

> Makina is the sound of the working-class North East, the sound of mobile phone speakers at the back of the bus, the sound of a late-night Metro. Makina is the sound of North Shields, Meadow Well, and Percy Main.[3]

The loquacity of makina can trace a lineage back to the pitmen's banter of the Great Northern Coalfield, with its obsession with rhymes and nicknames. The challenge matches that were arranged in pubs for the title of pitman's bard were uncannily similar to the rap battles that emerged from the Afro-Caribbean communities of inner-city USA, and verses had to be invented on the spot from subjects suggested at random by the crowd. In 1952 an eighty-year-old ex-pitman from West Stanley, Co. Durham, remembered:

> Making rhymes and songs used to run through the pit like a fever. Some of 'em seemed to go daft thinking up verses. Even us young lads used to answer back in rhyme. The men would get down, take a little walk, see what the last shift had done. The man who'd been working in your place had always left his smell behind him, and we'd even make a rhyme on that. One would say, 'Whe's been hewin' in maa place in the 'oors sin Aa've bin gan? As reckon it was aad Basher wi's lavender hair-oil on.'[4]

It's clear that much of this was a way of passing the time and cheering your workmates during hard and tedious graft in the pit. This 'patter' tradition gives us another insight into another distinctive feature of North East England: its notable sociability. Newcastle is well known in Britain and beyond as the hedonistic party city par excellence, with the Bigg Market as the Reeperbahn of Northern England. Newcastle is regularly voted among the planet's top ten party cities—and was named the best place to visit in the world in 2018 by Rough Guides. This sociability is lubricated by alcohol, and the history of Northumbrian drinking could fill a whole volume, but the amiability and much-commented upon friendliness of North East England— the local papers love to report stories like 'Government survey: Geordies revealed as 'kindest' people in the UK,'[5] 'Newcastle people rated the most polite'[6] or 'Geordie Accent Rated UK's Most Friendly'[7]—derives from both the border traditions of huddling together for warmth and safety, and the shared experience of extraordinarily hard and dangerous working lives. The consequence of this has been an enduring need for liberation through drink and debauchery, and, although there are of course exceptions to this, it has impelled a Northumbrian disposition towards conviviality and good humour.

Industriousness is a lasting leitmotif in Northumbrian history, from the toiling legionaries who built the Roman Wall, and the *Bararri Tigrisienses* from Mesopotamia (the earliest recorded watermen of the Tyne) who supplied them, to the beavering monks of Lindisfarne who transformed the skins of 1,500 calves into the pages of their famous Gospel, to the birth of arguably Britain's 'first industrial society' at Whickham on the Tyne in the seventeenth century, where, by 1700, over 75 per cent of the residents worked in mines and factories organised on rational lines.[8] In neighbouring Winlaton there was Sir Ambrose Crowley's ironworks, reputedly the greatest manufactory of ironware anywhere in Europe—churning out nails, chains, scythes, hoes, pots and pans—and where, in the early eighteenth century, £20,000 a year was paid in wages to Crowley's workforce who were housed in a proto model village at Winlaton Mill. The village of Whickham was built on an underground mountain of coal and it was the dominance of coal-mining in the region—'the hardest work under heaven'—that made the Northumbrian industrial classes so distinctive.[9] The North East became known as England's 'Black Indies,' where the layer of coal dust on Northumbrian faces 'seemed to horrify and alarm southern visitors, evoking colonial imagery.'[10] (The historian Robert Colls once told me that 'growing up in Shields I hadn't realised snot wasn't black until I moved to Uni in Brighton.').

By 1911 one in five of the working population of Northumberland was a miner, and in Durham almost one in three. This preponderance of the working classes among the local population, and the formation of a social and community structure strongly centred around work, was the rootstock of Northumbria's distinctive proletarian culture, where the hard working and hard living life was celebrated in the tunes and ballads that Thomas Bewick whistled in his workshop: *The Bonny Pit Laddie, The Brave Ploughing Boy*, and *The Miner's Garland*.[11] Think of the exultation of 'Byker Hill and Walker Shore—Collier lads for ever more!', or that hymn to hard work and the manliness required to cut coal written by Ed Pickford of Shiney Row, the self-styled 'Noël Coward of the Coalfields':

When Ah was young and in me prime
Ee aye Ah cud hew
Ah was hewin' aal the time
Noo me hewin' days are throo, throo
Noo me hewin' days are through.

...

Ah've worked with marras and they were men
Ee aye Ah cud hew ...

The term 'Stakhanovite' originated in the Soviet Union and referred to workers who modelled themselves on Alexei Stakhanov, a Russian miner whose strenuous efforts at digging coal earned him the accolade 'Hero of Socialist Labour.' A certain 'Stakhanovism' was widespread among Northumbrian pitmen: partly due to the innate competitiveness between men whose output was weighed and measured, and the relatively high pay that they could earn from increasing their output. As a writer in the 1850s observed of miners' conversations, 'the apple of discord' usually turned upon 'personal and professional prowess.'[12] Working in the coalfields shared some aspects with agricultural labour: the pitmen adapted the farming terms 'inbye' and 'outbye' to mean seams further into the pit, or towards the mine shaft, and Northumbrian farm labourers had a reputation for discipline and productivity. Where southern farmhands were often seen as downtrodden and pauperized, there is a record of one home counties aristocrat asking for 'not only a first-rate ploughman but the sort of fellow you have in Northumberland who can be trusted to overlook the other labourers.'[13] It is telling that the pitman artist Norman Cornish described the robust Durham colliers he painted as having 'peasant strength and rootedness' whose work involved having to 'wrench the coal out with picks, shovels and sheer muscle power. These men were industrial gladiators and I was to be part of its brutality.'[14] In contrast, surface workers, those who screened and sorted the coal for example, tended to have very low status in mining communities, whereas the strapping hewers stripped to the waist and swinging their 5lb picks at the coal face were idolised almost like sports stars. 'He couldn't be beat,' said a Durham miner of the appropriately named Bob Towers:

> By, he was a big man. Can you imagine? He was eighteen stone,—no fat, eighteen stone of man; what we called the County of Durham Big Hewer. He was like a machine when he was hewing. You could hear the pick, pick, pick, pick, as regular as the clock. He never used to seem to tire.[15]

There were a range of overseers in the pit, some of whom carried short sticks which were borrowed from the military as a mark of authority; but to understand the culture of the coalfields it is crucial to appreciate just how much coal-mining relied upon self-motivation. The surveillance, and what E. P. Thompson called the 'work discipline,' of the factories simply did not apply to the hewers who toiled in the confines of a coal seam. This was very different from the industrial work that predominated in the rest of the industrial North, or even in the shipyards (a Wallsend man, Gerry Scott, once told me about the harshness of the 'shithouse clerk,' that he endured at Swan Hunters, who would dish out sheets of *Evening Chronicle* and time the workers' toilet breaks). The coal-owners were not like other manufacturers, for they merely leased a portion of the coalface to the pitman's skill and experience, and the latter were paid for what they could win through their brawn and guile.

But as hard as it was, many pitmen found the work to be intensely stimulating. Henry Mess wrote that although coal-mining was

> strenuous physical work, probably much more so than in most manual occupations. It is not uninteresting. Its peculiar disadvantages are that it is underground and that it is very dangerous. It is a fact of some significance that

miners show no great desire to leave their occupation for another, and that there is no difficulty whatever about getting recruits.[16]

This was certainly true of my own grandfather, Ken Lawton, who loved to recount tales from the underground, in the club and at the dinner table (laced as it was with the baffling technicalities of pitwork—such as 'windy-picks' the 'bull's heed' and 'driving the caunch'). He was a great exponent of the romance of digging for coal, and even made the front page of *Coal News* in 1966 when he and his marra Tommy Rutherford discovered a quartz-lined cavern 'the size of a cathedral,' as he told me, under the North Sea near Blyth. The colliers of the Northumberland and Durham coalfield embodied what Eric Hobsbawm called the 'heroic' period of the Industrial Revolution, preserving their traditions like the seamen who transported the coal they dug up.[17] Consequently, they saw themselves as the aristocrats of the working class—not least because coal-mining traditionally paid so well. Adam Smith stated in *The Wealth of Nations* that 'a collier working by the piece is supposed, at Newcastle, to earn commonly about double ... the wages of common labour ... from the hardship, disagreeableness and dirtiness of his work.'[18]

The demand for coal gave the miners tremendous bargaining power, as in 1765 when almost all of the 4,000 miners in the North-East coalfield successfully struck for higher wages. By 1810 the *Newcastle Courant* noted that pitmen's earnings were 'far greater than those of any other class of mechanics' (on top which some owners made provision for the housing of the miners or made payment in lieu thereof, and miners were able to hew 'house coal' to take home, provided that they 'won' it in their own time). The 1834 Report into the Poor Laws was clear that there was barely any pauperism in Northumberland and Durham, largely because of the constant competitive demand for labour by the expanding collieries, ironworks and railways.[19] William Cobbett observed of Sunderland in 1832 that the miners' lives 'seem to be as good as that of the working part of mankind can reasonably expect.'[20] One account from the mid-nineteenth century well describes the affluent lifestyle of a typical Durham pitman:

> About eleven o'clock he has done his day's work. He gives over, puts on his clothes, goes to the foot of the shaft, and ascends. He then goes home, washes his hands, and his face and neck, wipes his body with a towel, and sits down to his baked potatoes and broiled ham. He may if he thinks fit put on his good clothes and walk about like a gentleman in the afternoon. He takes his tea a little after four, sits an hour or two by the fire, and then goes to bed and sleeps sound till the voice of the callman arouses him to his labour.[21]

The role of family breadwinner among miners (and in the North East it was a matter of pride for miners that their wives did not take on paid work outside the home) was a fundamental part of male self-evaluation. The status of a Northumbrian man 'lay in the size and regularity of his pay packet, and the manner in which he turned a proportion of it over to his wife.'[22] As a line of miners' verse had it 'maw wife an' bairns, need meat an' Sunday claes' and these should 'come oot what one man airns.' In the 1950s a letter was sent to the Newcastle *Evening Chronicle* that neatly summed up the miner's swaggering attitude to his earning potential:

Aa lit me pipe w' aad pund notes, an'hoyed away th' dottle,
An' bowt meesel a bran' new car, an' let 'or oot full throttle;
Aa travelled far fot hallidays, went sumtimes ower th' sea,
Oh! Whaat a time w' haad in France, th'Wife, an' Bairns, an' me.[23]

In their heyday, Northumbrian coal miners (and shipyard workers too) were probably the highest paid proletarians anywhere in the world outside the USA, and higher pay and higher output went hand in hand in what was the most productive coalfield in Britain. In the early nineteenth century, the northern hewer could cut coal at about 4.3 tons per shift or 1,160 tons per year—twice the rate of Scottish or Black Country hewers, and northern levels of output per man-year were always above the national average.[24] Hewing 'matches' were commonplace underground, and one Durham miner recalled men working 'like horses [and] going home after each twelve hours' shift with sore and tired bones.'[25] By 1911 the North East coalfield was producing more coal than any other coalfield, some 21 per cent of Britain's coal production, and in 1965 Lynemouth Colliery in Nortumberland was the first in Britain to produce 1,000 tons of coal in a shift off a single coal face. This productivity was reinforced by the unique 'cavil' system that held sway in the North East (a sort of lottery that meant each squad of miners had a fair chance of a turn at the seams with the 'softest' coal). This was a great motivating factor for the hewers and the 'putters,' the younger men who hurried to and fro in the bituminous darkness keeping them supplied with empty tubs to fill. Any perceived slacking was dealt with harshly. 'If one bloke was a bit slow there was always somebody right behind him ready to stick a boot up his arse,' recalled the South Shields miner Tommy Turnbull, 'everything came down to money.'[26]

We should, though, be wary not to glamorise these working men's lives. Catherine Cookson was once criticised for writing about the culture of the North East. 'What culture?' she replied. 'The only culture I knew was hard work'—adding that 'hard work doesn't kill you, but it helps along the way.' Coal-mines in particular had long been understood as a place of terror (and in 1786 the Home Department even considered imprisoning convicts in the gloom of the pits where the 'blackness would invite reflection on his soul, the labour would punish his body, and [the convict] would 'sigh in Perpetual Darkness, and the whole length of [his] Slavery, will be One Mournful Alternative, of insensibility and Labour.'"[27] And yet the Northumbrians took to coal-mining with a hard-nosed relish. The Northumberland and Durham miners' unions were the last to join the National Miners' Federation of Great Britain, partly because they saw nothing wrong in haulage boys working eleven hours or more to help keep the price of Durham coal down (this changed after the Eight Hours Act of 1909, after which they finally joined the Federation).[28] But mining coal was absolutely exhausting. The actor Robson Green recalled seeing his father come home to Annitsford 'dead shattered after his shift, his body so dirty and black. It was scary to see his bath water.'[29] Before the pits were fully mechanised absenteeism was often the only way a miner could sustain mind and body, and miners would be literally worn out if they reached their 50s, at which point, with lungs full of coal dust, they would typically seek a 'datal job' (work paid at a daily minimum wage, instead of piece work paid by the ton).[30] The poem 'A Miner's Advice to his Son' by the Durham pitman John Rickaby well sums up the utter enervation of pit work:

> Ye come back hyem, yor hands on yor belt
> Ye feel like faalin' to bits
> It's only yor belt that haads ye together,
> Yor sick o' the sight o' the pits.[31]

But gruellingly hard, unpleasant graft was by no means confined to the coal mines. Sid Chaplin recalled the 'brawny gang of coke-burners' that he saw at Ferryhill toiling away at the beehive coke-ovens, where the only measures they took to protect themselves from the heat were the sacks they wore 'draped over their heads like cowls' and 'a water-hose played continually upon them as they worked.'[32] Similarly infernal conditions were the norm in places like Consett, where the iron 'puddlers' stirred the molten iron to remove any impurities before rolling, and such dehydrating work was always a great stimulus to beer drinking. And writing of the coal ships of eighteenth-century Tyne and Wear in his *Treatise upon Practical Seamanship*, William Hutchinson claimed that the crews of colliers were the most efficient seamen afloat. 'In heaving up their anchor briskly they greatly excel other merchant ships' as they could do this with only seven men in half the time it took another ship to do it with eighteen men; and in addition to these sea-going vessels the 'nervous and muscular strength' of the keelmen, who transferred the coal from shore to ship, was a crucial part of the operation 'as they transferred their bulky, backbreaking cargoes up and down stream in all weathers and states of the tide.'[33] Although the coal trade was long established on the river, Tyneside did not see widespread manufacturing until the mid-nineteenth century. But, again, contemporary accounts give us a vivid sense of the extraordinary industriousness of places like Armstrong's great engineering works at Elswick, where, in an account from 1858, Walter White, librarian to the Royal Society, wrote that

> I saw brawny smiths forging chains link by link, and small mountains of fin-
> ished chains lying ready for transport not far from the ruthless machine by
> which their strength had been tested. I saw an iron bridge being built for India,
> and small iron steamers for the navigation of Indian rivers; and huge engines
> for sundry purposes, besides which the men looked dwarf-like; and gangs of
> rivetters wielding their hammers with deafening din.[34]

* * *

What of female labour in the industrial North East? A key feature has been the almost complete absence of female factory workers—in comparison to the mill workers of Lancashire and Yorkshire. By the turn of the nineteenth century there were only a handful of Northumbrian employers who hired women in any great numbers, such as the 'white mice' of Maling's vast pot-teries on the Tyne (so called because they were usually covered in porcelain dust). In Henry Mess's 1928 survey he thought it 'an asset of the area that its married women, for the most part, are not industrially engaged'; and in 1921 only 21% of women on Tyneside worked, compared with 34% nation-ally, and the region didn't catch up with the rest of the country until the 1980s.[35] Several factors explain this. Migration from the countryside to the pits and shipyards led to an acute shortage of men in farming areas. This in turn reinforced a unique pattern of agricultural work by which male 'hinds' (appointed at annual hiring fairs, much like coalminers until 'the bond' sys-tem was broken in the 1870s) were obliged to provide one or more women helpers to carry out the most back-breaking tasks—such as hoeing, weeding and digging up turnips. These 'bondagers' were usually, but not always, related to the hind who they lived with in tied-cottages, and the shilling a day they earned at harvest time was paid directly to the hind to whom she was 'bound' and who provided their bed and board. These women were a picturesque feature of Northumbrian rural life right up until the First World War, and their costume of a broad bonnet, hobnail boots and a wimple known as a 'heid hankie' was probably the last peasant costume worn in England. It was gruellingly hard life, but then there were few occupations for Northumbrian women that weren't.

The Coal Mines Regulation Act of 1842 that banned women and children under ten years old from working underground was part of a general wave of reforming zeal, inspired at least in part by moral concerns over scantily-clad women working at such close quarters with men as it was about saving them from the dangers and toil of pit-work. But such concerns were exaggerated: there were few, if any, women (as distinct from boys and girls) working underground by this time, but there were thousands of Northumbrian women and girls who laboured in such punishing and unrewarding trades as construction—'mounting high ladders and crawling over the tops of houses'—as well as the 'the lower and dirtier departments of factories on the Tyne.'[36] Instead, the Act was motivated by an impulse to discipline the coalfields following the unrest of the 1830s, and should be seen alongside the growing strength of Methodism in the pit villages which preached the virtue of respectable family life as much as salvation. For the sub-commissioners who gathered evidence to prepare the Act for Parliament were given clear instructions:

> In regard to female workers, you will inquire how far their employment during Childhood has prevented them from forming the domestic habits usually acquired by women in their station and has rendered them less fit than those whose early years have not been spent in labour for performing the duties of wives and mothers.[37]

The pit villages developed their distinctive character from the mid-nineteenth century, where order, hard work and strictly defined gender roles were the norm. The few concessions to femininity were the names of the pits themselves—as in the defunct Gloria and Hester collieries in New Hartley where I grew up, and Isabella and Ann collieries against whom we played football.

The standard mark of respectability for a pitman was that his wife should not have to go *out* to work, but the domestic realm that pitwomen inhabited was intensely laborious. Their day would typically begin with the painstaking work of getting the fire lit in the grate in the back-kitchen, the engine room of the pit-cottage, and the source of the hot water that was essential for making tea, boiling filthy clothes and washing the grimy bodies of sons and husbands.

'One of my jobs was to dad [strike] my Father's pit claes against the wall, to get the dust out,' recalled Florence Merihein of Ashington, 'then scrape the clarts off his beuts [boots] and wipe them over with dripping—to keep the wet out, for he was often working in wet conditions underground.'[38]

Men's work routines delineated the life patterns of women. Miners' wives in County Durham slept in snatches when they had shift-working husbands and sons, for these men would come in and out of the house requiring food and hot water, at regular intervals throughout the night and day … The mother of Jack Lawson would rise at three in the morning to get his father off to work at Boldon colliery and again at five to do the same for the boys. Lawson's mother did this in part because, such were the dangers of mining, 'it might be the last time she would see us,' for the miner's wife, it was 'unthinkable that we should go to work while she was in bed.'[39]

Coal-mining would have been simply impossible without this female reserve army of labour. Tommy Turnbull's description of his mother's Sisyphean routine in the back streets of South Shields, cleaning the accumulated grime of pitwork from vests, shirts, socks and pants is so evocative of the unrelenting hard work that was the lot of women in the coalfields.

> The clothes which are always of heavy material—they wouldn't last if they weren't—have to dadded [beaten] boiled, possed [pounded with a stick in a tub of water], boiled again, scrubbed, rinsed two or three times, put through the mangle a couple of times, carried out in a heavy basket and then pegged out on the line. And if it rains they might be in and out several times before they go onto the clotheshorse and then get ironed. This takes a lot out of everything. Underclothes, outer clothes, and woman.[40]

Hard work was as pervasive in the hearth and home as it was at the coal-face, and the fanatical cleaning and polishing of net-curtains and front-steps was often a source of competition in such close-knit communities. In 1977 John Ardagh wrote of the modest Tyneside homes he visited as having levels of 'almost Swabian cleanliness' and we can trace this back to a sort of professionalised domesticity that grew out of patterns of work and levels of pay that distinguished the coal industry.[41] William Morrison, a doctor 'engaged in the Countess of Durham's collieries,' reported in 1841 that the typical pit cottage was a 'well-ordered house' presenting 'a gratifying picture of social comfort'; and in an account of the Durham pit-village of Coxhoe one observer was struck that the cottages 'all appear exceedingly neat, and as like to one another as so many soldiers are like to each other [and] all was swept and clean,' and, as well as the gleaming brassware, tasteful calico decorations and four-poster beds he noticed that 'most of the women take pains to make themselves, as well as their houses, look very agreeable.'[42] (Domestic decorating, painting and paper-hanging was usually done by women as a money-spinning sideline.)

Away from the coalfields, there was a greater variety of experiences open to women. The rope-making industry—dirty, arduous and low-status work, but vital for the maritime trades—was almost entirely dominated by women who became notorious for their brash, and at times licentious confidence. One 1930s account of Hood Haggie's at North Shields recalls how terrified men were of being sent there as the ropery's female employees were 'practically dehumanised because of the conditions they worked and lived under. They'd strip him and they'd probably rupture him through their frolicking.'[43] As well as ropeworks, the North Sea fishing fleet required armies of female labour on shore to process the catch and hawk it round the streets. The picturesque fishing village of Cullercoats north of Tynemouth drew the American artist Winslow Homer to live and paint there in the 1880s. Here he found his muse studying the robust fisher lasses who plied their trade on the shore with their baskets of crabs and herring.

Aw's a Cullercoats fish-lass, se cozy an' free
Browt up in a cottage close on by the sea
An' aw sell fine fresh fish ti poor an ti rich—
Will ye buy, will ye buy, will ye by maw fresh fish?

The First World War was a watershed for women in the North East, who, for the first time, found employment opportunities in fields as diverse as window-cleaning and conducting trams. The labour-hungry armaments industry was the biggest new employer of women, with 21,000 taken on by Armstrongs alone—by then the biggest privately-owned arms company on the planet—in manufacturing guns and shells. These 'Munitionettes' were resented by some men, and the trade unions dubbed them 'dilutees' and ensured that they weren't paid men's wages. But released from pre-war strictures they explored other avenues hitherto barred to women, and football in particular became extremely popular. Blyth Spartans Ladies even won the national 'Munitionettes Cup' largely thanks to their lethal centre-forward Isabella 'Bella' Reay who scored 120 goals in one year. It is telling though that after 1918 the government, employers and unions conspired to ensure that women were quickly returned to the domestic realm and by 1921 the number of women employed on Tyneside was down to pre-war levels.[44] In 1920 the FA even banned their member clubs from hosting women's football with

'Under the Coaly Tyne', by John Hodgson Campbell (1887).

'The Fighting Fifth' ('Northumberland Fusiliers') after the Battle of St Eloi, 14–15 March, 1915. Official War Photograph published on a postcard. Caption on reverse: 'Assisted by the Royal Fusiliers, took with splendid dash the first and second link trenches at St. Eloi'.

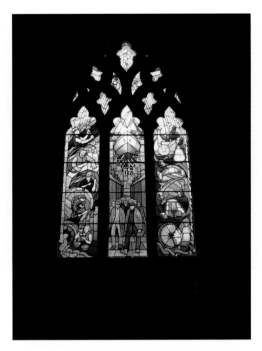

The 'Tyneside Industrial Heritage Window' (2006) by Joseph Nuttgens in St Mary's Roman Catholic Cathedral Church, Newcastle upon Tyne. It replaced a window damaged during the Second World War.

Edwardian View of Grey Street, Newcastle.

'Weel May the Keel Row', painted by Ralph Hedley in 1905 and later exhibited at the Bewick Club in Newcastle.

Second World War gun emplacement at Tynemouth Castle with the ruined priory church.

Exhibition Park, Newcastle-upon-Tyne, Tyne and Wear, May 1929. Aerial view of the North East Coast Exhibition, showing the Pleasure Grounds for the exhibition, including gardens, a lake and a funfair on the edge of the Town Moor. The exhibition attracted more than 4 million visitors over 24 weeks.

the cursory justification that 'the game of football is quite unsuitable for females and ought not to be encouraged.'

Well-heeled women felt the pressure to conform to traditional gender roles too, as in the case of Rachel Parsons, daughter of the famous Tyneside industrialist Sir Charles Parsons. She was a Mechanical Sciences graduate from Cambridge and President of the Women's Engineering Society, and during the war had been a director of her father's Tyneside engineering company, but at war's end Sir Charles insisted that Rachel stand down, causing a rift between them that was never healed. After female suffrage was introduced partially in 1918 and then fully from 1928 we do see women's participation in politics increase (Rachel Parsons stood for the Conservatives in Newcastle). It is telling however that the private lives of the women elected in the North East between the Wars gave them untypical of levels of independence. After the former 'Gaiety Girl' Mabel Philipson was returned for the Conservatives at Berwick in 1923 as the North East's first female MP, there came a succession of formidable women who were all either widows, unmarried or childless: Margaret Bondfield in Wallsend (who became, in 1929, Britain's first female Cabinet Minister), Dr Marion Phillips (Sunderland), Susan Lawrence (Stockton), Irene Ward (Wallsend), and 'Red Ellen' Wilkinson (Middlesbrough and then Jarrow).

* * *

The inherent danger in the industries that dominated the economy of North East England was a hugely significant factor in shaping Northumbrian culture. It's been estimated by the Mining Institute in Newcastle that 85,000 British coal miners were killed at work between 1873 and 1953. In 1862 one member of the Institute made the grisly calculation that if 184,000,000 tons of coal were won in Northumberland and Durham over the last ten years, at a rate of 157 mining deaths per year, then 8.7 lives were lost for every million tons.[45] Records are much sketchier before then, but pits were much deeper in the North-East counties, and this led to increased risks from both lethally volatile gases and the accidents that attended the use of gunpowder underground (the term 'pitfall' derives from mining). As early as 1705 an explosion at Gateshead killed thirty workers, and three years later another at Fatfield near Chester-le-Street killed sixty-nine. Between 1767 and 1815 there were at least seven explosions which each caused more than thirty deaths and in one two-year period at the beginning of the nineteenth century it is thought that as many as 600 miners were killed in pit explosions in North East

England (with a further 538 deaths between 1816–34).[46] In 1767, the Duke of Northumberland, whose coal income amounted to over £10,000 a year, pressured the *Newcastle Journal* to restrain itself from drawing attention to pit accidents, a request which the craven editor complied with: 'As we are requested to take no particular notice of these things, which, in fact, could have very little good tendency we drop the further mentioning of it.'[47]

The fatalities were shocking enough, but by 1914 there were over 150,000 serious mining accidents a year in Britain (those that required more than seven days' absence from work). The coal-owners were notoriously cavalier about miners' safety, and even fought a rearguard action against the introduction of twin shafts after the New Hartley Disaster in 1862. One review of *The Great Northern Coalfields*, a book that explores the mining collections at Beamish Museum, made the powerful point that given how frequent were the deaths of miners (accidents that killed five to ten were truly regular events and single deaths were seldom reported) is the word 'accident' accurate and appropriate 'since the frequency of disaster suggests they were entirely predictable. Is homicide too strong a word?'[48] One of the most moving accounts of the emotional impact that accidents underground had in mining communities was written by Jack Lawson in his autobiography *A Man's Life*:

> a friend of mine had a son of eighteen years working when the place caved in on him. Word came home to father, who lived near the drift. He did not run; he leaped to the place. A great raw-boned he was, a top-notch man. Straight into the low tunnel he went, where, behind, and under a great fall, lay the body of his boy. The father was a raving madman of energy, groans, splashing tears, wrestling with giant boulders, which would have defied even his great strength at ordinary times. To move an ounce of stone at such times sometimes dislodges a ton. Only one man could work at once, and all must stand back for this one man, a man of giant strength and craft; strength multiplied and craft more pointed because of the exquisite pain of the worker. It was agony to watch the man, for he neither spared himself nor cared for himself, while both for him and the workers there was the sure and dreaded knowledge of what he would find. And when he came at last to the broken, bleeding, lifeless body of his lad, he gathered him up in his great arms and stooping low carried him to the light of day.[49]

The communalism that so defined the pit villages of Northumberland and Durham grew from the simple facts that miners relied on each other for their safety at work, and the people who lived in these places shared a common purpose. The historian Eneas Mackenzie remarked in 1825 that 'the colliers form a distinct body of men, and seldom associate with others, they entertain strong feelings of attachment,' and the Labour minister (and MP for Seaham) Manny Shinwell wrote in the 1950s that the enduring characteristics of North East miners were 'courage [and] unselfish and heroic behaviour' for the greater good of the 'oppressed mineworkers and their families.'[50] This was undoubtedly a romantic view, but the sense of comradeship among communities which shared the same hardships is not surprising, as was a shared sense among some miners of doing exciting, heroic labour.

Although many miners were terrified by working 'doon the pit,' my own grandfather actually enjoyed his work: relishing the physicality, comradeship and even the dangerous thrill of mining for coal while the North Sea creaked and groaned above your head. There were pits in the North East nicknamed the Slaughterhouse and the Butcher's Shop, and 'granda' (who started work at New Hartley Colliery, where, in 1862, 204 men and boys had been killed) was badly mangled several times, saw men die underground and was present when his best pal lost an arm. (He also bore on his face and body miners' 'buttons'—old healed-over wounds with coal dust that turned blue over time and were worn by old pitmen like campaign medals). Indeed, it only struck me after he'd died that his usual words on parting—'watch what your dee-ing,' or 'keep a howld', grew from the fear of loss as described by the pitman poet Joseph Skipsey:

> 'GET UP!' the caller calls, 'Get up!'
> And in the dead of night,
> To win the bairns their bite and sup,
> I rise a weary wight.
> My flannel sudden donn'd thrice o'er
> My birds are kiss'd, and then
> I with a whistle shut the door
> I may not ope' again.

As if coal-mining wasn't enough of a danger to the Northumbrian working man, the other profession that dominated North East England—sea-faring—was even more hazardous. John Ruskin may have written romantically that not even the 'quay-sides of Carthage [that] glowed with crusaders' shields above the bays of Syria' could compare 'as much as a Newcastle collier beating against the wind' but transporting coal by sea was lethal.[51] In the first few months of 1800 no less than 69 out of 71 vessels laden with coals from the Tyne and Wear were wrecked on the passage to London. By the mid nineteenth century around 1,000 seamen were dying annually around the coasts of Britain alone. Even after Samuel Plimsoll's loading restrictions of the 1870s (and the three major cases cited by Plimsoll as evidence of systematic over-loading were all from the North East) such losses remained commonplace, reaching a peak in 1881 when almost 4,000 masters and men died including 2,552 by wreck, and 1,123 by being washed overboard). These horrendous casualties caught the attention of Joseph Chamberlain, President of the Board of Trade, who in a speech at Newcastle in 1884 noted that

> We know that the miner's is a dangerous and perilous trade, but the loss of life has never been even in the heaviest year, more than one in 315 of the persons employed. In the case of British shipping ... one in 60 of those engaged in it met with a violent death in a single year.[52]

Britain's first Sailors' Union was founded on the Wear in 1887 by the Sunderland-born seaman Havelock Wilson, a self-educated man who'd discovered trade unionism on a voyage to Australia. Wilson's union was born at a time when the old sailorly skills of block and tackle were becoming obsolete through the replacement of sailing ships by steamers, where the real requirement was for 'burly lads who could steer' and 'ship-navvies' who could shovel coal.[53] The greater reliability of steam ships meant that more men could be home-based, working in 'weekly boats' sailing to the Thames or across the North Sea and back. This gave the port towns of Tyne and Wear a particularly salty character, and for most of the nineteenth century shipping was the largest employer in Sunderland, employing almost one in four males over the age of twenty according to the 1861 census (it's likely to be higher as many seamen would be at sea on the enumeration night).[54] But like coal-mining, the physical debilitation and susceptibility to injuries that were typical of the maritime trades meant that Wearside was unusually burdened with exhausted seamen and the widows and orphans of men lost at sea (Sunderland had, on average, 800 of each in the middle decades of the nineteenth century, and 300 disabled seamen—and this accounts for the impressive sailors alms-houses in Tynemouth, South Shields and Sunderland). The sea remained a place of peril well into the twentieth century: wartime losses of shipping were huge, and in the Second World War the Merchant Navy had a higher ratio of casualties—at over 25 per cent—than any of the Armed Services (and it's thought that more than 3,000 merchant seamen from South Shields alone were lost at sea).[55]

The unusual dominance of the two most lethally dangerous occupations in Britain—coal-mining and seafaring—made working lives precarious in North East England. The response to what many would still see as egregious exploitation was certainly political (as we shall see in the following chapter), but also practical—there was seldom a shortage of volunteers for rescue attempts whenever there was a disaster underground or at sea. The classic 'self-right-ing' lifeboat was invented in South Shields by William Wouldhave in 1789, and the world's first volunteer Life Brigade was founded in Tynemouth in 1864—but a certain stoicism, even fatalism was just as commonplace. Frank Atkinson, the Yorkshiremen who founded Beamish Museum, observed that one of the most remarkable things about talking to old miners was 'their lack of bitterness,' and that 'one almost becomes more bitter on their behalf than the men themselves, who seem to have developed a special kind of gentleness through their hard experience.'[56]

This expressed itself through a distinctively Northumbrian appetite for sentimentality—one thinks here of Billy Elliot's macho father weeping at the picket line, Ralph Hedley's much reproduced painting of a miner and his baby 'Geordie Ha'ad the Bairn,' or the touching farewell scene in the midst of grim-visaged Northumberland Fusiliers marching to war in 'The Response.' It's possible that an intensity of emotion stemmed from danger-ous, precarious, soldaristic lives, and it's illustrative that Charles Dickens loved to do readings in Newcastle, whose audiences he thought were 'indi-vidually rough [but] unusually tender and sympathetic ... while their comic perception is quite up to the high London average,' adding that 'a finer audi-ence there is not in England and I suppose them to be a specially earnest people, for while they can laugh till they shake the roof, they have a very unusual sympathy with what is pathetic or passionate.' Considering the banality of industrial tragedy in the industrial North East, this inclination towards mawkishness is understandable—and could be heightened by hor-rific events like the crushing to death of 183 children in Sunderland in 1883 at the end of a variety show in the Victoria Hall. It also found expression through the enduring popularity of nostalgic 'Geordierama' on the regional stage and the canon of lachrymose Northumbrian songs, whose usual subject matter—Geordie's been press-ganged/Faither's drunk again/Dozens were killed at the pit today—milk the tear ducts with both hands. This in turn built on deep traditions of folk song and poetry that were unusual in England, where the men 'spoke English but had the outlook of Afghan tribes-men' and 'prized a poem almost as much as plunder, and produced such an impressive assembly of local narrative songs that some people used to label all our greater folk poems as 'Border ballads.''[57] G.M. Trevelyan noted the predisposition that those who live with great danger have towards emotional expressiveness when he wrote of the Border Reivers that

> like the Homeric Greeks, they were cruel, coarse savages, slaying each other
> as the beasts of the forest; yet they were also poets who could express in the

147

grand style the inexorable fate of the individual man and woman, and infinite pity for all the cruel things which they none the less perpetually inflicted upon one another.

An Anglo-Scottish friend of mine from Barrow is less impressed by all this and likes to mock lachrymose Geordies for 'greeting' at the slightest provocation. It's significant that 'Gresford,' the weepy 'miners hymn,' although written for a Welsh mining disaster, was composed by an army bandsman (and former pitman) from Hebburn, Robert Saint. But it wasn't all moping around. The main coping mechanism favoured by Northumbrians for the trials of life has always been the drink.

* * *

The history of Northumbrian drinking—one of the most recognisable clichés in the national consciousness—goes back a very long way. Newcastle has been famous for its beer for centuries and claims to be the first town in England to brew ale.[58] The expression 'Newcastle hospitality' was once widely used and was defined in M. A. Denham's *Folk Lore of Northumberland* as 'roasting a friend to death' or killing a person with kindness. 'The saying, no doubt, alludes to the ancient drinking customs of Newcastle and Northumberland.'[59] Drunkenness was so ingrained in the local culture that the 'Newcastle cloak' was a well-known punishment for inebriates in the seventeenth century, and an account from 1655 describes groups of men in the town being driven 'up and down the streets, with a great tub, or barrel, opened in the sides, with a hole in one end, to put through their heads, and to cover their shoulders … and so make them march to the view of all beholders; and this is their punishment for drunkards, or the like.'[60] When John Wesley lived and ministered in eighteenth-century Newcastle he was appalled by the prevalence of drunkenness (while also noting the 'pure love and kindness' of the local population). The Portuguese novelist Eça de Queirós, who lived and worked in Newcastle as a diplomatic consul in the 1870s—once describing the region as a 'melancholic coal pit'—has left us a vivid account of the sort of debauchery that the town has long been known for:

> An enormous brutish crowd, rough and noisy, fills the wide streets, harshly lit by shining gas lamps and shop windows; the bars, the gin palaces are ablaze with light… drunks stagger about, punching each other; on a street corner a preacher … howls verses from the Bible… Prostitutes pester insolently, demanding money… two enormous policemen drag an old woman away, drunk and cursing; groups of miners, pipes in their mouths, greyhounds at

heel, talk in the rough speech of Northumbria; amorous couples go by, arms round each other, kissing shamelessly; the whistles of locomotives pierce the thick air… and in the squares and alleys, on restaurant pianos, drunken patriots sing the new war song We don't want to fight, but by Jingo if we do…! shouting that the Russians shall not have Constantinople![61]

Newcastle had the highest concentration of taverns and beer-shops in the North East, and this beery vortex pulled in thirsty farmers who'd converge on the Bigg Market, while the sailors' and keelmen's saturnalia would take place on the Quayside. In the early nineteenth century Newcastle had so many pubs that the liberalising Beer Act of 1830 did not lead to the spectacular eruption of beer houses that other towns witnessed. By 1876 researchers have calculated the average consumption of male beer-drinkers was 16 pints per week.[62] In 1854 the Newcastle Temperance Society argued that drink was 'no affectation but part of the city's economic and social fabric,' with 425 pubs, 76 beer-shops and the colossal sum of £130,000 being spent a year on alcoholic beverages, which would be worth anything up to £368 million in today's prices.[63] And there was another practical reason behind frequent visits to the pub: public houses were usually the only place where men (and women) could escape the cramped and overcrowded housing that so prevailed in the North East.

In the late nineteenth century drunkenness proceedings averaged 62 per 10,000 persons across England but stood at 207 per 10,000 for Newcastle. In 1901, when the average rate for ten similar 'seaports' was 88, Newcastle's equivalent rate was 225. Newcastle was simply 'the most drunken town in England,' and woe betide any do-gooding temperance campaigner who tried to interfere.[64] In the 1892 general election at Newcastle the popular Tory candidate, Charles Hamond, ran an effective campaign by appealing publicly for the support of 'all who loved a glass of beer.'[65] It's instructive that one of the arguments put forward by the campaigners for the 'nine-hours movement' in the engineering works on the Tyne in the 1870s was that

one of the most seductive agencies of drunkenness has been the long duration of the hours of labour, and its consequent effect in the almost total exhaustion which it has produced upon the vital energies of the working man.[66]

Although the distilling of bootleg whisky was not unknown in the hills of Northumberland, beer was always the tipple of choice. Indeed, if called back to the pit to carry out additional work coal miners would be paid a 'lowens'—literally a tankard of ale. In 1830 it was estimated that 70 per cent of the beer sold in Newcastle was considered 'strong,' and the Newcastle antiquarian John Collingwood Bruce, looking back on the late Georgian period, thought that later generations could have 'no idea of the heads and stomachs of men in those days ... prodigious was the quantity they drank.'[67] Newcastle Brown Ale is now the most famous beer brand associated with the North East (although Sunderland's own Double Maxim Ale—so named by a Boer War veteran at Vaux's Brewery who thought it had a kick like the eponymous machine gun—was older); but the potency of local beer was the lifeblood of Tyneside's popular culture. It was even eulogised in classical verse by the eighteenth-century poet John Cunningham, where Mars summons the Gods to Olympus to celebrate Britain's success in war.

> And freely declared there was choice of good cheer
> Yet vowed to his thinking,
> For exquisite drinking,
> Their nectar was nothing to Newcastle beer
>
> ...
>
> Your spirits it raises,
> It cures your diseases
> There's freedom and health in our Newcastle beer.

The preference for strong waters wasn't confined to Newcastle though. I've heard it said locally that 'North Shields is a drinking town, with a fishing problem,' but similar things might be observed of other Northumbrian places. In the early 1890s there were nearly 500 public houses in Sunderland, about 250 at South Shields, and national figures of convictions for drunkenness in 1911 saw Northumberland top of the county league with 127.31 per 10,000 population, Newcastle at 97.91 and Middlesbrough 117.51.[68] In the First World War Tyneside was considered the second most drunken district in Britain after Clydeside, where a shortage of cinemas to entertain the growing munitions workforce meant that the rest would just 'drink their pay packet,' and to make matters worse, the press ruefully noted, 'light beer is not popular in Newcastle.'[69] Indeed, when the Armistice was declared in 1918 the workers of Tyneside were given two days off and returned to work on the 13th, but many apparently took the whole week off to attend so-called 'Victory Teas,' street parties, which in the words of the local prosecuting constable 'had developed into drunken orgies.'[70]

But why was there such a tradition of dipsomania in the first place, and why in a study from the 1980s did researchers note that 'the strongest tradition followed by the young adults we knew was drinking alcohol,' with the 'importance of drinking to the local community reflected in the large number of words used for being drunk, including "stottin," "mortal," "pissed," and "smashed."'[71] In Joe Sharkey's recent book he wonders why drinking and fighting are still considered 'Geordie life skills' and cites Freud's view that 'the life imposed on us is too hard to bear, it brings too much pain.'[72] As Terry Collier once said to Bob Ferris in the Tyneside TV comedy *The Likely Lads*, 'I'd offer you a beer but I've only got six cans.' This may well have been the view of the 'pit sinker' that Thomas Bewick remembered from his childhood in the Tyne Valley who spent his working life working in flooded pits up to his chest in water, who would save up his wages for a monthly blow-out on the beer in Newcastle which he called 'lowsening his skin.'[73] One account from 1951 of the Durham Miners' Gala (not long after a disaster at Easington colliery) by the Labour MP for Huddersfield, J.P.W. Mallalieu—who thought the platform speeches were merely incidental and 'mixed with the sounds of the fair, of late-arriving bands, of sandwich papers and of popping corks'—well-describes how the Dionysian instinct of the mining communities was a reaction to hardship and sorrow:

> Suddenly there was silence. The colours still danced, but everything else was still. For the banner we now saw was draped in black. It carried a flag sent by the miners of Yugoslavia. It carried also the name of Easington Colliery. In that colliery, 52 days earlier, 83 miners had lost their lives [as the result of an explosion]. Through the silence the Easington band began to play. It played 'Gresford', the tune which a miner himself had written in sorrow for the great Gresford disaster [of 1934 near Wrexham in North Wales, when an explosion had killed 266 miners]. When the tune came to an end there was again stillness and silence until Old Elvet gently relaxed his hold and there was space to move. With the first movement the great crowd set up a storm of cheering that could be heard in Paradise, dancers cavorted again and sunshine wiped away all thought of tears. 'Miners rub shoulders with death,' concluded Mallalieu. 'They know how to face death. Last Saturday I saw, too, that they will not let death spoil life.'[74]

This mixture of mourning and celebration may have been an inheritance from the older Northumbrian tradition of the 'lake-wake' (*lic* was Anglo-Saxon for corpse), which featured the rowdy singing of psalms and hymns round the bed of the dying, but which by 1898 had become a 'hard-drinking excuse for 'indecent revelry' around the flower decorated coffin.'[75] Perhaps understandably, Northumbrian drinking is often described with a certain purse-lipped disapproval, what the seventeenth-century Newcastle puritan John Pigg described as 'riotous prodigalitie,' and the twentieth-century feminist Beatrix Campbell bemoaned as 'incontinent, marauding masculinities—the football, the drinking … Andy Capp, the Toon Army and Viz Magazine, the signifiers that infused Geordie identity with misogyny.'[76]

One might argue with some of this, but such disdain misses so much of what is good-humoured and carnivalesque about the Northumbrian pursuit of hedonism at all costs. In the 1990s when *Viz* took over the sponsorship of Blyth Spartans FC they asked to have the legend 'Drink beer smoke tabs' emblazoned on their shirts, until overruled by the local football association. This goes back at least as far as the Middle Ages where Newcastle Corporation kept a 'company of fools,' a unique instance of a civic company, and the mystery plays performed at Corpus Christi were, by all accounts, 'vulgar, foul-mouthed and sensational, the leads often performing completely naked.'[77] We might add here that the drunken riot that followed Newcastle Corporation's unwise decision to install 'wine pants' (fountains) in several places in the town to mark George IV's coronation—where one celebrant washed 'his posteriors' in the civic claret whilst another paraded the broken fountain spout 'as if it was a huge penis'—was typical of the bacchanalia that I first saw as a child on Bank Holiday Mondays in Whitley Bay.

The manic frenzy of Northumbrian drinking has been both the lubricant of and inspiration for verse and song for centuries. Take the Newcastle poet Edward Chicken's extraordinarily pungent celebration of 'The Collier's Wedding' from 1729, with its unforgettable passage

> *Dead drunk, some tumble on the floor,*
> *And swim in what they'd drunk before.*
> *'Hiccup' cries one. 'Reach me your hand.'*
> *The house turns round. I cannot stand.'*
> *So now the drunken senseless crew*
> *Break pipes, spill drink, piss, shit and spew.*

Or consider Johnny Handle's 1960s ballad 'The Collier Lad,' who, as the song goes:

> *… is a canny lad,*
> *An' he's aalwes of good cheor,*
> *An' he knaas how to wark,*
> *an' he knaas how to shork,*
> *An' he knaas how to sup good beor.*

This exuberant *joie de vivre* has long been accompanied by a canon of distinctive Northumbrian music, unusually vibrant for an English region, and with its emphasis on pipe and fiddle closer in form and spirit to the traditions of Ireland and Scotland. The local repertoire has been embellished by the unique Northumbrian smallpipes, smaller and more mellifluent than the Scottish variety, and best suited to fireside and alehouse, rather than mountainside and battlefield. In the hands of expert players such as Jack Armstrong, the Duke of Northumberland's piper from 1948–71, or the contemporary performer Kathryn Tickell, the smallpipes are capable of energetic jigs and reels and complex arpeggios. But sentimental laments are not unknown either: 'you should be able to hear the bairns crying' was how the noted Northumbrian piper Billy Pigg described the instrument's expressive potential. Northumbrian music and song were further amplified by the strength of local printing and publishing which could rapidly collect and disseminate popular ballads as they emerged from the streets and taverns. Printed collections of local music were very popular, and expressed a pride in native eloquence and musicality, as the preface to *The Tyne Songster* of 1840 put it:

> No pompous strains, nor labour'd lines are here,
> But genuine wit and sportive mirth appear;
> Northumbria's genius, in her simple rhymes,
> Shall live an emblem to succeeding times.

Similar works, such as the bestselling *Northumbrian Minstrelsy*, compiled by John Collingwood Bruce, reflected subject matter both heroic—'The Battle of Otterburn,' 'Derwentwater's Farewell'—as well as the workaday—'The Bonnie Pit Laddie,' or 'Small Coals an' Little Money.' Alongside this there was an incredible flowering of Victorian singer-songwriters, who expanded the existing canon of popular Northumbrian ballads by chronicling the lives of ordinary people during a time of tumultuous change. Men like Joe Wilson, Geordie Ridley, and Ned Corvan had something of Robbie Burns and Charles Dickens in their talent for humour and pathos, and the output of minstrels such as Billy Purvis has been described as blending 'hardy realism and stoicism, precisely those Brechtian values which his audience needed in order to endure the harsh conditions on the river, at sea and in the pits.'[78] These local musical traditions were rejuvenated by the many Irish migrants of the nineteenth century who brought with them a rich stock of melody. Their rousing 'come-all-ye' folksongs had much in common with the heroic border ballads of Northumbria, and found fresh expression in the music halls and in the work of 'disaster-balladeers' like Tommy Armstrong of Tanfield Lea, always on hand to versify when men were lost underground, and whose son noted that 'me dad's muse was a mug of ale.'[79]

Tyneside developed its own sound in the era of twentieth-century popular music. The rhythm and blues rock band The Animals were part of the British invasion of the USA in the 1960s, but their transatlantic hit 'The House of the Rising Sun' was based on a much older border-ballad that the band's vocalist Eric Burdon had first heard sung by the Northumbrian folk-singer Johnny Handle (who spent his days working at the Rising Sun Colliery in Wallsend), and was probably the first 'folk-rock' to top the charts. The Animals' 'uncompromising image matched the grittiness of their music,' and their penchant for denim workwear stood 'in contrast to the squeaky clean modernity of the early Beatles and stylishness of the Small Faces.'[80] That sense of roistering, hairy-chested hedonism in their music was carried on by Brian Johnson, the Gateshead-born son of a sergeant-major in the Durham Light Infantry, who took over as the screeching frontman of AC/DC after Bon Scott drank himself to death. AC/DC's 'Back in Black'—'the apex of heavy metal art' according to *Rolling Stone*—is the second best-selling album of all time.[81]

These Northumbrian musical traditions owed something to the vigour of the language itself. Bill Lancaster has observed Geordie dialect terms seem preoccupied with movement and energy 'gannin tappy lappy doon the lonnen, passin yem, howay wah gannin tu the toon, we flew past, aw went, an teuk.'[82] Such dynamism is typified in the euphoric verses of the Blaydon Races, Tyneside's national anthem composed by the disabled ex-pitman Geordie Ridley in 1862, with its account of inebriated working men and women on their way to a *horse race*:

> *The rain it poor'd aall the day an' mayed the groons quite muddy,*
> *Coffy Johnny had a white hat on—they war shootin' 'Whe stole the cuddy.'*
> *There wis spice stalls an' munkey shows an' aud wives selling ciders,*
> *An' a chep wiv a hapenny roond aboot, shootin' 'Noo, me lads, for riders.'*

In a British Movietone short film from 1953, *Heritage of Song: Northumbria*, the narrator explains that 'the charm of Newcastle lies in its virility. Virility with a capital V' and describes the centrality of boisterous gatherings of all kinds to Northumbrian identity from the 'Hoppings' festival on the Town Moor—the name derives from an Old English word for dancing, and it's still the largest travelling funfair in Europe—to the Pitmen's Derby at Newcastle Races. The biggest, and oldest, of these gatherings was Stagshawe Bank fair in the Tyne Valley, once the greatest livestock sale in the north, held at Whitsun and midsummer, but there was a whole calendar of such events that drew out the masses, from the civic processions that turned out to meet the judges at Sheriff Hill in Gateshead and escort them into Newcastle, or the brutal boxing matches—such as the huge crowds that thronged Blyth Sands in 1846 to watch William Gleghorn beat Michael Reilley to death. Public executions at

Gallowgate were popular too, where in 1829 a condemned woman was conveyed to the gallows on the Town Moor in a cart sitting above her coffin before a crowd of 20,000, 'more than half of whom were women,' and the crowd that attended the last public execution in Newcastle in 1863 was so dense that many people fainted.[83]

The annual hiring and binding days of pitmen and farm-labourers were huge occasions—and a frequent source of trouble as in 1875 when a police sergeant was beaten and killed amidst a crowd of nearly 3,000 who had gathered at the Alnwick hirings.[84] Even when meetings of miners became more civilised, as in the Durham Miners' Gala (pronounced 'gay-lah') and Northumberland Miners Picnic, they were principally a drinking spree where 'shop windows would be boarded up [while] the pubs keep their doors open.'[85] The Durham Big Meeting has reinvented itself of late as a festival of uncharacteristically earnest Corbynite politics, but in the 1950s the Durham Miners' Union leader Sam Watson saw it as a celebration of free people:

> There were no orders rapped out from the Miners' Hall. The people could shout, sing, dance and drink all day, and members of the Association were free to attend or to absent themselves from the gala as they chose. No thought of regimentation. They could criticize or even ridicule their leaders or the political speakers who addressed them. There were no secret police, indeed the Durham police, led by their Chief Constable (Mr. A.A. Muir) seemed to be enjoying themselves just as much as the miners.[86]

* * *

The other great means of release for the Northumbrian working classes—cooped up as they so often were underground or in the bowels of ships—was sport in general, and football in particular—a game that was once as dominated by Northumbrians as table tennis is by the Chinese and volleyball by the Brazilians. The origins of ancient sport in Northumbria began with the rough-and-tumble football played by whole villages on Shrove Tuesday. These games were once widespread but by 1830 only survived at Chester-le-Street, Sedgefield and Alnwick (where to this day the Duke of Northumberland kicks off the annual game by hoofing a football off the battlements). Into the nineteenth century and the athleticism of Northumbrian pitmen was an important factor in the growth of organised sport. In a parliamentary debate in 1844 on creating an armed militia to keep the peace, Lord Howick urged that they be 'well fed and clad, for it was quite possible they might come into conflict with strong athletic bodies of working men, for instance the Colliers!'[87]

The main Victorian outlet for local muscularity—and the working-class sport par excellence—was competitive rowing. This grew out of the potent commercial rivalry between the Tyne and the Thames and provided Tyneside with its first mega-star sporting heroes. In July 1845, the Clasper brothers, Harry, Robert and William, with their Uncle Ned Hawks, snatched the world championship crown from the London watermen at the Thames Regatta, arriving back in Newcastle to huge crowds and the pealing bells of All Saints.

> *Ov a' your grand rowers in skiff or in skull,*
> *There's nyen wi' wor Harry has chance for to pull*
> *Man he sits like a duke an' he fetches se free,*
> *Oh! Harry's the lad, Harry Clasper for me!*
> *HAUD AWAY HARRY!*
> *CANNY LAD HARRY!*
> *HARRY'S THE KING OF THE TYEMS AN' THE TYNE.*

Clasper's success was based on rigorous training and a controlled diet. 'What Frederick the Great was of military matters, Harry Clasper is in boat racing,' wrote a contemporary; and he turned rowing into a major spectator sport, winning him £2,600 in prize money during his career, and the owner-ship of eight pubs. There were two other Tyneside rowing greats: Bob Chambers, whose work as an iron-puddler (someone who stirs the molten pig iron with a ladle to release the impurities) grew an impressive muscula-ture which helped him win 89 out of 101 professional races and the world sculling championship in 1863; and James Renforth, a real bruiser who'd built his physique from an early age as an apprentice anchorsmith and then as a soldier, before a stellar career on the water, which saw him win international laurels like Chambers before him. While racing an American crew on the Kennebecasis River in New Brunswick in 1871 Renforth died tragically, probably of heart failure—'the oar dropped from his stricken hand, his brawny arm fell like a withered branch in a storm' (although given the prize money at stake there were rumours of foul play). His melodramatic memorial in his native Gateshead, paid for by public subscription, describes him simply as 'Champion Sculler of the World.'

But sport in North East England was not just a matter of cheering from the side-lines: it was hugely participatory. A guide to Newcastle issued in 1863 noted that the local pitmen 'take great delight in bowling, foot-racing and quoits, at all of which games they are most expert.'[88] This may have grown out of the isolated nature of pit-village life, where distractions were limited for athletic and restless working men—other than the ale-house.

Miners' amusements included traditional pastimes such as throwing quoits (metal rings or horseshoes) and pitching pennies, and where the Occitans had pétanque, the Northumbrians had 'potshare bowling,' more golf-like than crown-green, where men tested their strength by throwing a whinstone 'bool' over a mile-long course. But such games were mere bagatelles compared to football. Although one of the game's first great administrators, Charles Alcock—who, as FA secretary, established the first FA Cup in 1871—came from Sunderland, professional football came relatively late to the North East. The amateur Northern League covering Northumberland and Durham—founded in 1889 at the Three Tuns Hotel in Durham—may be the second-oldest football league in the world, but Northumbrian participation in national and professional football did not arrive until Sunderland joined the Football League in 1890.

So why did the game explode in popularity? Some have argued that 'football satisfied them by its combination of great drama, combining cunning skill and brutal effort, in an atmosphere which joined companionship and conflict.'[89] In his peerless 1994 football book *The Far Corner* Harry Pearson posited an intriguing theory that the reason rugby never really took off in the North East was that there was no need for the Northumbrian working classes to prove their toughness; that was a given. What these men did want was a means of expressing their skill, even their artistry—and the beautiful game provided that like no other; and one thinks here of Chris Waddle and Paul Gascoigne, some of the most graceful ball-players England has ever produced. There are some flaws in this argument—not least the rugby-playing coalminers of Yorkshire and South Wales—but what is certainly true is that the heyday of Northumbrian industry corresponded with the dominance of the North East's football clubs, and its native footballers who plied their trade elsewhere.

After Sunderland joined the Football League in 1890 they won the title five times before the First World War (narrowly missing out on the double in 1913). Their manager in the 1890s, the Newcastle-born Tom Watson, then became the first man to win league titles—five in total—with two clubs, after joining Liverpool in 1899. While in the same period Newcastle United won the league three times and the FA Cup once (whilst losing in three finals). Indeed, the first ever football 'World Cup', held in Turin in 1909, was won by West Auckland, an amateur team of Durham pitmen invited to Italy by the grocery magnate Sir Thomas Lipton. They retained the trophy two years later, beating Juventus 6–1 in the final.

Some of the all-time greats of British football were the sons of miners, or had been miners themselves: Herbert Chapman of Huddersfield and Arsenal, and the Scottish colossi Matt Busby, Jock Stein and Bill Shankly who all sprang from the Ayrshire and Lanarkshire coalfields, where stamina, skill and team-work at the coalface transferred naturally onto the football pitch. The same was true of the North East, where three of the most successful English man-agers of all time were all the sons of Durham coal miners Bobby Robson, who worked as a pit electrician as a young man and even wired the Royal Festival Hall while he played for Fulham; Howard Kendall, who played in the same school football team as Bryan Ferry before he won the league as a player and then a manager with Everton; and Bob Paisley, who led Liverpool to six league titles, and was one of only two managers in history to win the European Cup three times. Paisley's first European victory took place in Rome in 1977, a place he'd last seen 'through the dusty wind-screen of an army truck' in 1944, joking that it was second time he'd beaten the Germans in the Italian capital. To this list of greats, we might add Brian Clough and Don Revie from just over the Tees in Middlesbrough, and it is little known that Bobby Robson was only the *second* Durham pitman to manage Barcelona, after Jack Greenwell, a former miner from Crook, who was the longest serving manager of *Barca* before Johann Cruyff, and remains the only non-South American coach to win the South American Championship when he steered Peru to glory in 1939.

From the beginning of professional football in the North East it was the burly and swashbuckling centre-forwards that were seen as the heirs to Clasper and Renforth. In 1905 prolific goal-scorer Alf Common, the son of a Wearside ship-riveter, became the world's first £1,000 player when he transferred from Sunderland to Middlesbrough, and there is a genuine pan-theon of idolised forwards that includes Horatio 'Raich' Carter and Bobby Gurney of Sunderland to the Newcastle heroes Jackie Milburn and Alan Shearer. But Northumbrian players in other positions made their mark, not least Jack and Bobby Charlton, lynchpins of England's 1966 World Cup winning team (their father was at work underground at Hirst Colliery in Ashington while they were collecting their medals). I was conscious too that the only famous alumnus of the high school I attended in Seaton Delaval was the supremely gifted footballer Ray Kennedy. In Michael Walker's study of North East football, *Up There*, he illustrates the fame and glory of North East footballers with two vignettes: the first when Arsenal secured the 'Double' at White Hart Lane in 1971, and a cross from Hebburn's George 'Geordie' Armstrong was met by the imperious Ray Kennedy, and at the Parc des Princes in Paris in 1981, Kennedy, then playing for Liverpool, takes a clever throw-in to find his rampaging namesake Alan Kennedy from

Shiney Row, near Sunderland, who smashes the ball past the Real Madrid keeper to seal Liverpool's third European Cup, and all under the manager-ship of a man from Hetton-le-Hole. And, in 2019, Liverpool were led to Champion's League victory by their hard-working captain from East Herrington near Sunderland, Jordan Henderson.

These traditions continue and in 2011 it was revealed that County Durham has produced more English-born Premier League players than any other county (over nine per 100,000 of its population since 1992), with both Northumberland and the modern county of Tyne and Wear also in the top ten. What is more, of the ten FA Vase finals played at Wembley between 2008/9 and 2017/18 an astonishing eight of those finals were won by Northumbrian teams, who were the losing finalists in the other two. (This echoes the total dominance of the old FA Amateur Cup by two North East sides—Bishop Auckland and Crook Town—with fifteen wins between them.) When I asked a friend of mine, Adam Sadler, who coaches in the Premier League, why this should be so, he was convinced that this was because this tier of football is the highest standard one can play without having your weekends spoiled by long away trips over the Pennines. 'You can turn out for South Shields, say, on a Saturday afternoon—and get paid for doing it,' he told me, 'and still be back home in time to go out on the lash.'

* * *

This sense of Northumbria *en fete* may linger on at big events like the Durham Miners' Gala, but the most vivid expression of the Northumbrian love of crowds is still to be found among the ebullient supporters of Newcastle United and Sunderland AFC. 'Wor Baal!' howl the football terraces of Tyneside,' observed the playwright Tom Hadaway, 'all cow-horned, and bris-tling with spears.'[90] A group of supporters—those 'seated army of convicts' according to the poet Sean O'Brien—who are, perhaps uniquely in England, more famous than the teams they support. 'The north-east's deep feeling for football is part of the region's character. It is riveted to the game,' wrote Michael Walker in *Up There*. 'The same can be said of Merseyside, Manchester, areas of London and elsewhere in England, but if there is a difference, it is that the North-East's attachment has not been maintained by success.'[91]

Tribalism is another part of football's appeal, and it's not fanciful to trace terrace *braggadocio* back to the tradition of border feuding or the rivalries between foundrymen, such as the legendry clashes between 'Crowley's Crew' and 'Hawks' Blacks' at events like the Swalwell Hoppings, where wrestling and

foot races often spilled over into fisticuffs.[92] The communality of football supporting suited the Northumbrian working classes very much, and has been a
wellspring of deep emotion and occasional violence. Crowd trouble at Tyne-
Wear derby games began as early as 1901 where a Good Friday fixture at
Newcastle had to be abandoned, and Sunderland's 'Roker Roar' and Newcastle's
'Toon Army' has made Northumbrian football fans famous for their passionate
loyalty and swaggering machismo—as a popular chant would have it:

> We are the Geordies, the Geordie boot boys,
> For we are mental, we are mad,
> We're the loyalest [sic] football supporters, the world has ever had.

The sartorial creativity that distinguishes football's 'casual' subculture, so
prominent among North East supporters, can trace its heritage to a male
interest in fashion that goes back centuries (indeed, North East football fans
in the early 1970s were probably the first in the country to wear the team
shirt to matches, rather than just scarves and rosettes).[93] An Act of the
Newcastle Merchant Adventurers of 1554 thundered against the 'gay dress'
and 'tippling and dancing,' and in 1603, the local youths are again enjoined
'not to dance or use music in the streets at night': nor are they to deck themselves in velvet and lace—or to wear their 'locks at their ears like ruffians.'[94]
The pitmen themselves developed a tradition of dressing up for big occasions—what Welbourne in his history of the Northumberland and Durham
Miners called the 'height of his outward splendour'—that lives on in the
Friday and Saturday night rituals of North East England.[95] One account from
1811 described the colliers' turnout for Binding Day when the coal-owners
would compete for their signature:

> In their dress they often affect to be gaudy and are fond of clothes of glaring
> colours; their holiday waistcoats (called by them 'posey jackets') are frequently
> of very curious patterns, displaying flowers of various hues; and their stockings
> mostly of blue, purple, pink or mixed colours. A great part of them have their
> hair very long, which on workdays is either tied in a queue, or rolled up in
> curls; but when dressed in their best attire, it is commonly spread over their
> shoulders. Some of them wear two or three narrow ribbons round their hats,
> placed at equal distances, in which it is customary with them to insert one or
> more bundles of primroses or other flowers.[96]

This style of dress—common among pitmen and keelmen alike—adver-
tised both their affluence and emphasised their sexual attractiveness; as the
verse goes in the 'Keel Row,' 'wha is like my Johnnie/So leish, so blithe, so
bonny.' 'Leish' meant lissom and athletic and may even share a common root

with 'lush,' a term still much favoured by Northumbrian women to describe masculine eye-candy. There are sexual overtones to working-class songs like the The Quayside Shaver, where keelmen and 'pitmen with baskets and gay posy waistcoats/Discourse about nought but who puts and hews best' and subject themselves to the sharp edges of female barbers' razors and tongues as the usual prelude to a 'bonnie pit laddie's' Saturday night on the lash. The lasses too joined in with gusto in this culture of bawdiness, particularly those Northumbrian *poissardes*, the 'fish wives,' who enjoyed a reputation for quick wit, bawdy humour and a capacity for drink that matched their menfolk. Women like 'Cushy Butterfield' of Gateshead, immortalised in song by Geordie Ridley as 'a big lass and a bonny lass [who] likes hor beer' which became the 'anthem to local feminine raucousness.'[97]

The sexual license inherent in Northumbrian culture was noticed by out-siders. The future Pope Pius II (Aeneas Sylvius Piccolomini), who passed through Northumbria while serving as a papal diplomat in the fourteenth century, observed that while the men were 'small, bold and forward in tem-per,' the women were 'fair in complexion, comely and pleasing,' and 'not distinguished for their chastity, giving their kisses more readily than Italian women their hands.'[98] In the nineteenth century the future Bishop of London Mandell Creighton wrote, priggishly, of his Northumberland parish that 'the unchastity of Embleton was terrible—low, animal,' which he deduced from the numbers of illegitimate births; but this was a fact of life, even in Victorian England.[99] Furthermore, Newcastle alone was said to contain over 100 broth-els, and pregnant brides were commonplace.[100] Again it is in local songs where we find the racier side of nineteenth-century Northumbrian life, as in this post-coital episode from 'The Pretty Girls of Sunderland':

> I then fill'd up another glass,
> Saying take this, and so begone,
> She tapp'd me on the back and said
> I believe you're up-to-snuff, young man;
> I see that you're a sporting blade,
> And on shore have lately come,
> To sport and play your time away
> With the pretty girls in Sunderland.[101]

Many of these habits are now seen as archetypally North Eastern. It was almost inevitable that when the flashy American reality TV series Jersey Shore was to be remade in the UK, Tyneside was chosen as the setting. Since 2011 *Geordie Shore* has showcased a world of buff and perma-tanned young Northumbrians, who flaunt a hyper-glamorous working-class aesthetic where ostentatious grooming is much-admired as 'a sign of the *work* and *time* you put into yourself,' and 're-traditionalises gender' with hyper-feminine girls and pumped-up boys from the gym thrown together for heavy drinking and heavy petting.[102]

These themes were brilliantly captured in Grayson Perry's two giant Sunderland tapestries 'Agony in the Car Park' and 'Adoration of the Cage Fighters' in which he venerates the exaggerated feminine and masculine aesthetics that often characterise working-class taste, as well as the joy of living in the moment where getting ready to go out is as much fun as going out itself. It is instructive that back in the nineteenth century the dress of Northumbrian fisher lasses attracted as much attention as their confident demeanour. Writers would rhapsodise that 'nothing could be more becoming than their costume,' with their figure-hugging print bodices, brightly coloured neckerchiefs and distinctive blue flannel skirt 'worn short and with a profusion of tucks (the more tucks a Cullercoats belle has the better style she is counted)' topped off with 'home-knitted stockings, and strong, but neat, shoes.'[103] Making a fashion statement from practical workwear may have begun with the pitmen in their ribbons and corduroy, and taken to new heights of elegance by the lasses of Tyne and Wear—but its most lasting legacy has been the global success of the chic waterproof jackets manufactured by a South Shields firm who now dress the royal family, but who started out supplying oilskins for Tyneside merchant seamen and waxed cotton trench coats for HM forces: J. Barbour & Sons.

This leads us to another legacy of hard work and hedonism: the Northumbrian love of consumption—and not just of beer and baccy either. In 1635 the Cheshire baronet Sir William Brereton described Newcastle as 'beyond all compare the fairest and the richest town in England, inferior for wealth and building to no city save London and Bristow [Bristol].'[104] In William Gray's *Chorographia* of 1649 he asserted that Newcastle's Flesh Market was the greatest of its kind in England. Lorna Weatherill's study of changing consumption patterns from 1675–1725 reveals that Durham and Northumberland were only surpassed by London and Kent in the possession of the 'new goods' of the age: clocks, china, cutlery, paraphernalia for consuming hot drinks and so on. This was no accident, as Daniel Defoe had noticed in the 1720s that Newcastle had 'the largest and longest key [quay] for landing and loading goods that is to be seen in England.'[105]

But Newcastle was always more of a centre for consumption than an industrial town like Manchester, instead it was 'the capital, the head office, the cultural centre, the playground and shopping mall for Tyneside.'[106] 'The Toon,' as it is still known, enjoyed almost complete dominion over a prosperous industrial hinterland on both sides of the Tyne, sucking in the growing middle classes, as well as the well-paid pitmen and their wives for fortnightly binges where 'it was not considered improper for colliery women to smoke, drink, and be noisy, in city pubs,'[107] and men showed off their spending power by spoiling their wives and children—as recorded in Henry Robson's *The Colliers Pay Week*, of 1840, where

> Those married jog on with their *hinnies*,
> Their canny bairns go by their side;
> The daughters keep teasing their minnies
> For new cloaths [sic] to keep up their pride.[108]

Growing levels of disposable income provided the impetus for ground-breaking developments in retailing. The vast covered Grainger Market in Newcastle was considered the 'the most beautiful in the world' when it opened in 1835, but only a few years later a local draper called Emerson Bainbridge opened a store across the road on Market Street that retail historians consider the world's first department store.[109] The Bainbridge name was lost after a takeover by the John Lewis Partnership, but another Tyneside retail pioneer continues to thrive. John J. Fenwick established his store on Northumberland Street next to the Methodist Chapel where he worshipped (and which John Wesley himself had founded). Fenwick aimed to emulate the *Grands Magasins* of Paris, like the famous Bon Marche, and specialised in aspirational fashions (he soon opened an off-shoot on London's Bond Street) and, through fancy window displays and clearly marked goods, made the experience of high class retail—'fantasy, adventure and cornucopia'—accessible to the masses.[110] Retailing developments in the nineteenth century weren't just confined to Newcastle department stores: Binns of Sunderland were similarly successful, with stores across County Durham, and the Co-operative Societies—with their branches in every pit village—had a hegemonic dominance of the coalfields. But the later twentieth century saw an even greater concentration of what the property developers now call 'destination retail' in Newcastle, with the opening of Europe's largest shopping precinct at Eldon Square in the 1970s (for a while only Oxford Street in London had higher retail ground rents), followed in the late 1980s by the Metro Centre—built a mere three miles away on Church-owned land near Dunston, which was at the time the largest out-of-town shopping mall in Europe.

The Northumbrian love of shopping is of a piece with a highly sociable working-class culture where buying a 'gannin oot' outfit in the Toon—inexpensive and disposable for the more frequent female shopper, branded and saved-up-for for the lads—is as much part of the ritual weekend as the drinking itself. John Ardagh noted in 1977 the local preference for cheap clothes was part of a 'hedonistic' local culture that preferred to 'blow their own money on the pleasures of boozing, gambling and dancing.'[111] All the jokes about Geordies not wearing coats stem not just from their expense, and the inconvenience of taking them off and on between bars (plus the death of the cloakroom), but that urgent need to show off figure-hugging outfits—for both lads and lasses. Professor Rachel Dwyer, on a visit back up north to her native Tyneside in 2019, pointed out to me something distinctive about Northumbrian drinking culture: first, that one rarely sees multi-generational groups of women out drinking together elsewhere the way they do in the North East; and that the sartorial finery and meticulous hair and make-up of these women—often in homage to Newcastle's own Cheryl Tweedy, international style icon (and the first British female solo artist to have five number-one singles in the UK)—seem to be as much about impressing each other, as they are to attract any male interest.

This sort of commitment to the rituals of social drinking make the city centres of the North East so exciting. Take a walk down Grey Street in Newcastle through High Bridge and the Bigg Market to Collingwood Street—the so called 'Diamond Strip'—and beyond to the gay quarter of the 'Pink Triangle' and the Hogarthian scenes of flesh and excess that one still encounters in Newcastle every weekend, and in all weathers, are highly unusual in chilly Northern Europe, and closer in spirit to the Rio Carnival or the New Orleans Mardi Gras. The London-based writer on place and culture Luke Turner was blown away by a recent visit to the city and tweeted on 10 November 2018 that

> I love the energy of Newcastle on a Saturday night—Slayer fans from their big gig, Sea Power crew, inter-generational groups on the piss, a bloke dropping his doner, laughing his head off, getting the poppers out for his mate. It's easy to moan these days about the homogenisation [...] of the UK, but Newcastle always feels like it's a bit of an exception to that. It is such a great city.[112]

Weekend hedonism is just the most colourful example of a more quotidian culture of sociability borne out of hard lives where warmth and comfort were sought from the company of friends and neighbours. See for example the Gloucestershire-born war poet Ivor Gurney's description of his time recuperating in the General Hospital at 'Canny Newcassel,' as he called it, 'where people have very kind hearts and very rough manners,' and 'hospitable in a manner almost unknown in the South,' or Thomas Bewick's recollections of the open-handed generosity he met everywhere as a child at Christmas in the Tyne Valley, where, heightened by sword-dancing and the 'exhilarating wild notes of the Northumberland pipes … the countenances of all, both high & low, beamed with cheerfulness.'[113]

One should not be blind to the downsides of a culture where alcohol has long been Northumbria's chosen social lubricant. Catherine Cookson's memoir of her dismal childhood surrounded by adults mired in alcoholic desperation—'I longed for such poverty that there would be no money left for drink'—can stand for many lives made miserable by heavy drinking.[114] In 2018 the NHS-sponsored 'Alcohol Control for the North East' states baldly that 'our drinking is damaging the health, wealth and safety of people and communities in the North East,' and notes that the North East has the record highest rate of alcohol related deaths in England, with 48% of men and 29% of women drinking above the daily recommended limits and 50% of all violent crime being alcohol-related. But are they waging a futile battle? For better or worse Northumbrian culture has been irrigated by beer for centuries. It amuses my Liverpudlian wife that the question 'where does he [and it's usually 'he'] drink?' is still a key question to ascertain someone's soundness in Northumbrian society. The formulaic response to this is typically 'oh he *gets in* [the Wooden Doll/the Dun Cow/the Top Club etc],' and 'we had a good drink' remains the mark of a canny night out.

* * *

There aren't many places in the world whose staple industries have ended up being sung about on Broadway. But in Lee Hall's 'Billy Elliot' and 'The Pitmen Painters,' and Sting's 'The Last Ship' it seems that Northumbrians emoting about lost worlds of mining and shipbuilding is big at the box office. For despite the death and danger, the work itself was some of the most romantic and rewarding ever undertaken by the working classes. This was not like making hats, or lace, or jute-sacks or any of the other myriad trades that British towns once specialised in. Nothing could compare to the thrilling satisfaction of winning a new coal-seam or launching a battleship—and there is a sense that the North East still hasn't got over the loss of these industries. In 2015 a statue by Ray Lonsdale was erected in the former Durham pit village of Horden. 'Marra' depicts a nine-foot miner, slightly stooped and carrying a pick, with what looks like a gunshot wound in his chest. In brutally literal terms this is to represent a community with its heart ripped out—a feeling most keenly felt in the moribund coalfields of East Durham. The 2018

Netflix documentary 'Sunderland Til I Die' covering the recent decline of Sunderland AFC is made all the more bittersweet for supporters of the Black Cats by its emotional theme tune 'Shipyards,' written by the local singer Marty Longstaff as a tribute to his grandfather who worked as a rivet catcher at Austin & Pickersgills on the Wear. Longstaff was born after the last of Sunderland's shipyard's and collieries had closed, but the elision of industrial identities into passionate football allegiance fits with the observation of the club's former player and chairman Niall Quinn that 'the football club is no longer part of Sunderland's identity, we are the identity.'[115]

In the nineteenth and twentieth centuries the twin pillars of Northumbrian identity were heavy industry and heavy drinking. The heavy industry of smokestack, graving-dock and pit-wheel may have transformed into more hi-tech enterprises, but the cult of hard work lives on in places like Nissan's huge plant at Washington near Sunderland—as of 2016 still the single most productive factory in the country, where they make more cars than the whole of Italy. The habit of hedonistic heavy drinking has barely changed in several centuries. The titles of Brian Bennison's three volume history of Newcastle pubs—*Heady Days*, *Heavy Nights* and *Lost Weekends* give a sense of the cherished place of sociable drinking in Northumbrian culture, not least as what Colls and Lancaster have described as the beery 'carnivalisation of popular culture' has always provided a 'vital emotional prop for coping with rapid change.'[116]

This was a point made strongly in a 2001 case-study of Tyneside youth culture in which it was observed that 'elements of an industrial heritage were embodied in an appreciation of skilled physical labour over mental agility, a collective sharing of heavy, often sexual, adult humour, and an established drinking capability,' where acting the 'Geordie hard man' was still much-esteemed and 'football and public-house drinking' helped to sustain community in the face of social change.[117] But its conclusion was stark, and might make any Northumbrian wince in recognition. The young people studied by the author lived in a culture that had become 'petrified in the hardened solution of an older period from which their values descended,' and these lads with their emblematic love of drinking, graft and banter seemed trapped forever 'like flies in amber.'[118]

6

COME LET US REASON TOGETHER

We, the Shipwrights in the town of South Shields ... taking into serious consideration, that man is formed a social being, and that the Sovereign Ruler of nature has pleased to place us in life dependent upon each other, and in continual need of mutual assistance and support, do severally agree to form ourselves into a Friendly and Benevolent Association to aid and assist each other.

RULES, ORDERS, and REGULATIONS,
of the South Shields Shipwrights Union, 1824

Attlee was in hospital—demanding a snap decision about Britain joining the coal and steel community, the original EU. Grandfather thought for two seconds, and said 'No, the Durham miners will never wear it.'

Peter Mandelson on his grandfather Herbert Morrison

How did the particularities of Northumbrian society shape the politics of the region, and what might be considered as characteristic and consistent in its political outlook? Although the radical and reforming movements of the North East (and the occasional riot) have tended to catch the eye of historians, its conservative traditions have been just as durable. The twentieth century record shows that the region was dominated by the Labour Party, but its *modus operandi* (in government at least) was usually pragmatic and moderate and rarely revolutionary. To understand Northumbrian politics, we need to appreciate the centuries-long interplay between a shared experience of living in extremely close-knit communities (and the expectation to conform that this placed on individuals), and how the dependence of those communities on a handful of powerful landlords, oligarchies and institutions—from Lord Wardens and Prince Bishops, coal-mining cartels and industrial autocrats, to the nexus of monolithic employers and unions—in both the private and, latterly, the public sectors—has contributed to a consistently corporatist outlook in Northumbrian public life, and the weakness of entrepreneurialism in contrast to the rest of the country.

The often-oppressive closeness of life in the industrial communities of the North East shared some striking similarities with pre-modern patterns of living. The cohesive kinship of the 'English Highland Clans' supported otherwise vulnerable families to make their living from grazing and reiving in the perilous fells and valleys of Tynedale and Redesdale.[1] A deep, tribal loyalty to their local chieftain was also fundamental to such clanship and, as well as occasionally causing consternation in London, provided a 'highly effective adaptation to a world of violence and chronic insecurity.'[2] What is more, research by the University of Oxford into the genetic diversity within the British Isles revealed the extraordinary stability of the British population, with the Northumbrians of 2016 still living within the same *Angelfolc* 'tribes' that first settled Bernicia from Northern Germany in the seventh century.[3] But even in the industrial era it was noted that because of their 'clannishness, their fighting qualities … their 'peculiar traits and habits,' and even their ethnicity, it was possible to look into the coalfield and see a folk'—as Bede himself would've understood the term to mean a people united by a shared ethnicity—'rather than a proletariat.'[4]

The kibbutzim-like quality of pit villages had deep roots in the patterns of settlement, building styles and agriculture that characterised the North East of England. The Norman conquest and the punitive campaigns which devastated the existing towns and villages meant that the new Norman overlords sent north by Duke William had a much freer hand to develop new settlements than was typical in the rest of the country. Niklaus Pevsner noted that the medieval archaeology of County Durham reveals three basic types: two rows of buildings on either side of a street or green, four rows of buildings around a square central area, or substantial farmsteads, often known as 'steadings' in the North of England. This represented 'a deliberate policy—the reconstruction of the county, to a clear plan imposed from above' following the 'Harrying of the North' in 1069–70.[5] This practice of constructing planned settlements would continue into the eighteenth and nineteenth centuries, beginning with those model Northumbrian villages put up by enlightened aristocrats at places like Blanchland, Capheaton, Ford and Etal—when William Cobbett visited Northumberland he noted that farm-labourers lived in a 'sort of barracks; that is to say, long sheds with stone walls' where the workers 'seem altogether to be kept in the same way as if they were under military discipline'—and then most obviously with the proliferation of iden-tikit mining villages erected by the coal companies with their long rows of pit cottages themselves based on farm-buildings, and then the New Towns of the 1950s and 60s.[6]

Patterns of living in the industrial North East had deep roots in traditional forms of Northumbrian agriculture. During the long wars with Scotland, Northumbrian lairds granted long land tenures, low rents and rights of inheritance in return for the military service they regularly needed to defend the border. Such martial discipline would also come to characterise Northumbrian miners, who contemporary observers thought worked 'more as a machine, or a soldier.'[7] This was reinforced by the hated 'Durham system' of bonded labour which prevailed in North East England until as late as 1872—under which miners were contracted to work for an annual term for a single 'master' in return for a cash bounty (a deal typically lubricated with alcohol at the aforementioned boisterous 'hiring days'). The great aristocratic coal-owners felt very proprietorial of 'their' men and expected their loyalty as much as any medieval warlord. As Richard Fynes recorded, in his first great history of the Northumberland and Durham miners, a foreign visitor to Tyneside at the end of the 1700s was struck by the number of notices in local newspapers by masters 'offering rewards for knowledge of the whereabouts of runaway miners and threatening to prosecute whoever might employ them.'[8]

Perhaps the most striking continuity between the agricultural past and the industrial period was the 'cavil,' a quarterly lottery whereby names were drawn from the foreman's hat to allocate self-selecting pairs of workers ('marras') to positions on the coalface (the parts with 'softer' coals were much sought after). One study of this system has called it a 'wise compromise which blunted some of the worst de-humanising aspects of industrialisation found elsewhere.'[9] We can detect similar principles at work in mediaeval Northumbrian agriculture which in organisation was closer to the Scottish *run rig* system than to the 'three-field' system of the English lowlands.[10] *Run rig* worked by demarcating cultivable 'in-bye' land near the township from larger areas of pasture and rough grazing. This in-bye was divided into strips which were then periodically reassigned among local tenants so that no one person had continuous use of the best land. What is more, national trends to divide and enclose open pasture were resisted in the North because of the value placed on unrestricted grazing by cattle and sheep during the winter months. The campaign to prevent the enclosure of the Newcastle Town Moor was championed by the Tyneside radical Thomas Spence, described by E.P. Thompson as being preoccupied with communal 'agrarian socialism,' a nostalgic view that 'Thompson (like Marx) casts as the Achilles heel of English popular radicalism.' Nevertheless, Spence's vehement opposition to what he saw as the malign 'Private Property in Land' had a great influence on Karl Marx who cited him in his *Theories of Surplus Value* of 1861.[11]

Here we had a civilisation where the land—both above and below ground—had consistently been seen as a shared resource to be managed and allocated on the principles of fair shares and co-operation. This collectivist outlook was shaped by a Durkheimian process of socialisation, whereby social norms and values were determined by the experience of living first on a perilous frontier and then latterly in what became a harsh and unforgiving industrial region where seven year apprenticeships for young men taught them a trade, as well as how to behave. In the walled town of Newcastle there was an elaborate system of regulating communal life, with numerous accounts of punishments for drunkenness, fornication and even witchcraft (fifteen so-called witches were hanged on the Town Moor in 1650). A fixation on such delinquencies was typical in early modern Europe, but we should note how lower-level transgressions against the harmony of society were punished. In 1596 Newcastle Corporation paid 4*d* 'for carrying a woman through the town for scolding with branks'—a term used in Scotland and Northern England for a 'scold's bridle,' an iron helmet-like contraption which left the face exposed but inserted a length of iron into the mouth to suppress the tongue—and in the same year Alice Carr was ordered to purge herself of the offence in All Saint's church for calling Elizabeth Hayning an 'arrant witch, common slut and a curtailed knave.'[12]

A more edifying side to Northumbrian communitarianism has been the impulse towards charity and philanthropy. We might begin with the Medieval endowments for church and chantry building—the latter especially popular as prayers of redemption from Purgatory would be said there for their bene-factors (there were twenty-seven chantries in Newcastle alone before the Reformation). One recent study conducted by Newcastle University's 'Centre for Research on Entrepreneurship, Wealth and Philanthropy' con-cluded that 'the North East has a long and rich history of philanthropy,' noting that it is 'remarkable that philanthropic initiatives taken during the first cen-turies following the Norman Conquest are still bearing fruit today' as in the two ancient 'hospitals' Sherburn House near Durham, founded in 1181 by Bishop Hugh du Puiset, and the Hospital of God at Greatham near Hartlepool, founded in 1273 by Bishop Robert de Stitchell, which still provide accom-modation for the elderly.[13] Well-endowed almshouses were a particular fea-ture of Newcastle society, as in the Trinity Almshouses, founded in 1584 to support twenty-six aged seamen or their widows, likewise the Holy Jesus

Hospital, for thirty-eight 'freemen' of the city and their wives, and the Keelmen's Hospital for fifty-four aged and infirm keelmen, their wives or their widows. There were also philanthropically-funded dispensaries, infirmaries and hospitals at Bamburgh (1792), Sunderland (1794), Darlington (1808), Hexham (1815), Gateshead (1832), Durham (1853), Jarrow (1871) and Monkwearmouth (1874). Ecclesiastical benefactors were especially active, such as the two bishops of Durham: Thomas Langley, who founded the still extant Durham School in 1414, and Nathaniel Crewe, whose will in 1721 left his extensive northern estates to found a charitable trust—'Lord Crewe's Charity'—which thrives to this day.

The same study of North East philanthropy concludes that charitable giving in the region had three key features: first, the unusual wealth and power of the Palatine Bishops of Durham meant that their foundations—which include the University of Durham, founded in 1832—were well-established. Second, 'elite cohesion' among Northumbrian industrialists and businessmen 'created a sense of common purpose and the capacity to mobilise in support of philanthropic initiatives, often in advance of other towns and cities,' and the Newcastle Infirmary (1751), the Lying-in Hospital for Poor Married Women (1760), and the College of Physical Sciences (1871) exemplify this impulse. And third, the vertiginous de-industrialisation in the post-war North East created the 'economic and social problems in the North East that are more severe than in other parts of Britain,' which cried out for philanthropic action. It is illustrative then that the 'Community Foundation Tyne & Wear and Northumberland,' a grant-making organisation that connects philanthropists to local good causes, is the largest foundation of its type in Britain.[14]

We might add another dimension to this history of philanthropy, that of a certain affection for and loyalty to the places where the wealthy came from or made their money. Certainly, much charitable activity is (still) driven as much by the pursuit of tax efficiency as it is by altruism. But a certain *noblesse oblige* animated the likes of Lord Armstrong and his extensive endowments to his native town of Newcastle, or the shipbuilder Sir John Priestman in Sunderland, whose charitable trust was established to 'feed the poor in times of distress.' Present-day Northumbrians-made-good are just as generous—with important charitable enterprises set up by Dame Catherine Cookson, Dame Margaret Barbour, Ian Gregg, of the baking dynasty, the football manager Sir Bobby Robson, and the Sunderland-based car-dealers Sir Tom Cowie and Sir Peter Vardy. The town of Bishop Auckland is lucky to have two major benefactors in the billionaire hedge-fund manager Jonathan Ruffer—who saved the Zurbarán paintings for Auckland Palace, while investing heavily in local regeneration initiatives—and the manufacturer John Elliott, who handed over his multi-million pound dehumidifier business Ebac to a local philanthropic trust—to, in his words, 'deliver substantial reoccurring sums for community initiatives and enshrine our community ethos for the benefit of all.' It is striking that the language of obligation does seem to recur as an explanation for Northumbrian philanthropy, as in the case of the footballer Alan Shearer who was inspired to establish a charitable foundation for disabled children because he wanted to 'give something back to the region and country that has served me so well'; or the IT entrepreneur Graham Wylie, co-founder of the Sage multi-national software company, and major funder of the Sage music centre in Gateshead, whose motivations are derived from being brought up in the North East and founding a business there 'so it's incredibly important to me to launch this Foundation [and] give back to the region in a very significant way.'[15]

Historically, acts of charity were as much an opportunity for fellowship as they were for doing good to the less fortunate. The elder brethren of the 'Guild, Fraternity or Brotherhood of the most Glorious and Undivided Trinity of Newcastle' shared control of the River Tyne with the Corporation of Newcastle, and a coastal jurisdiction that covered every single port and creek from Whitby to Holy Island. The brethren utilised income from the light-houses and pilotage services they provided to further charitable work: teaching the craft and mystery of seamanship to nautical apprentices and running an almshouse for 'aged and impotent seamen.'[16] Not far from Trinity House and overlooking Sandgate stands the Keelmen's Hospital, built in 1701 for £20,000—a remarkable sum considering that it was paid for with funds raised by the keelmen themselves. The Bishop of Ely was caused to exclaim that 'he had heard of and seen many hospitals, the works of rich men; but that it was the first he ever saw or heard of which had been built by the poor.'[17] In the eighteenth century associationalism began to flourish in the North East and by 1801 5,000 working men, and perhaps as many women in Newcastle, were members of over thirty benefit societies with names such as the Flourishing Society of Women, the Good Intent, the Love and Unity, the Peace and Unity, and the Unanimous Society of Men, reflecting a 'groping desire for community and the deep moral earnestness of the age.'[18]

In the nineteenth century this predisposition towards mutuality found fresh expression through the extraordinary growth of workingmen's clubs in the North East. The Club & Institute Union (the CIU) continued something of the social side of the medieval guilds or mysteries, and as well as providing cheap beer (eventually establishing their own production via the famous

Federation Brewery) their charitable ethos was just as important. The Clubs instituted saving schemes for Christmas and day trips for members (my own grandfather always looked forward to the 'auld men's trip' from Seaton Terrace to Seahouses). We can also see how this instinct for altruism was expressed through practical action. Charitable resources could also be mobilised impressively to meet pressing temporary needs. The New Hartley pit disaster of 1862 is a good example of this, where, in addition to the volunteer rescue party who thronged the pithead from surrounding villages, a public subscription for the benefit of dependents of those killed was quickly established. Queen Victoria herself sent a donation of £200, but the whole fund raised an astonishing £81,838 (which depending on how one calculates these things could be worth anything between seven million and two hundred million pounds at 2019 prices), the vast majority of which came from within the region.

This selflessness was of a piece with a culture where duty to one's neighbour was expected and reinforced by formal and informal systems of social control. Abraham Crowley's famous works in the Derwent Valley was unique in England in having a written constitution, 'The Law Book of the Crowley Ironworks,' compiled around 1700. This document detailed a scheme of industrial welfare whereby both employer and employees contributed to a system of insurance that paid for medical services and compensation in case of injury, and a weekly pension for widows and aged workers. However, those in receipt of benefits had to wear a badge inscribed 'Crowley's Poor' on their left shoulder, and any employees housed in company property were expected to go to bed on the stroke of a nine o'clock curfew. Furthermore, 'Order Number 85' made clear the company's disapproval of those employees whose dissolute behaviour 'rendered themselves unfit for any business, and reduced themselves into extreme poverty [by] pride … by gameing … by sotting and … by trading … and in going much abroad, particularly to Newcastle which hath been the ruine of several.'[19]

Such discipline and regulation became typical of industrial communities—but could be exploitative. The practice of being paid in vouchers which could then be exchanged for goods at colliery owned grocery stores known as 'Tommy Shops' (at exorbitant prices) was a great cause of resentment in the nineteenth-century coalfields—not least as the miners' wives had no way of taking their custom elsewhere. Even when this system was overturned following union pressure, the Co-operative Wholesale Societies that replaced them were similarly monopolistic. So too was the Durham Miners' Association, which by 1900 had become the largest miners' union

in Britain with over 80,000 members. The DMA didn't just agitate for better working conditions, it was hugely influential in all the pit villages in the
county, where it had already created a mini-welfare state while William
Beveridge was still a schoolboy at Charterhouse. Each DMA lodge provided
a 'Colliery Welfare and Institute' funded through membership subscription
and providing educational and welfare resources as well as convalescent
homes to deal with the constant stream of mining injuries, and 'Aged
Miners Homes' in every village.

This was a highly ordered society, ironically suspicious of nonconformity
given the preponderance of Primitive Methodism in the coalfields. Such a
puritanical strain of Christianity offered both the hope of salvation, and,
through its promotion of a strict moral rectitude based on industriousness
and temperance, it fulfilled an important role in disciplining the workforce.
It is a cliché but nonetheless true that the early Labour Party owed more to
Methodism than it did to Marxism. It is notable how many Miners Lodge
banners have biblical themes, especially the parable of the Good Samaritan
and the stern injunction to 'Go Thou and Do Likewise.' And when, in 1906,
the twenty-nine newly-elected Labour MPs were asked for their favourite
authors, none cited Marx, although fourteen chose the Bible, and eight men-
tioned John Bunyan.[20]

But the Methodists' message of 'the democratic gospel of Jesus Christ
and the brotherhood of man' faced stiff competition from the pub and
workingmen's club for the attention of the miner; as one Durham clergyman noted, the 'brutal pugilism, beastly drinking [and] degrading gambling
often yielded to the potency of love's evangel.'[21] The Catholic Church too
achieved a strong foothold in the coalfields, largely on the back of mass Irish
migration in the nineteenth and twentieth centuries. Coalfield Catholicism
was just as austere and straight-laced as Methodism, and its clergy were if
anything even more authoritarian. Stories are still told in Consett of Fr
Francis Kearney surveilling his parish on horseback in the 1850s, and of his
decisive role in breaking up the 'Battle of the Blue Heaps'—a pitched battle
between cudgel-wielding English and Irish ironworkers. And yet such min-
istration was consistently valued and noted by Henry Mess in the 1920s
who recorded how, in addition to paying for explosives and pick-sharpen-
ing, other deductions from wages included 'sums for light, doctor, orphan-
ages, and various other benefit funds, and even in some cases for the Roman
Catholic priest.'[22]

Such regimentation wasn't just confined to the pit villages and working-
class suburbs. The Russian novelist Yevgeni Zamyatin lived in Jesmond in the

First World War (he was supervising the construction of icebreakers on the Tyne for the Tsarist navy). His work was much influenced by his time on Tyneside, especially his satire of middle-class conformity in Newcastle, 'The Islanders,' which opens with a vicar intoning that 'life must be like a well-run machine and lead us to our goal with mechanical inevitability.' His dystopian novel *We* was read with fascination by George Orwell and inspired much of *Nineteen Eighty-Four*. One Zamyatin expert notes that the all-seeing time-discipline of the shipyards must have sparked the idea for the 'Table of Hourly Commandments' in the walled-city of his 'One State' where privacy is non-existent and every hour is accounted for, and outside the walls the 'gaunt ruins have a Northumbrian feel of castles and pele towers, while remains of ovens and industrial flues recall more recent episodes in the history of the area. Zamiatin [sic] conflates all this into the debris of the 'two hundred years war,' a powerful echo of the centuries of Anglo-Scottish conflict.'[23]

No doubt there were many that truckled against such societal constraints but they help us understand why 'solidaristic self-perception [is so often] embodied in the art of the north,' certainly in contrast to the more entrepreneurial stereotypes of Londoners 'ducking and diving and blurred boundaries of criminality.'[24] It was noted of the Northumbrian miners that 'exposure to common dangers and trials helped to develop a strong sense of solidarity among pit-men,' and it's telling that if miners ever took risks underground with their own safety for 'the lives of their comrades,' they were 'very particular.'[25] Such factors may have been the seedbed from which grew the stereotype of Northumbrian affability, something that is impossible to prove, but is anecdotally credible. In a 2005 *Readers Digest* survey which involved a series of experiments such as help from strangers and politeness of taxi drivers, Newcastle came top of the courtesy list with 77%, beating Liverpool into second with 70%.[26] The experiences of the great Austrian philosopher Ludwig Wittgenstein who spent time living in Newcastle in the 1940s (he was working as a laboratory assistant at the Royal Victoria Infirmary) can stand as a good example of the unaffected warmth of ordinary Tynesiders—he recounted one incident when he asked a bus conductor where to get off for a certain cinema, and was told by several passengers that the film was not worth seeing.

One can imagine 'Wey man, you don't want to see that pitcha, it's arful—you should see Erroll Flynn at the Essoldo'; there followed an argument on the bus about which film he should see and why. W[ittgenstein] valued such Geordie friendliness.[27]

One visitor to the North East in 1979 thought that the strength of the matriarchal extended family in the North East, 'generally a facet more of Latin than Nordic countries,' was important to note, and that 'archaic this society may in some ways be, but any visitor is also impressed by its friendli-ness—too effusive for some tastes—and its very real human concern.'[28] One habit of my own grandparents in Northumberland was to present any baby they were introduced to with money—a legacy perhaps of the 'Ammiss bundle' tradition which usually included a silver coin, a candle, an egg and some salt to bring luck on the journey through life[29]—a custom I last saw in 2015 when an old man in Jarrow town centre delighted a young Asian woman by squeezing some pound coins into the tiny paw of her pram-borne child.

The downside of such communitarianism was its claustrophobia. Not only was the population of North East England unusually concentrated into flats but the scale of colliery house provision in the Great Northern Coalfield was also unique.[30] Even though the coalfield employed nearly one quarter of all the colliery workmen in Great Britain, by 1913 it contained almost one half of all colliery-owned houses.[31] Thus the Northumbrian society of the nine-teenth and twentieth centuries was the very opposite of atomised; this was a people who really were in it together. In such communities gossip was a currency—I can still remember the instruction from my grandmother: 'div-vunt let anybody know your business.' This was made more acute by a highly judgemental attitude towards anyone perceived to be lacking in industrious-ness. Indeed, in the 1980s I also recall how 'he's never done a bloody hand's turn', was the ultimate calumny against any perceived scroungers. Nor do we have to look hard in the historical record to find these attitudes recurring time and again. In early nineteenth-century Sunderland, for example, the Poor Law Guardians published lists of applicants for poor relief, and encour-aged ratepayers to scrutinise the lists and inform them—anonymously—of any paupers with undeclared income, so as to awaken

> a decent and becoming pride, to stimulate industry, to create disposition to economy as regards the future, in opposition to a *lazy and despicable habit*—that of existing on the industry of more provident neighbours ... undistinguishing benevolence offers a premium to indolence, prodigality and vice.[32]

The working-class novelist Jack Common wrote of the stifling conformity of suburban Heaton, where the pursuit of respectability, through a clean front-step and a spotless rent-book, was pursued fanatically, and all under the watchful eyes of one's neighbours. 'And there by the slight fold of a lifted curtain, he encountered an Eye,' wrote Common in his autobiographical

Kiddar's Luck. 'It was Mrs Rowley's, and there was no doubt about it, the woman was a natural overlooker.'[33] The North East has never really lost that slightly oppressive sense of community, and a certain suspicion of individualism. 'He'd always thought of the community as a sleeping, good-humoured giant,' reflects 'Tiger' Mason in Sid Chaplin's novel *The Watchers and the Watched*, 'hard-drinking, hard-working and hospitable. Now that comfort was cracking.' The crime-writer Martyn Waites commented that 'Newcastle … though a city, it feels like a market town … there is always 'somebody who knows somebody.'[34] It's perhaps not surprising that some of the more restless locals couldn't wait to leave—Bruce Welch of the Shadows has spoken of the appeal of the old sign on the Tyne Bridge declaring 'THE SOUTH,' and Bryan Ferry (who viewed himself in his youth as 'an orchid born on a coal tip') was determined not to 'stay in the North East all my life … ashamed.'[35]

Moving away from the North East can still be met with bafflement (why would anyone want to leave?), but it's not just geographical mobility that is met with suspicion, the merest hint of social-climbing is too. Writing of his childhood in 1970s Newcastle, the founder of *Viz*, Chris Donald, recalled that after his uncle Jack got a job as the Lord Mayor's chauffeur (requiring him to dress 'in fancy suits') Donald's working-class grandmother in Shieldfield took to calling him 'Lord Shite.'[36] Deracinated Northumbrians—especially those who move to London and try to disguise their accent—are still the subject of much ridicule back up North; one thinks here of Catherine Cookson (who attempted an RP drawl in later life), or the footballer Steve Bruce and the actor Robson Green whose vowels have all been through the mangle to unintentionally comic effect. Indeed, having a North-Eastern identity—in all of its subtle Geordie and Mackem variations—is still seen as synonymous with being working class. In 2018 the satirical website 'The Daily Mash' ran the amusing headline 'Geordie with posh voice baffles workmates,' with the comment from a colleague, 'It is almost like he is middle class. But that is clearly impossible.'[37]

Despite the social mobility of the last fifty years whenever Northumbrians gather they celebrate an identity that is rooted in shared working-class experience and a need to recreate that sense of belonging. Football crowds can still give that dopamine hit like nothing else; this is especially true given what has been described as their recent 'turn to history' with regular commemorations of dead players and managers.[38] But for the most transcendent evocation of community we must return to the Durham Miners' Gala. 'The Big Meeting' has always had a political element, but at its core remains the representation of the communities themselves as they parade their lodge banners through the city in a manner similar to the flag-waving 'Alfieri' that process through Siena before the Palio from the city's seventeen *contrade*. The banners themselves, eight feet high and six feet wide, are made of silk and painted on both sides— sometimes on top of older images which give them a sacred, palimpsestian quality. On gala day itself these holy relics make a sacral passage through the vast nave of Durham Cathedral. Nye Bevan once wrote of his distaste for 'the most conservative of all religions—ancestor worship,' but such venerations are hard to avoid in Britain. David Starkey has described the whole panoply of Armistice Day and Remembrance Sunday as a sort of 'English Shinto,' and there are strong overtones of this in the annual ceremonies at Durham, which have only grown in popularity within the now post-industrial mining communities, in what has been described variously as a 'complex process of emotional regeneration,' and a form of 'social baptism' and a rite of passage 'where comradeship was consummated.'[39]

The world that these events commemorate is slipping further and further into the past. The last coal mine in Durham (at Wearmouth) closed over twenty-five years ago, but the social fabric that knitted together the old coalfield communities had begun to tear decades earlier. A patriarchal system based on an heroic coalmining breadwinner and his diligent helpmeet back at home may once have been an efficient division of labour, but it was soon caught by a pincer movement of economic and social liberalism, which undermined large-scale coal-production and the strict gender roles that the whole system relied on. It is striking, for example, that after the liberalisation of the 1960s Newcastle became known as the 'abortion capital' of the United Kingdom, with Walker Park Hospital carrying out 411 terminations in the first nine months of 1969, more than any other hospital in the country.[40]

No one analysed these changes more trenchantly than the sociologist Norman Dennis who grew up in Sunderland in the moral world of the 'respectable working class' and mourned the passing of a socialism first theorised by his hero R. H. Tawney, one based on fellowship and co-operation between strong chapel-going families and enabled by a benign and active state. Dennis differentiated between what he called 'ethical socialists'—co-operators who nonetheless hold that individuals are personally responsible for their own actions—and 'egoistic socialists' who contend that society causes individuals to behave as they do, and that individuals should live whatever lifestyle they choose. Dennis, who never moved from the Millfield council estate in Sunderland he grew up in (despite holding a string of high profile academic posts), firmly believed that the causes of family breakdown and delinquency that he saw across the North East came from a dominant philosophy that relies 'on the State—which means other people—to pick up the bill for their folly,' but the ultimate corruption, he thought, derived from elevating 'individual will above one's obligations to the wider community.'[41]

* * *

If the centrality of communalism helps us to understand Northumbrian society, then so too does an appreciation of how power was wielded in the North East, and by whom. 'The feudal tradition is strong in Northumberland,' wrote Henry Mess in 1928, 'and there is not the sharp divorce between it and the new industrialism which is found in most areas.'[42] If we take the OED definition of feudalism as a system where peasants 'were obliged to live on their lord's land and give him homage, labour, and a share of the produce' then it's possible to see an interlinking pattern of Northumbrian feudalism that connected the aristocratic families who held the medieval border for the Crown with the power of the coal-owning oligarchies, the so-called 'Lords of Coal' and the handful of industrial and then trade union barons who so dominated the eighteenth, nineteenth and twentieth centuries.

As a military frontier zone, the North East was governed differently, and with uncharacteristic autonomy, in an English nation state that had centralised much earlier than the rest of Western Europe. Beyond the reach of London, northern office-holders such as the Lord Wardens of the Marches had the authority, among other things, to turn out all the able-bodied fighting men of the Marches for their defence, to hold Courts, punish disobedience, grant safe-conducts and to meet his counterpart Warden over the border 'to make a truce with the Scots for any period up to two months, without previously consulting the King.'[43] As Parliament treated the defence of the border as a purely local affair, and never raised any taxes for this purpose, they relied on the few northern magnates and their retainers, whom they compensated by adding 'barony to barony and office to office until by the fourteenth century the greater part of England north of the Trent was held by three great families, the Percies, the Nevilles, and the House of Lancaster.'[44]

Although the Tudor Royal Council in the North would eventually absorb these border jurisdictions, the unparalleled power base that these offices of state had given to the great northern houses of Percy and Neville gave them almost princely power and made them formidable rivals to the Crown. In his *Chorographia* of 1649 the antiquarian William Gray had made the point that the nobility and gentry of the North:

are of great antiquity, and can produce more ancient Families than any other part of England ....The Noblemen and Gentry of the North hath been always imployed [sic] in their native country, in the warres of Kings of England, against the Scots; all of them holding their land in Knights service, to attend the warres in their own persons, with horse and speare, as the manner of fighting was in those dayes.[64]

As late as 1900, 50% of Northumberland was held in great estates (of more than 10,000 acres), which was the largest proportion of any county in the country, other than tiny Rutland, and a further 35% of the county was owned in 'gentry' estates of one to ten thousand acres.[45]

The distinctiveness of border governance was made all the more unusual by the semi-regal position of the Bishop of Durham, whose County Palatine was the only Prince-Bishopric in the British Isles. '*Quicquid rex habet extra, episcopus habet intra*' (the King's prerogatives outside are the Bishop's inside) was the maxim of the time, and as 'King in Durham' *Dunelm* had his own council, exchequer and courts (where, uniquely for a prelate, the bishop could pronounce sentence of death), his own steward, sheriff, and chancellor, his own hunting ground and his own parliament; indeed, Durham sent no MPs to Westminster till 1676. As royal writ did not run in the county the Bishop had his own coroner, Judges of Assize and Justices of the Peace, and it was he who granted licenses to crenelate (build castles). The 'liberty of Durham' was simply the greatest feudal franchise in the country, where the bishop's vassals—the haliwerfolc—pledged to defend St Cuthbert's shrine, and kept not 'the King's Peace' but 'the Peace of St. Cuthbert.' What is more, the bishop minted his own coinage, which bore his image, not the king's, and all the mines in the county belonged to him, which provided a huge source of episcopal income, and made him one of the richest men in England (when in 1802 Bishop Shute Barrington renewed the lease of the London Lead Company's Weardale holdings, he charged them £70,000—the equivalent of over £70 million in 2019—with an annual rent on top of £4,000).[46] The grandeur of the title was such that the Bishop of Durham, Anthony Bek, was appointed by Pope Clement V as the Patriarch of Jerusalem in 1305. The authority of the office was so well-known that the powers granted to Lord Baltimore by King Charles I to govern the American colony of Maryland were modelled on the Durham Palatinate charter of the fourteenth century and gave him all the 'rights and privileges enjoyed by any bishop of Durham.'

The temporal authority of the Prince-Bishopric lasted until 1836 (although they zealously maintained their coal and lead mining interests), after which time the Marquesses of Londonderry and the Lambton Earls of Durham assumed a more prominent role in the county. But the greatest of the blue-blooded Northumbrian magnates were the Earls, and later the Dukes, of Northumberland. One history of the House of Percy has noted that in the tumultuous North, the 'Southern king's writ hardly ran. In Percy country, there was Percy law backed by a Percy army paid for by Percy money.'[47] (The French writer Marcel Proust was fascinated by the sonority and evocation of high lineage of certain ancient titles and was always delighted when he came upon the name of the Duke of Northumberland, which he thought had a 'sort of thunderous quality.')[48]

The dynasty began with a Norman knight from Calvados who was granted lands in Northern England by William the Conqueror. In the following centuries the family's fortunes rose and fell with the vagaries of court politics, but they always had their Northumbrian stronghold at Alnwick Castle from which they dominated Northumberland from the Tweed to the Tyne. By the eighteenth century the male line had died out, and, in an aristocratic sleight of hand, Sir Hugh Smithson—an obscure but wealthy Yorkshire baronet who had married a descendent of the last Percy Earl of Northumberland—assumed the famous surname and was elevated to ducal status. The Dukes of Northumberland's vast land-holdings—including some of the richest seams of coal in the world, which by 1919 were earning him £82,000 a year (worth up to £31 million in 2019 prices)—had made them utterly pre-eminent in the county. 'The Duke of Northumberland is dead,' observed the black-bordered *Newcastle Journal* in 1865; 'it will spread a gloom and sorrow in the north whose dark shadow will fall upon a generation to come.'[49] The deceased duke in question was 'Algernon the Benevolent, the greatest of all the Percies,' whose 'practical efforts for the poor and for the welfare of his county had earned him the love of the humblest cottagers,' some 7,000 of whom shuffled past his bier as it lay in state for two days at Alnwick. The social position of the Northumbrian landed interest was well-described by a meeting of Percy tenants in the late nineteenth century who seemed to revel in ducal munificence:

> ...Those relics of the feudal yoke
> Still in the north remain unbroke:
> That social yoke, with one accord
> That binds the peasant to his Lord...
> And liberty, that idle vaunt,
> Is not the comfort that we want;
> It only serves to turn the head,
> But gives to none their daily bread.

We want community of feeling,
And landlords kindly in their dealing.[50]

Percy influence in politics was such that Northumberland saw only three contested county elections between 1760 and 1830, and even after that local candidates had to secure the ducal imprimatur to get elected. When Sir William Beveridge stood for the Liberals in 1945 in the Berwick constituency (which covered most of North Northumberland), the Durham miner Sid Chaplin, on holiday in Alnwick, wrote to a friend describing the 'the shadow of Percy Hotspur ... the Politics of the Duke are the Politics of the Town,' and that when the Duke 'spoke for the Tory nincompoop that settled the interloper Beveridge!'[51] Alnwick has retained its feudal atmosphere, and Percy influence extends across the county where the Duchess is the current Lord Lieutenant and the Duke's property portfolio extends from Cheviot grouse-moors to Tyneside trading estates. Few other places outside Liechtenstein and Luxembourg could match the Ruritanian splendour of Lady Melissa Percy's marriage to Thomas van Straubenzee in 2013 when she travelled through Alnwick with a retinue of bicorned footmen in the yellow state coach which had carried the 3rd Duke of Northumberland (as George IV's personal representative) to the coronation of the Bourbon King Charles X in Reims in 1825.

With the expansion of the coal trade there emerged new rivals to the Northumbrian nobility. The burgesses of Newcastle had been quick to capitalise on the economic potential of coal and had managed to assert the right of the town's Freemen burgesses that they must 'host' any stranger coal-merchants that came to the Tyne to do business. These 'hostmen' became an important and distinctive part of Tyneside's commercial life, and in the late sixteenth century two of these, Henry Anderson and William Selby, used municipal funds to buy up most of the leases in the Tyneside coalfield on behalf of twenty other burgesses. This near-total monopoly of coal-production and municipal government became known as the 'Grand Lease' and was confirmed in a charter of Elizabeth I in 1600. Through their control of the twenty-five most important collieries on Tyneside, and their role in providing the capital for ship-building ventures and the coal-hungry new salt, lime and glass industries, these Hostmen were soon being called the 'Lords of Coal' and arrogated to themselves jurisdiction over the River Tyne and representation of the borough in Parliament. By 1700 the Newcastle Company of Hostmen was dying but a new generation of coal-owners stepped forward to create an even more powerful cartel called 'the Vend' which established arrangements for agreeing prices and output which lasted until the 1830s. London's demand for coal in the eighteenth century was insatiable and the coal-merchants on the Thames bitterly resented this system for keeping prices high, nicknaming the vend 'The Newcastle Parliament.' The grandest member of this 'Grand Alliance' of coal-barons was the stupendously wealthy Sir George Bowes of Gibside, and thanks to the marriage of his daughter and heiress Mary Eleanor—perhaps the richest woman in Europe at the time—to a Scottish aristocrat called John Lyon in 1767, the present Queen carries the DNA of hard-nosed Tyneside coal-owners.

This associational and proto-corporatist approach to conducting business was typical of the North East. One notices this in the centralising instincts of Robert Stephenson who made speeches against the messiness of the free market in railway provision, or Sir George Elliot's proposals in the 1890s to amalgamate all the Northumbrian collieries into a huge semi-public enterprise to control output and fix prices and fair wages (and, to be fair, establish a miners' welfare fund). Nor was the North East's economic growth ever based on the individualist free enterprise of small craftsmen: note well the baronial control of key industries in the hands of very few individuals, starting with Ambrose Crowley, whose works on Derwentside were described in 1768 as 'among the greatest manufactories of the kind in Europe,' employing several hundred hands to supply the East India Company with hardware; or Sir James Joicey and Company which by 1896 operated twenty-seven collieries in Durham producing between four and five million tons of coal each year; and most famous of all, Lord Armstrong's vast concerns on the north bank of the river, which teemed with 25,000 workers in 1914, and by the end of the First World War had extended to employ over 62,000 Northumbrians.

But then no other town in Northern England had an older system of guilds than Newcastle—the oldest of which, the Merchant Adventurers' Company, was founded in 1216 (the crests of the twenty-eight extant guilds adorn the ceiling of the Banqueting Hall in Newcastle Civic Centre). A man could only be a full citizen, or a 'Freeman,' of medieval Newcastle if he was admitted to one of these guilds or 'mysteries' after serving an apprenticeship. By the early modern period such Freemen made up about one third of all the men in the town, and this provided Newcastle with 'an usually high electorate.'[52] (When Jean Paul Marat published his *Chains of Slavery* in 1774 he sent copies up from London to the incorporated companies of Bricklayers, Cordwainers, Plasterers, Wallers, Goldsmiths, Skinners and Glovers, 'so that a large section of the electorate had ample opportunity of imbibing his doctrine').[53] It was these Guilds of Freemen that controlled all branches of local government and river trade and directly elected the town's members of parliament. The historian Bill Purdue has observed that 'One man's monopoly is, no doubt, another's co-operative enterprise,' and that the town's history was 'in large part that of layers of monopolistic influence and power.'[54]

To be outside this charmed circle of business and patronage was an almost insurmountable disadvantage and eighteenth-century Newcastle was run by an oligarchy of families such as the Blacketts, Andersons, Fenwicks and Claytons, and perhaps most dominant of all, the Ridleys, three generations of whom were returned (usually uncontested) as the town's MPs from 1747–1835. This oligarchic arrangement continued well into the late nineteenth century, where Beatrice and Sydney Webb noticed that municipal elections in Newcastle were not subject to party contests (as was also the case in nearby Tynemouth Borough until as late as the 1950s). This was something that, in their view, gave off the whiff of corruption as local capitalists could exploit the Corporation and obtain favourable terms as 'buyers and lessees of its land and port facilities, and in their arrangements for the composite payment of town dues, and in the control of the gasworks, water works and tramways.'[55]

Such was the cohesion of Newcastle's upper echelons that one distinguished local Freeman and coal merchant, Ralph Carr (1711–1806)—a man so wealthy that he was able to lend the government £30,000 in 1745 to pay the troops of the Duke of Cumberland's army in Scotland—was able to raise enough capital locally to establish Newcastle's first bank, arguably Britain's first proper bank outside London and Edinburgh, in 1755.[56] (In the 1960s his direct descendant, Sir Ralph Carr-Ellison, demonstrated the enduring influence of these old families by chairing both Northumbrian Water and Tyne Tees Television—and commanding the Northumberland Hussars.) This close-knit community of merchants, coal-owners and local gentry had established their own club on graceful Pall Mall lines in Eldon Square in Newcastle in 1828. 'The Northern Counties'—which has since moved to Hood Street—is one of the oldest private members' clubs in the world. A painting on the Club's main staircase shows a gathering of red-tailcoated Northumbrian grandees in the 1950s, with all the old families represented: the Duke himself, with Viscounts Ridley and Allendale, as well as Field Marshal Sir Francis Festing (whose son Matthew became, in 2008, the Prince and Grand Master of the Order of Malta), as well as assorted members of the local squirearchy: Straker, Pease, Riddell, Bigge and, inevitably, Carr-Ellison.

The tenacious grip of this cosy group of families was noted in a provocative study by a Community Project from the West End of Newcastle in 1978 which observed, in a chapter entitled 'The Making of a Ruling Class,' that despite the decline of the industries that had made their fortunes, their dynastic power, wealth and authority had lived on—not least through the control of banks and building societies. The slightly incestuous *modus operandi* of the Northumbrian elite was to have a significant impact beyond just the North East of England. When the Newcastle-based Northern Rock began to run out of money in 2007 it led to the first run on a British bank in over 150 years, heralding a global financial crisis the consequences of which we are still living with. It was noted at the time that the board of the Rock—whose members included a number of the same old gentry families—did not seem fully understand the complex world of sub-prime mortgages and securitisation, with particular criticism levelled at the chairman—a zoology graduate and man of letters in the Northumbrian Enlightenment tradition who just happened to be the 5th Viscount Ridley.

* * *

The hegemony of these Northumbrian plutocrats was by no means always benevolent. In the market place in Durham city there stands an extraordinary over-life-sized statue of an Anglo-Irish aristocrat: Charles William Vane Stewart, the 3rd Marquess of Londonderry. In his youth Londonderry had been a dashing cavalryman—his nickname in the Peninsula, where he was Wellington's adjutant, was 'the Bold Sabreur'—but after leaving the army he gained a reputation as a loutish libertine, whoring and scrapping his way around Vienna in 1814 with his brother Viscount Castlereagh, the British minister at the peace congress. After he inherited the marquessate in the 1820s he then settled down to become a gouty and despotic owner of Durham coal mines, and in Raffaele Monti's fantastical, gothic sculpture, Londonderry—elaborately attired in hussar uniform and plumed busby—is shown with the curling lip and contemptuous look that he so often showed to the men who worked on his estates and in his collieries. In Ellen Wilkinson's famous *j'accuse* against the capitalists who had laid waste to her constituency of Jarrow, *The Town That Was Murdered*, she cited Londonderry's strike-breaking actions as the sort of ruthless tyranny that long abounded in the coalfields, and quoted from the threats he published widely in the coal strike of 1844:

> I superintended many ejectments … it had no avail. I warned you next I would bring over more men from my Irish estates and turn more men out … you heeded me not. I have now brought forty Irishmen to the pits and I will give you all one more week's notice. And if by the 13th of this month a large body of my pitmen do not return to their labour, I will obtain one

hundred more men and proceed to eject that number who now are illegally and unjustly in possession of my houses, and in the following week another one hundred shall follow.

I will be on the spot myself; the civil and military power will be at hand to protect the good men and the strangers; and you may rely upon it the majesty of the law and the rights of property will be protected and prevail.

Believe me, I am your sincere friend,

VANE LONDONDERRY

If the rights of property were well-defended then it was clear to many Northumbrians that serious organisation was required to safeguard the rights of labour. The North East of England had some of the oldest trade unions in Britain, and by the 1890s Northumberland and Durham were the most strongly unionised counties in the country. This fact would determine the socialist nature of popular politics in the region—in Henry Pelling's classic study *The Social Geography of British Elections* he noted that the region had 'the strongest and best organised working-class electorate in Britain'[57]—but so too did the implacable nature of their opponents and the salutary experience of major defeats at the hands of organised capital. This birthed a characteristically Northumbrian political outlook that was cautious and incremental and, after the tumults of the 1830s and 1840s, seldom if ever revolutionary.

Much of this organisation began not in the collieries, but on the rivers Tyne and Wear. Here the keelmen and crews of the collier ships 'closely knit by a common calling and dialect, celebrated in song [and] inured to hardship beyond even the standards of their time' were drawn together in work and leisure, and their gatherings in the riverside drinking houses led to the first stirrings of if not a class consciousness, then certainly a self-awareness of being a community apart with a vital place in the life of a seafaring nation.[58] Their first industrial action—or 'mutinies' as the authorities called them—is recorded in 1768 when hundreds of North Shields seamen marched with colours flying to Sunderland and prevented any vessel from leaving port until their grievances over pay were met. The chief complaint of the collier seamen was often against the unique threat of the press-gangs (which was even employed by the civil authorities in peacetime to assist in strike-breaking as late as 1822); indeed, in 1793 over 500 armed seamen had attacked the *Eleanor* at Shields in an attempt to rescue the impressed men aboard, and Royal Navy ships (much to the chagrin of their officers and men who hated the task) were regularly sent North to intimidate the colliers and keelmen back to work.

Around this time the shipbuilders themselves also started to unionise. The South Shields Shipwrights' Association was perhaps the first such union in Britain and dated its foundation to 1795—making it the oldest antecedent body of the much amalgamated GMB Union. The Association was established to provide 'mutual relief' for members and their families, with provisions for any member suffering unemployment, 'shipwreck' or 'being taken by the enemy' (as well as penalties, and even expulsion, for any members who caught a venereal disease or were found guilty of 'notorious immoralities' such as adultery, theft, murder and fornication). This was essentially a conservative craft-based union (although it was sufficiently affluent that by 1826 it was able to finance a ship-building project for its unemployed members) and was strong enough to secure reliable day wage rates when the majority of the British shipbuilding industry had moved over to a system of piecework. In 1851 the *Sunderland Herald* noted that the Tyne shipwrights 'were pretty well known as close unionists,' and so too were the Wearside men for in the census of that year it was recorded that there were 1,372 shipwrights in the town, and nearly 1,200 of them were members of a union.[59]

As for the pitmen, Samuel Smiles wrote in 1868 that '"the lads belaw" are a people of peculiar habits, manners and character, as much so as fishermen and sailors,' adding that fifty years earlier they were undoubtedly 'hard workers, but very wild and uncouth; much given to 'sleeks,' or strikes."[60] Some of the first recorded instances of industrial action in British history took place in the Northumbrian coalfields as in 1740 when the colliers joined the poor of Newcastle in the corn riots, or in 1765 when 4,000 miners made their 'Great Stand' against the hated yearly binding. The strike was a limited success, and if nothing else the pitmen had proven that they were not, as one letter to a London paper put it, 'a rabble of Coal-heavers.' They were pitmen, and they also conceived themselves to be 'free-born Englishmen.'[61]

The early 'combinations,' as miners' unions were called at the time, shared much of the same spirit that animated the watermen: they pooled their resources to provide relief for widowed and orphaned colliers and compensation for injury, and they shared too a propensity for enforcing solidarity. For example, when impressed seamen returned to port in Sunderland in 1783 they sought out those who had informed on them to the press gangs; these informers were then mounted on a 'stang' (a long pole) 'and carried through the principal streets, exposed to the insults and assaults of an enraged populace, the women in particular bedaubing them plentifully with dirt etc,' and it's telling that the Tyne seamen who refused to join the strikes of 1792 and 1815 were humiliated in a similar fashion.[62] Similarly, when the miners struck in 1810 they were solemnly pledged to secrecy under penalty of being 'stabbed through the heart' or 'having bowels ripped out,' and an account of the time notes that 'when they combine or stick for the purpose of raising their wages, they are said to spit upon a stone together, by way of cementing their confederacy.'[63] Such visceral commitment was perhaps best described in the lyrics to 'Blackleg Miner,' a traditional ballad written to commemorate the fightback against the strike-breaking labour brought into South East Northumberland in 1844.

> And divvunt gan near the Seghill mine,
> Across the way they stretch a line
> To catch the throat, and break the spine
> of the dirty blackleg miner.

There was a febrile atmosphere throughout the first five decades of the nineteenth century, with regular strikes intermingled with 'monster demonstrations' against the Peterloo Massacre, and growing Chartist agitation. There has been a tendency in the historiography of the North East to think of the radicalism of this period teleologically, as part of the inevitable growth of class consciousness and onward march of socialism. To be sure, radical politics are an important strand in Northumbrian history. The concept of 'free-born rights' first posited by Sunderland's own John Lilburne in the 1640s had a profound effect on the development of the American Constitution—especially the Fifth Amendment of 1791 and the right to avoid self-incrimination. In John Baillie's eighteenth-century *History of Newcastle* he saw the Saxon origins of the town's 'Moot Hall' (court-house) as the place 'from which the glorious palladium of British freedom, trial by jury, took its origins.'[64] The leading reformer John Wilkes was much feted in the North East too, where an 'Ode to Liberty' was performed in his honour in 1770 that drew on widespread assumptions about the Northumbrian love of freedom:

> But hark! what grateful sounds salute my ear?
> Behold *Northumbria's* freeborn sons appear.
> Their souls with inward greatness soar on high
> And bear bright freedom's banners to the sky.
> They know the wish'd-for crisis is at hand,
> When *Britons* ought to make a glorious stand;
> With virtuous zeal to check oppression's rage,
> And *slew* the *venal torrent of the age.*[65]

This Northumbrian love of liberty was also manifest in anti-slavery campaigning where Newcastle, it was said, was 'among the foremost' in demanding that Parliament stop the slave trade, with numerous petitions to that effect emerging from Newcastle and Gateshead from the 1790s onwards. (Wedgwood's famous anti-slavery medallions—'Am I not a man and a brother'—were probably based on an engraving by Thomas Bewick, who himself subscribed to anti-slavery causes.) After the freed-slave Elaudio Equiano came to Newcastle in 1792 he wrote to the local newspapers offering his 'warmest thanks of a heart growing with gratitude to you, for your fellow-feeling for the Africans,' and the testimony of the Sunderland-based actor and merchant James Field Stanfield via the horrors he recorded in his 1789 *Observations on a Guinea Voyage* did much to advance the cause of Abolition in the North.

Much of the strong feeling against slavery was influenced by a Northumbrian who was one of the most effective Abolitionists in British history. Granville Sharp was born in Durham, the ninth son of the Archdeacon of Northumberland, and after an education at Durham Grammar School he became a noted scholar of Greek and Hebrew, publishing several works of Biblical criticism. From there on Sharp became active in the anti-slavery movement, becoming the first chairman of the Society for Effecting the Abolition of the Slave Trade. It was after his brilliant *pro bono* defence of a black immigrant, James Somerset, that Lord Mansfield made his famous judgment of 1772 that slavery was 'so odious, that nothing can be suffered to support it' and therefore, as soon as any slave sets foot in England, they become free men and women.

The torch of Abolition was carried well into the nineteenth century, not least by the extraordinary efforts of Northumbrian women—such as the 'Female Inhabitants of Newcastle upon Tyne, Gateshead & their Vicinities' who sent a petition with 6,288 signatures to Parliament in 1833 calling for the abolition of slavery in the West Indies (slavery was indeed banned in the British Empire in 1838), or the 'Newcastle Ladies' Free Produce Association' founded in 1846 to boycott goods produced through slave labour in the Americas. It was fitting, therefore, that Martin Luther King received his only honorary degree outside the USA from Newcastle University in 1967, where, in the Armstrong Building, and in front of the Duke of Northumberland presiding as Chancellor, Dr King brought a message that struck a chord with his Northumbrian audience of the 'inescapable network of mutuality,' and the 'beautiful symphony of brotherhood' that would hasten the day 'when all over the world justice will roll down like waters and righteousness like a mighty stream.'

There were certainly prominent Northumbrians who championed the cause of political reform. Charles Grey, the 2nd Earl Grey, was born at the family seat of Fallodon in Northumberland and represented the county in parliament in the Whig interest. During his career he was a consistent advocate of electoral reform and Catholic Emancipation, and in his four years as Prime Minister from 1830–34 he steered both the Abolition of Slavery in the British Empire and the Great Reform Act of 1832 through Parliament that enfranchised the growing industrial towns (and of the 130 new seats created by the Act, only South Shields has never returned a Tory MP). In addition to the blend of tea that still bears his name, he is also commemorated by a grand monument in Newcastle which bears the fulsome tribute that he was 'the fearless and consistent champion of civil and religious liberty.' Grey was supported in the drafting of his Reform Bill by another Northumbrian: his son-in-law—and possessor of a massive coal-fortune—John Lambton, 1st Earl of Durham. 'Radical Jack,' as he was known, was the most prominent and influential standard-bearer for radicalism in the 1830s where he campaigned for the secret ballot, a vote for every householder and a general election at least every three years.[66] He later became a reforming Governor-General of Canada and his *Report on the Affairs of British North America*, commonly known as 'Lord Durham's Report,' was a landmark in Canadian history in its recommendations for responsible self-government.

The biggest beast in later nineteenth-century Northumbrian radicalism was the industrialist and newspaper proprietor Joseph Cowen. The son of a self-made colliery owner who had sat as a Liberal MP for Newcastle, Cowen Junior also represented the town in parliament, and via his ownership of the *Newcastle Daily Chronicle* he was able to broadcast his worldview—radical, liberal, internationalist—to the burgeoning population of Tyneside. He transformed the *Chronicle* into a popular but serious paper, influential and international in its reach—it was one of the very few newspapers to support the Union during the American Civil War, and in its uncompromising support for Irish Home Rule the government judged the *Chronicle* to be dangerously seditious and prohibited its circulation in Kilmainham jail. Cowen was a personal friend of a number of leading European nationalists and revolutionaries—Mazzini, Orsini, Louis Blanc, Herzen, Bakunin and Kossuth—and Giuseppe Garibaldi even came to visit him on Tyneside to raise funds and volunteers to fight for Italian reunification.

With his personal wealth and charisma, and his populist instincts (he was no doctrinaire: being an Imperialist supporter of Disraeli in matters of Foreign Policy—a smart move given the dominance of the arms trade on Tyneside), Cowen had something of the William Randolph Hearst about him. Away from Westminster Cowen maintained a powerbase in the North East through his newspaper and connections with all the various friendly societies, trade unions, mechanics' institutions, and co-operatives uniting their voices into what he called a 'militant democracy' and amplifying their voices first regionally, and then nationally as he did via the Northern Reform Union (NRU), and its petitioning of Parliament for universal male suffrage, abolition of the property qualification and the secret ballot. The petition compiled by the NRU in 1859 was six hundred yards long and bore 34,456 signatures from across the North East (an estimated fifty per cent of the enfranchised adult male population of Northumberland and Durham).[67] This 'Aurora Borealis of Reform,' as it was known, represented a distinctly liberal voice that would dominate North East politics until the 1920s, weaving the Free Trade instincts of the Tyneside industrialists together with the reforming, rational and internationalist outlook of the Northumbrian bourgeoisie that finds an echo in the enduring influence of the Fabian Society in North East Labour politics and the strength of pro-Remain opinion among the region's Labour MPs.

Cowen's Irish Nationalist sympathies also played an important role in strengthening Anglo-Irish relations in the North East itself, which, after Liverpool, London and Glasgow, was the fourth largest centre of Irish migration to England in the nineteenth century. Works such as *When Paddy Met Geordie* have demonstrated that this encounter was usually a cordial one—certainly in contrast to the sectarian cauldrons of Clydeside and Merseyside. This was aided by a buoyant local economy, and the strength of local non-conformity which was as hostile to Anglican ascendancy as the Irish were, but also the liberal political traditions that Cowen did so much to foster. This allowed the Irish to take a prominent place in public life, and when Bernard McAnulty was elected in All Saints ward in Newcastle in 1874 he became the first Catholic Irishman ever to sit on a town council in England. Moreover during the First World War the Lord Mayor of Newcastle was an immigrant from Tipperary, Sir John Fitzgerald, who had established a chain of pubs in the city (that still exists).[68] Fitzgerald was a driving force behind the raising of the Tyneside Irish Brigade in 1914, a uniquely successful volunteering initiative among the Irish communities of Britain, and testament to the depth of their integration into Northumbrian life.

It is useful to note here too the experience of other immigrant groups, especially on Tyneside where Germans and Scandinavians started to settle in large numbers from the 1800s. These were joined from the 1880s onwards by the 'lascars' from Aden and elsewhere who came to the Tyne on British vessels (their tolerance for extreme heat was said to give them an aptitude for working as firemen and stokers). One study of migration to South Shields by an American author concluded that these migrants 'encountered not simply tolerance or co-existence but mutual cultural accommodation into local kin, occupational and other social networks.'[69] As a consequence, South Shields has one of the oldest settled Muslim populations in Britain, a Yemeni community that has been notably successful at integration; indeed the mosque in the town was the venue for a marriage blessing for the boxer Muhammad Ali and his wife on their visit to Britain in 1977. Jewish migrants from the later nineteenth century onwards experienced similar toleration, with grand synagogues built in Newcastle and Sunderland to serve a community which has produced important figures in British public life including Aaron Gompertz and Sir Jack Cohen, post-war mayors of South Shields and Sunderland respectively, as well the Chief Rabbi from 1948–65, Sir Israel Brodie; the Lord Chief Justice from 1992–96, Lord (Peter) Taylor of Gosforth; the doctor and advice columnist Miriam Stoppard; and the eminent professor of War Studies (and panel member of the Chilcott Inquiry), Sir Lawrence Freedman. Indeed, it is striking that Gateshead Talmudical College is the largest Yeshiva in the world outside Israel and the USA, and sits at the heart of an 8,000 strong Charedi community in the town, and Gateshead has become, in the words of Jonathan Arkush, the president of the Board of Deputies, 'the Charedi equivalent of Oxford: a unique university town for the very devout and a citadel of Orthodox intellectualism.'[70]

* * *

In the study of British social and political history there is often a tendency to over-emphasise the radical and liberal over more traditional and conserving movements. This may owe something to the predominant political sympathies within the academy, but it can present an unbalanced view of the past as one long march towards class or gender consciousness. But Northumbrian political traditions are as conservative as they are radical—even when they were nominally 'left wing,' as embodied by the characteristic socialism of the coalfields which was a sort of 'Blue Labour' *avant la lettre*. By taking the long view we can see the deep roots of this conservativism.

The 'Pilgrimage of Grace,' the failed Northern rebellion that began in 1537 in protest at Henry VIII's suppression of the 'old religion,' garnered much support in Durham where the pilgrims joined the revolt under the legendary banner of St Cuthbert (although after the rebellion was put down, and Henry VIII entered Yorkshire in triumph, the mayor of Newcastle was astute enough to send the King a gift of £100 as a token of the town's loyalty). The 'Rising of the North' in 1569 was inaugurated at Raby Castle in Durham where the Nevilles and Percys gathered 700 knights for the purpose of overthrowing Elizabeth I in favour of Mary Stuart and restoring a Catholic supremacy. These northern earls detested the 'new men,' Protestants like the Queen's advisor William Cecil, and the Calvinist Dean of Durham and his wife who had ritually burned St Cuthbert's iconic banner. So after marching to Durham Cathedral, they tore up the new English Bibles and Prayer Books they found there and celebrated a solemn mass in Latin before heading south to Nottinghamshire where Mary Queen of Scots was imprisoned. But their nerve didn't hold, and as in 1537 the Crown was able to suppress the rebellion, with harsh reprisals. Eight hundred of the rebels were hanged, sixty-six of them in the city of Durham, and the Earl of Northumberland was beheaded at York in 1572.

How did the North East navigate the turbulent seventeenth century? Firstly, Puritanism was much less marked among the Tyne merchants than it was in the other towns of the East Coast. Tyneside was characterised by a rather low-temperature Anglicanism in religious matters (conversely, only Lancashire had more 'recusant' Roman Catholics than Northumberland). As a town of vital strategic importance, and the epicentre of the coal trade, Newcastle was a key prize—even so (and despite how vulnerable it was to Scottish incursions) the town was, with King's Lynn, the only important seaport in the country that fought for the King—and this seemed to be as much a matter of hostility to the Presbyterian Scots, the ancestral enemy, as it was due to loyalty to the Stuarts. Sunderland, in contrast—as the bailiwick of the Puritan Lilburne family—declared for Parliament and allied with the Scottish Covenanters, whose lifting of the North East Coast blockade in 1644 turned the Wear into a vital source of coal (and coal revenue) for the Scottish Covenanting army and Parliamentarian forces. It's probable that the Tyne-Wear skirmishing of that period, including the victory of the Sunderland-based Scots Covenanters over the Marquess of Newcastle's Royalist forces at the Battle of Boldon Hill in 1644, laid the foundations for the Newcastle-Sunderland rivalry that still pre-occupies Northumbrians to this day, on the football terraces and beyond.

The Restoration of the Stuarts in 1660 coincided with a period of growing coal-based prosperity, such that the North East was even less inclined to support anything that might disrupt its economic progress. The reaction of the Newcastle mob to the demise of the Stuarts showed their flexibility: at James II's coronation they had 'shouted and drank the claret'; but at the accession of William of Orange they tumbled James's statue into the Tyne, and cheered for the new regime.[71] The town was similarly equivocal when the Stuarts attempted a return in 1715. A portion of the Northumbrian gentry declared for the Jacobites, and the Earl of Derwentwater raised the Jacobite standard at Warkworth (he was later captured and beheaded, and his estates in Northumberland were confiscated and given to Greenwich Hospital as a source of income), whereas Newcastle's position was ambiguous: it showed no inclination to support the rebellion, but it showed no great zeal for the Hanoverians either, and unlike Carlisle, Chester and Berwick, they waited until Jacobite defeat was certain before submitting a loyal address to George I.

In 1745, the position was more clear-cut. Field Marshal Wade was quickly sent north with 20,000 regular troops to garrison Newcastle—which had already rounded up suspected Jacobites, strengthened the town walls and inducted 800 volunteers into the local militia in defence of 'King Geordie.' The failure of 1745 finally closed the chapter on the Border instability that had so disrupted the economic life of the region, and the Hanoverian peace that followed ensured the uninterrupted growth of the highly lucrative coal trade. There was no more potent representation of this new generation, with its acceptance of the Protestant Settlement and militant defence of the rights of capital, than John Scott, the 1st Earl of Eldon. The son of a Newcastle coal-broker, Eldon—after serving his time on the northern legal circuit as an expert in property law—ascended to become an arch-reactionary Lord Chancellor for some twenty-five years. A staunch Tory and ally of William Pitt, he opposed the Abolition of Slavery, Catholic Emancipation, and the Great Reform Act, and embodied, perfectly, the harshness of *ancien regime* Britain (given a copy of Milton's *Paradise Lost*, Eldon was asked later what he thought of Satan: 'Damn fine fellow, I hope he wins!'). Shelley, in his *Masque of Anarchy*, mocked Eldon's supposed sympathy for the dead of the Napoleonic Wars with the famous lines:

> *Next came Fraud, and he had on,*
> *Like Eldon, an ermined gown;*
> *His big tears, for he wept well,*
> *Turned to mill-stones as they fell.*

For the liberal historian G.M. Trevelyan he represented, simply, the worst of 'the stupid old Tory party.'[72]

Eldon died at the height of the turbulent 1830s, when the Tories were riven by debates about how to respond to the changing world around them. Sir Robert Peel's vision of political reform without the 'perpetual vortex of agitation' would prevail and both the old 'throne and altar' Tories and the aristocratic Whigs began to embrace political reform and heed the views of a growing middle-class electorate. This still left in place an unenfranchised swathe of working men and women, and the clashes and compromises of that period cast a long shadow on Northumbrian politics. For although the miners in particular did taste victory in 1831 when the Pitmen's Union of the Tyne and Wear (known as 'Hepburn's Union,' after their leader, the self-taught and redoubtable Tommy Hepburn) forced the employers to concede a maximum working day of twelve rather than eighteen hours, and ensured that payment for labour was always in money, rather than credit in the hated 'Tommy Shops,' this triumph was short-lived. The strikes of 1832 and 1844 were crushed, pitilessly, by the coal-owners via strike-breaking labour, blacklisting union-leaders (Hepburn was reduced to hawking tea around the pit-villages as the owners banned him from their collieries) and the 'full majesty of the law' as Londonderry had it. This was a humiliating experience for the miners, and from the mid-century onwards a new generation of leaders emerged who were more inclined to accept Harriet Martineau's advice to Hepburn in 1832: 'combine against ill fortune instead of against the masters.'[73]

The quintessence of this new temperament can be found in the life of the Northumberland Miners' leader Thomas Burt. Despite his humble beginnings, Burt—who had started his working life underground at the age of ten—was an intelligent and industrious Methodist, who built a career first as a trade union secretary, and then by becoming, after his election at Morpeth in 1874 as a 'Lib-Lab' MP (a Liberal elected with union backing), the first working class man ever elected to Parliament. Burt's biographer called him the 'great conciliator,' and although he was a radical in terms of his support for universal suffrage, for men and women (he once addressed a crowd of 80,000 on Newcastle Town Moor on the subject), in labour relations he was an undoubted moderate who utterly rejected class conflict. Burt described the miners' unions of the North East as

> something more than fighting machines. Whilst they have stood up for the right of labour, they have ever been reasonable and conciliatory in their methods, preferring to settle their differences by friendly conferences rather than by the arbitrament of force in the shape of strikes.[74]

As a Methodist, Burt represented the principles of 'conscientiousness, sobriety, industry and regularity of conduct,' and he firmly believed in hierarchy, reciprocity, and justice for working people.[75] To achieve this he was determined to make the working classes respectable in how they conducted their politics and collective bargaining, turning away from the direct action and strikes of the earlier half century, and towards Parliament as the legitimate means of redressing social and economic grievances. 'One thing gives me unqualified satisfaction,' William Gladstone was supposed to have remarked of the miners, 'it is that the workmen know how to select their leaders. They do not choose charlatans to represent them in Parliament.'[76]

The Durham Miners shared this political outlook, and a procession of formidable trade unionists and MPs wielded huge influence in the county. Those frock-coated and chapel-going pitmen Liberals of the later nineteenth century were well-represented by men like their General Secretary, John Wilson, who ensured that arbitration and conciliation prevailed over class militancy, and would use his authority to put down demands for what he saw as 'suicidal' colliery strikes from 'hotheeds' and 'socialists.'[77] Then came the Methodist lay-preacher Peter Lee (1864–1935), another powerful figure who, via his leadership of the Durham Miners Association and the first Labour county council in the 1920s, assumed the role of 'chief of the civic life of Durham and leader of its people,' who, through his oversight of public works—building houses and hospitals, even a reservoir in Weardale to supply clean water to the pit villages and fight typhoid—espoused a 'demotic social-ism focused on practical solutions to everyday problems,' and sought 'accom-modation with capitalism rather than its overthrow.'[78] The Durham Miners showed their appreciation and built him a spacious pile—Bede's Rest—over-looking Durham Cathedral, but the County Council went further and, thanks to the Labour Government's *New Towns Act*, they named the new town of Peterlee after him.

The Northumbrian coalfields in the nineteenth century were unusual in their adherence to Liberalism, where most politically conscious miners remained moderate 'lib-labs,' and 'the new socialist currents hardly touched them.'[79] As most North East colliery ouput went for international export, the Northumbrian miners' unions understood how sensitive the industry was to the selling price of coal, and accepted that wages should reflect that changing demand—in contrast to the other inland coalfields who supplied the more predictable domestic market, and were thus bolder in their demands. As a consequence, the Northumberland and Durham miners' unions didn't affili-ate to the more radical and syndicalist Miners Federation of Great Britain—a union that had long sought nationalisation—until 1907–08.

It has been noticeable of late how frequently the modern Durham Miners' Association display the lodge banners of Chopwell and Follonsby with their hammer and sickle imagery. The pit village of Chopwell, near Gateshead, was certainly a hotbed of revolutionary socialism—and even had a Marx Terrace and a Lenin Terrace—but this outlook was far from typical in County

Durham. Biblical devices on lodge banners were much more common, and the motto on the Monkwearmouth banner—'Come Let Us Reason Together'—as well as the design of the 'Pitmen's Parliament' in Durham, headquarters of the DMA, part debating chamber, part Methodist chapel, embodied their strict adherence to conciliation and liberal democracy. As Henry Mess explained, the leaders of the Miners' Federation of Great Britain aimed at replacing private capitalism, whereas 'the leaders in Northumberland and Durham, and a great many of their followers, had aimed at improving conditions within the existing system of ownership and management.'[80]

Similar attitudes predominated in other local industries. Despite one engineering strike on Tyneside in 1917, the North East—in contrast to other areas—was relatively free from industrial unrest throughout the First World War; industry was booming with war-work and disputes were usually settled by arbitration rather than strikes. But the Great War did provide the Northumbrian working classes with an insight into the effectiveness of state control, and even the potential for nationalisation—a policy taken up enthusiastically by Labour but not by the Liberals. Indeed, the Morpeth Liberal Party thought that the war had fatally weakened the cause of Liberalism in the coalfields:

> The war required considerable state involvement in the lives of the people and as a consequence a large section of the community looked to the state rather than to themselves for any improvement in the lot of the people and thought that the improved conditions of life ought to come out of the state.[81]

This awakening followed the earlier affiliation of the MFGB with the Labour Party in 1909, which foretold the end of the old Lib-Lab consensus. But the dislocations of the First World War helped to create a more assertively self-conscious working class, and one that rejected the traditional accommodations with capital championed by Burt and Wilson. From the 1920s onwards, the North East emerged as one of the Labour Party's firmest heartlands, building on the history of coalfield community and co-operation and pioneering a municipal socialism that delivered massive improvements in living standards for ordinary people.[82]

This new approach would be sorely tested by global economic forces. The recession of the mid-1920s caused unrelenting gloom in the North East, with catastrophic effects on wages. In 1921 Northumbrian miners had been paid nineteen shillings for one shift underground, but by 1926, that rate had plummeted to nine shillings and sixpence. Where once the Northumbrian miners had seen themselves as the aristocrats of labour, with money to spend on beer and baccy and 'shoes for the bairns,' the declining demand for coal had made them the worst-paid pitmen in Britain—with wages down below the official level of subsistence. Tommy Turnbull recalled how to supplement family incomes in South Shields kids went out in the streets and 'collected dogshit and sorted it into black piles and white piles and put it into little bags for those that wanted different types for their garden.'[83]

The antiquated system of Poor Law administration struggled to cope, and, in 1926, to take one example of many, the Chester-le-Street Board of Guardians managed 14,000 cases of outdoor relief by flouting Whitehall regulations and paying generous allowances to desperate mining families.[84] But despite this miserable hardship, the political reaction was muted. The Flying Scotsman may have been derailed by striking miners at Cramlington, and a destroyer was moored on the Tyne in case of civil unrest, but in the end the miners were forced back to work as they had been in in 1832. To be sure, Labour would go on to win the 1929 General Election, with Ramsay MacDonald newly elected in Seaham as Prime Minister, and a former Party Leader Arthur Henderson (a former-lay preacher and foundryman from Newcastle) as the first working-class man to hold the post of Foreign Secretary full time (MacDonald had combined the post with the Prime Ministership in 1924). But this was a cautious and unimaginative administration that floundered in the face of a world-wide slump. Even as the 'hungry thirties' dragged on there was surprisingly little unrest, or much in the way of Communist stirrings. This was met with disbelief from those who knew how miserable conditions were for the unemployed, and caused the Labour MP Ellen Wilkinson to muse 'if not Jarrow, then where?'[85]

Two of the most imaginative responses to the inter-war Depression emerged from the North East, and tell us much about the Northumbrian preference for stoicism over revolution in the face of desperate circumstances. The North East Coast Exhibition was a world's fair-type event held in Newcastle, which ran from May to October in 1929. In his chronicle of the event, *Northumbria's Spacious Year*, the Lord Mayor of Newcastle recorded in meticulous detail how 2,048 local guarantors had stumped up £174,000 between them to stage the event—including pledges as varied as £1,000 from Newcastle United FC, £500 from the Duke of Northumberland and £5 from New Brancepeth Co-op. Their purpose was to encourage local heavy industry by showcasing their products in a 125-acre Art Deco theme park with Palaces of Arts, Engineering and Industry designed in spectacular Cecil B. de Mille style by W. & T.R. Milburn of Sunderland. The exhibition was opened by the Prince of Wales and visited by King Alfonso XIII of Spain and the Sultan of

Zanzibar, and was a huge success with the paying public. 'Come to Newcastle,' implored the London *Times*, 'the centre of the Romance, History and Industry of Northumbria.'[86] But for all that the Exhibition may have drawn the crowds it did not improve the region's economy that was almost entirely geared towards heavy industries—the export of coal and the manufacture of ships and heavy armaments—enterprises that were acutely vulnerable to the vagaries of global trade and government cutbacks. And this brings us to Jarrow.

There were at least seven long-distance protest marches to London between the wars; some involved many thousands of marchers, and some were met with violence, but the only one we tend to remember is the 'Jarrow Crusade.' From 1851 to 1930 the Tyneside town of Jarrow had literally launched a thousand ships, from tankers and colliers to cruisers and battleships, but Palmers shipyard was forced to close in 1931, putting thousands of men out of work. By 1936, as crippling unemployment dragged on, and government support failed to materialise, Jarrow Borough Council arranged for 200 out-of-work local men to march to Parliament and petition Stanley Baldwin's government to provide work for the town. The strategy of the marchers was astute: they knew that unless handled cautiously, political demonstrations can repel as much as they can galvanise. Therefore, the march organisers were careful to demonstrate discipline and dignity in their demand for *work*, not handouts. Conditions in Jarrow were so desperate that 'reaching out' had to be taken seriously, so churchmen were courted, Communists were wheeled out, and as over 60 per cent of these unemployed riveters and platers were Great War veterans, they presented a disciplined picture of men marching smartly in step, blankets tightly rolled, and demonstrating their endurance and good order in a deliberate appeal to Middle England. The march's immediate impact was limited (the old joke in the town is that it was Hitler who saved Jarrow—through war-work for the shipyards). But as A.J.P. Taylor put it, middle-class people had felt 'the call of conscience,' and the immiseration of Jarrow and places like it were uppermost in many voters' minds when they cast their votes in the Labour landslide of 1945.[87]

* * *

The 1945 Labour government—statist, militarist and socially conservative—was almost perfectly calibrated to appeal to Northumbrian voters. Attlee's 1945 cabinet included several prominent North East MPs: the Chancellor, Hugh Dalton (who sat for Bishop Auckland), the Home Secretary James Chuter Ede (South Shields), Education Secretary Ellen

Wilkinson (Jarrow), Manny Shinwell (Seaham), who had the increasingly important Fuel and Power portfolio, and Jack Lawson (Chester-le-Street) as Secretary of State for War. Attlee's most recent biographer has described Lawson as a 'personal mentor' to the Labour leader, and 'his closest friend in politics,' giving him invaluable insight into the trade union movement and the northern heartlands.[88] Labour's agenda of nationalised coal and steel, National Health Service and massive house building programme was hugely popular: indoor toilets and running water in the new council houses were a revelation for Northumbrian families who had endured some of the worst housing in the country, and when the signs went up at every pit on New Year's Day 1947 stating that 'This colliery is now managed by the National Coal Board on behalf of the people' there was much satisfaction that the years of struggle had ended in victory. 'We are all one family,' declared NCB chairman Lord Hyndley at Murton Colliery in the heart of the Durham Coalfield, and 'if they all worked hard and worked together they would make nationalisation a great success.'[89] The Ellington Colliery miners banner (designed by Oliver Kilbourn of the Ashington group of 'Pitmen Painters') summed up this contentment with its contrasting images of pit-rows giving way to spacious semis above the legend 'Close the Door on Past Dreariness. Open up to Future Brightness.'

The Northern coalfields of the 1950s came as close to Nye Bevan's ideal of working class 'serenity' as any other time in their history. The property tycoon Sir John Hall grew up in Ashington and recalled how pit village life in the 1940s was

> structured, your life was set out for you and ruled by the colliery manager, the headmaster and doctor, they controlled your life … I was a strong left-winger. I could never understand why my father and other miners didn't vote Communist. He was a Labour man, he wasn't left-wing. The miners were never extreme.[90]

But they didn't need to be: they had full-employment, decent housing and free healthcare. This was a sort of paradise, with the added satisfaction that their jobs were fundamental to Britain's greatness—as Labour's Foreign Secretary Ernest Bevin said to the miners at the time: 'give me a million tons of coal and I'll give you a foreign policy.'[91] All this made the North East a stronghold of what was known as the 'Old Labour Right': authoritarian, corporatist, pro-NATO and dominated by deeply conservative trades unions who maintained a narrow focus on their own hard-won rights and privileges. This partly explains Labour's rejection of membership of the nascent

European Coal and Steel community in 1951 because of the perceived opposition of the Durham miners. When the Conservative Prime Minister (and MP for Stockton) Harold Macmillan claimed in 1957 that working people had never had it so good, this was echoed by the Labour establishment in the region, well represented by men like the flinty ex-army officer, and Newcastle MP, Ted Short, who 'ran the Parliamentary Labour Party like the Durham Light Infantry.'[92]

But with such consensus came calcification and complacency. The region's continued reliance on a handful of traditional heavy industrial sectors made the North East unusually vulnerable to economic shocks and innovation elsewhere, as was the case when the Tyne and the Wear began to lose out to the mass-producing shipbuilders of the Far East who had no time for the inefficiency of bespoke shipbuilding. The sense of stagnation in economic and public life was compounded by the North East tradition of exclusionary closed-shops, where defensive trade unions specialised in 'who does what' industrial disputes that stymied modernisation, and where heredity could still be the main entry criteria for certain trades and professions. We could go back at least as far here as the careers of Nathaniel Clayton, Town Clerk of Newcastle from 1785–1817, who was succeeded by his son John Clayton who served as town clerk for forty-five years from 1822; or the coal trimmers and Tyne Pilots who handed down their professions from father to son until the 1960s. Such webs of patronage linked Labour Party officials, trade union shop stewards, even the 'committee-men' of local CIU clubs, and was ripe for exploitation. This was exemplified by the greasy world of municipal corruption that saw the Newcastle Council leader T. Dan Smith and the Durham councillor Alderman Andrew Cunningham sent to prison in the 1970s for their part in shady property deals for council-house building—so memorably dramatised by the Jarrow-born scriptwriter Peter Flannery in the 1996 TV series *Our Friends in the North*.

A persistent Northumbrian conservativism has long been a disappointment to those with more radical politics. The Attlee government's nationalisation agenda also served to obscure its old-fashioned patriotism. It committed Britain to punching above its weight on the world stage and squeezed welfare and NHS budgets by spending 10% of GDP on defence—a huge boon to the shipbuilders and coal-miners of the North East. This robust outlook was embodied by Sam Watson, the all-powerful and fiercely anti-Communist Durham Miners' Leader in the 1950s, who was such a significant supporter of NATO that he even invited the American Ambassador to the Durham Miners' Gala (allegedly at the instruction of his CIA handlers); and such attitudes were matched by a widespread caution and traditionalism in industrial and social affairs. In his 1982 hit 'Shipbuilding' Elvis Costello expressed a certain Leftist frustration with the durability of the old system, and what they regarded as the conservative docility of the British working classes, as the yards worked overtime readying the ships of the Naval Task Force to recapture the Falklands. 'The Devil's Destroying Angel Exploded' by the radical Tyneside poet Tom Pickard was even fiercer in its denunciation of the timid and reactionary Old Guard who ran the unions and the Labour Party in the North East:

> producers of heat
> confused in the cold
> the coal you hewed
> should have burnt them alive
> instead you begged another shilling
> you should have thrown it
> in their faces like a bomb
> fed your children joyful stories

The miners' confrontation with Margaret Thatcher's government in 1984–5 was the last stand of the old coalfield communities. The Ridley Plan of 1977—drawn up by the right-wing Tory, and son of a Northumbrian peer, Nicholas Ridley—had convinced Thatcher how the next Conservative government could defeat a major walk-out in any of the nationalised industries. The decision to strike by the Durham Miners was cautiously taken after a knife-edge vote by their NUM Area Executive Committee, but despite much impressive community organising—especially by groups of miners' wives— and a riot at Easington Colliery, the miners returned to work defeated just as they had been in 1926. Within nine years every pit in Durham had closed.

While coal-mining was in steep decline, new institutions were taking their place. The public sector had grown massively in the North East and by 1971, there were 210,000 jobs of this kind on Tyneside, representing 53 per cent of all employment, rising to an astonishing 63 per cent by 1981. Where once the pits and shipyards had been the destination for Northumbrian school-leavers, by the mid 1980s fully 8,000 people were employed at 'The Ministry,' the local name for the vast bureaucratic complex at Longbenton, in suburban Newcastle, which processed millions of pensions and benefits claims for the Department of Health and Social Services. As with Attlee's government, the Labour cabinets of the Tony Blair era were packed with North East MPs, and Blair himself sat for Sedgefield in County Durham. But there were no ex-miners and few trade union officials among their ranks: this new generation of Labour politicians represented the *hauts fonctionnaires* of the public sector establishment, and they oversaw a period of massive government spending in regions like the North East. For Labour to have working majorities in Parliament and access to the proceeds of a growing economy was unprecedented, and may explain why John Prescott's 2004 proposal for a North East Assembly was defeated in a referendum. For one thing it was hard to explain why such a body was necessary when a Labour government, full of North East MPs, was in power and investing millions in the region. And, as with every attempt to develop a coherent system of regional governance for the North East from the 1930s onwards, progress was stymied by parochial rivalries and suspicions of an overweening Newcastle, especially in Sunderland and on Teesside.

A key architect of the campaign against the North East Assembly proposal was the Durham-born and educated political strategist Dominic Cummings, a man who would go on to play an even more momentous role as Chief Strategist for Vote Leave in the 2016 EU referendum. Other than Newcastle with its wealthy suburbs and middle-class salariat—the comedian Gavin Webster once observed that 'Jesmond is so pretentious that the ice cream van plays Rachmaninov'—every single local authority area in the North East voted to leave the EU. As the results came in on 23 June 2016 it was the strength of the Leave vote in Sunderland that first alerted the country that Remain might lose. Such complacency was badly shaken by similar results across much of the post-industrial North, a surprise to many who had assumed that EU largesse and the dependency of manufacturers such as Nissan at Sunderland on frictionless access to the Single Market would win the day. But a rising dissatisfaction with stagnating living standards and government austerity, alongside a decoupling by the old working class from an increasingly bourgeois Labour Party, and a growing unease with social change (in part exacerbated by the issue of migration from the EU) had been missed by many, though not by Cummings himself. 'Why is almost all political analysis and discussion so depressing and fruitless?' he wrote after the event. 'I think much has to do with the delusions of better educated people. It is easier to spread memes in SW1, N1, and among *Guardian* readers than in Easington Colliery.'[93] That Northumbrian voters failed to behave as expected, in both 2004 and 2016, would suggest that, to Westminster, the far North of England still remains a source of incomprehension.

7

UPON A BLEAK NORTHUMBRIAN MOOR

*What the "North East" does it ever does with a will. Circumstances—frequently grim—
have, from earliest times, demanded of its people exceptional vigour and resource.
Fighters, rulers, builders and craftsmen, though cradled in a cockpit of war, they yet
managed to establish themselves one of the great trading communities of the kingdom.*

North East Coast Exhibition programme, 1929

Every year, on New Year's Eve, in the Northumbrian village of Allendale in
the North Pennines, forty-five men in fancy dress and soot-blackened faces
gather before midnight to lift whisky barrels full of tar onto their heads which
are then set on fire. The men, known as 'guysers'—all of whom must have
been born in the Allen valleys of Northumberland—then process through the
town led by a brass band, before hurling the flaming barrels onto a huge communal bonfire, while the well-oiled crowds shout 'Be damned to he who
throws last.' The origins of the Allendale Tar Bar'l are obscure. Some believe
it to be a medieval custom, others insist it was simply a Victorian lark that
caught on, an invented tradition like the annual 'Up Helly Aa' festival in the
Shetland Isles. But whatever its beginnings, such fiery festivals owe much to
the Northern European impulse to gather around midwinter fires to commune and drink heavily. With its emphasis on community and co-operative
effort, masculine strength and beer-fuelled fearlessness (the guysers have
been compared 'to "infantrymen waiting to go 'over the top' into battle", so
tense is the aura of the occasion')[1] the Tar Bar'l could scarcely be more
Northumbrian.

But does such distinctive *Northumbriana* live on outside of the moors of
Hexhamshire? I can still detect it in the work-ethic of the men I play football
with every week at Gateshead, with their shouts of 'ha'way lads, lets put a shift
in! Keep working for each other!' Or in that whiff of back-country Tennessee

when the ruddy-cheeked farmers and rural toughs gather at their agricultural shows at Stocksfield, Glendale and Stanhope. Northumbrian sociability certainly seems as strong as ever—with performers such as Ray Spencer, stalwart of the popular South Shields Customs House panto, embodying the bawdy music hall spirit of Wilson, Ridley and Corvan—but such merriment can still spill over into over-exuberance. 'Black Eye Friday' (the last Friday night drinking session before Christmas) is now a fixture on the region's social scene, and in 2013 Newcastle became the first city in Britain to apply a 'Late Night Levy' on the city's pubs and bars to meet the cost of policing night-time disorder. But less raucously, the North East craft-beer scene, with its myriad independent microbreweries, has grown quietly from the ashes of the once-dominant giant brewers, like Scottish and Newcastle, Federation, and Vaux, to become one of the strongest in the country. Sunderland now has its own 'Music, Arts and Cultural Quarter' centred around the town's precinct of splendid Edwardian buildings: The Dun Cow and Peacock pubs and the colossal Sunderland Empire theatre, whose foundation stone was laid by Vesta Tilley in 1906. Of the ten most beautiful gig venues in Britain as identified by the BBC in 2017, two are in Newcastle—the former Palace of Arts in Exhibition Park and 'the Boiler Shop,' part of Stephenson's former Locomotive Works behind the Station. 'The Toon' has long-revelled in its party city status. The *Rough Guide* characterised the prevailing local culture as 'weatherproof warmth,' adding that 'If there's one Geordie stereotype that rings true, it's disarming friendliness.'[2] This sort of bonhomie is embodied in the Newcastle-born TV duo, 'Ant and Dec' (Anthony McPartland and Declan Donnelly), whose genial on-screen banter remains so popular with British viewers that they have voted them the nation's favourite TV presenters for an astonishing eighteen consecutive years (from 2001 to 2019).

The pursuit of this sort of cosy communalism is typified by the enduring popularity of Beamish Museum. In 2017 a plan was announced to invest £18 million in developing a '1950s town' alongside the existing pit village from 1913.[3] The former Grand Electric Cinema from Ryhope, in Sunderland, is to be dismantled and rebuilt there as well as 1950s 'pre-fabs' and council semis, a Welfare Hall, bowling green, Fish and Chip Shop and some Aged Miners' Homes from South Shields are to be re-purposed for people living with dementia. Beamish is already the most popular paid-for visitor attraction in the North East with over 700,000 annual visitors, and despite the £20 entry fee it claims to welcome more visitors on lower incomes in comparison to free museums.[4] The whole place is an immersive time-travelling experience, the very definition of accessibility, and, with its

My great grandfather Patrick McCormack (1881–1957), a migrant from County Mayo to the Northumberland coalfield. Northumbrian miners typically wore short trousers known as 'pit hoggers'.

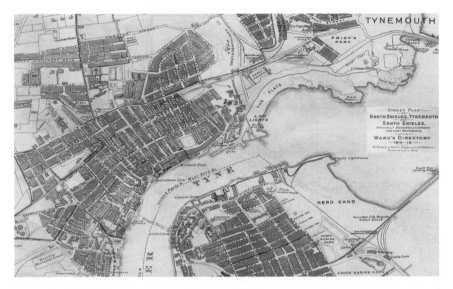

Map of First World War deaths in Tynemouth Borough (which included the town of North Shields). Each dot corresponds to the known address of a man whose death was attributed to war service. Over 1,700 men from the Borough lost their lives—either in the armed forces or in the Merchant Navy and fishing fleet.

King George V with General Sir Julian Byng in 1917 at the memorial to the officers and men from the 6th Battalion, Durham Light Infantry who fell capturing the Butte de Warlencourt on the Somme.

Miss Ellen Wilkinson MP, January 1936 with the Jarrow Marchers on route to London.

The Newcastle United team in their dressing room at Wembley celebrate their victory over Arsenal in the FA Cup Final, May 1952.

Hugh Percy, 10th Duke of Northumberland (Chancellor of Newcastle University) with Dr Martin Luther King, after the award of an honorary degree to Dr King, Newcastle upon Tyne, 1967.

The Animals pop group, 1964.

World Cup heroes Bobby and Jack Charlton get a royal reception back in Ashington, Northumberland as they return to visit their parents, 22 August 1966.

'My Plot', a painting by the author's grandfather Ken Lawton (1924–2013) of his allotment garden at Seaton Delaval.

'Whippets' (1939) by the Ashington 'pitman painter' George Blessed (1904–1997).

'Gordon in the water', gathering sea-coal at Newbiggin, Northumberland, by Chris Killip.

'Angel of the North', by Antony Gormley, 1998, Gateshead, Tyne and Wear.

'The Northumbrian Riviera', the bay at Cullercoats with Longsands and Tynemouth beyond.

refusal to label everything and tell the visitor what to think, completely non-patronising towards those may feel nostalgic for such places. For many Northumbrians it transports them back to a time and place that many still recognise as a sort of spiritual *heimat*.

In 2016, the Ken Loach film *I, Daniel Blake*, won the Palme D'Or at the Cannes Film Festival (where its Geordie dialogue was subtitled for an international audience). With great pathos the Geordie comedian Dave Johns, in the lead role as a Newcastle joiner recovering from a heart-attack and trying to get back to work, shone a light on the enduring misery of those who have to navigate Britain's dehumanising benefits regime. Some of the scenes in the film are pure Kafka, and perhaps without realising it the film becomes less a critique of government austerity *per se*, than a morality tale about vast, unfeeling state bureaucracies; and, tellingly, it's the neighbours and local voluntary organisations who seem the most sympathetic and responsive. The traditions of communitarianism in the North East are finding fresh expression in charities like Family Gateway, an organisation founded on Tyneside that recruits parents directly from deprived communities to support their own neighbours out of poverty; an implicit criticism of the remoteness and credibility of the state emissaries that these neighbourhoods are used to dealing with. The local NHS has noticed this too, and in places like South Tyneside, local clinical commissioning groups are increasingly interested in 'social prescribing,' where instead of reaching for the prescription pad doctors are encouraged to refer patients suffering from depression (which is often exacerbated by unemployment and what public health experts call an 'epidemic' of social isolation) to so-called 'community assets,' those voluntary networks, clubs and services that often have a greater reach than the state itself.

It is notable that volunteer-run foodbanks have become a feature of British cities over the last ten years. In 2019 the *New York Times* reported the efforts of Newcastle United supporters to raise money for the city's West End Foodbank, noting the £200,000 they'd raised from rattling buckets outside St James' Park for 'the largest institution of its kind in Britain.' They reported the views of one stalwart fundraiser outside the ground in words that speak to a fierce local altruism that remains one of the region's most admirable features. 'We can't have people in this city starving,' Bill Corcoran said. 'It is a badge of shame.'[5]

The uplifting sight of fundraising football supporters does not however present a completely rounded picture of Northumbrian culture in the twenty-first century. If the rest of the world notices the region at all it has been through unedifying spectacles such as the tawdry reality series *Geordie*

Shore, where research has found that nearly 80% of all scenes in the hit MTV show concerned alcohol.[6] Or in the crowd trouble that followed a 2013 Tyne-Wear derby match where a police horse was assaulted by a disgruntled Newcastle supporter prompting an earnest piece in *Vice*, entitled 'Masculinity in Crisis, or: The Curious Geordie Tradition of Punching Horses,' where it was argued that, in the North East, 'the concept of man is in crisis ... With no guide to life, no anchors in the storm, you kick and you scream and you fight. You punch horses. That's what men do.'[7] The troubling story of the rampaging Newcastle bodybuilder Raoul Moat—who shot three people in two days after his release from Durham prison in 2010, before taking his own life after being cornered by Northumbria Police—seemed to conform to that sense of masculine crisis. The whole squalid episode was recounted in Andrew Hankinson's 2016 book *You Could Do Something Amazing With Your Life* which revealed details about Moat's life that fit almost too perfectly into Northumbrian stereotypes: the childhood being brought up by a grandmother who'd left Moat's grandfather, a champion boxer in the British Army, because he was so dangerous; Moat's self-perception as being a 'grafter' whilst never being around for his family; the obsession with his 'hard-man' status and the lust to avenge his wounded pride with extreme violence after his partner had left him for another man.

Moat's denouement, with its bizarre cameo from the ex-Newcastle United and England footballer Paul Gascoigne, who arrived at the police lines with a fishing rod, some cooked chicken and four cans of lager, was like a macabre version of an Andy Capp comic strip, that creation of the Hartlepool-born cartoonist Reg Smythe. Both 'Capp' and Smythe were ex-regulars in the Northumberland Fusiliers, and to this day the armed forces remain dedicated consumers of the young male surplus of North East England. A leaked Ministry of Defence briefing on their twelve 'focus locations' revealed that a quarter of them were in the North East (Newcastle, Sunderland, and Middlesbrough) even though the region only accounts for 4% of the UK population. *The Guardian* reported that the armed forces' latest recruitment drive explicitly targets 'adrenaline-seeking teenagers' in areas where employment opportunities are limited 'as a cynical exploitation of the shortage of adequate career and training choices for all young people in society.'[8] And on television and cinema screens in 2019 a glossy advert shows a boisterous young man trading in his motorbike before signing up for a life at sea with the strapline 'Born in Blyth. Made in the Royal Navy.'

Britain has led the world in losing industry just as it had led the world in its development. This has generated a real sense of dislocation in the North

East as the heavy industrial staples of shipyard, coal-mine and steelworks have all but disappeared. The economy that is taking its place may have different features but the Northumbrian tradition of working for someone else lives on as strongly as ever. The career of the self-made property tycoon and former Newcastle United chairman Sir John Hall would be unremarkable in the South of England but has always seemed freakishly entrepreneurial in the North East (*The Viz* mocked him as 'Sir Wynyard Hall' after he bought the Marquess of Londonderry's stately pile of the same name in South Durham), and the region has the lowest concentration of registered businesses and business start-ups in the country. Where once it was Armstrong, Palmer and Parsons that were the great employers, 229,000 Northumbrians now work in the public sector—Newcastle upon Tyne Hospitals NHS Foundation Trust employs 14,000 people alone—fully 20% of the North East's working age population, and the highest percentage of any region in England.[9]

Even in the private sector, there are a still handful of dominant employers. Consider the extraordinary success of software company Sage, the only FTSE 100 company to have its origins and headquarters in the North East, and which has created some 2,500 jobs at its Newcastle Great Park base (and a further 10,000 in the rest of the world). Or the 8,000 employed at Nissan's Washington plant (now the biggest factory in the history of the British car industry). There are also the huge transport conglomerates Arriva (which began as Tom Cowie's Sunderland motorcycle dealership, and now employs 54,000 people across the world), and the Go-Ahead Group that grew out of the Gateshead-based Northern General Transport Company and now employs 28,000 across the country and has a fleet of 721 buses in the North East alone.

This is not to say that the older industries have entirely vanished. The North East is exceptional among English regions in having recorded a positive balance of trade for most of the past twenty years, and much of this is down to the export of manufactured goods. In Sunderland alone Rolls-Royce has two aerospace plants, near to Snorkel's factory, where they manufacture aerial work platforms and spider lifts, which in turn isn't far from Liebherr, who build huge maritime cranes. As shipbuilding declined on the Tyne and disappeared on the Wear in the 1980s and 1990s an oil-rig building boom briefly took its place—taking Northumbrians all over the world from Aberdeen to Azerbaijan—and from this fertile soil a local offshore sector has become world-leading. Where once the Tyne was known for its oil tankers and destroyers, firms like Soil Machine Dynamics in Wallsend now build remotely operated underwater vehicles, and its 'Ultra Trencher 1' with its high pressure jet 'swords' that carve channels into the sea-bed to lay cables, is the world's largest submersible robot. The global pursuit of underwater reserves in oil and gas and precious metals has led to the creation of the National Centre for Subsea and Offshore Engineering, the first of its kind in the United Kingdom, and builds on Newcastle University's traditions of naval architecture. 'Tyne Sub-sea' is now being described as the 'NASA of the underwater world.'[10]

But the outlook for the regional economy is by no means rosy. For all its strengths in manufacturing, and strong connectivity to important domestic markets, a greater proportion of the North East's trade goes to the EU than that of other English regions. Much was made of Nissan's decision in early 2019 not to expand operations at its Washington plant, with many blaming the uncertainties of post-Brexit trading with the EU as a decisive factor. But the great car manufacturers are at an inflection point anyway, and changing consumer demands, new technologies and green policies are all putting traditional manufacturing under serious pressure. There is, too, a tendency to over-exaggerate any economic green-shoots, as in the case of the burgeoning tech cluster in the North East, which has undoubted strengths but, as one local tech journalist observed, around which there is a 'current of embellishment [and] hyperbole,' for although the North East may be 'the fastest growing tech hub in the UK ... really, after Wales, we're the second smallest!'[11]

Whatever economic virility the region claims for itself, 'the North East's statistical demerits are stubbornly ever the same,' wrote Richard T. Kelly in 2011, describing a litany of depressing statistics from the lowest incomes and highest unemployment in England to the poorest A-Level results, but adding (with tongue-in-cheek Northumbrian bravado) 'Haven't we weathered worse? Aren't we a hardy people, resilient in our own way as the Frosterley marble in Durham Cathedral, the Whin Sill rock under Hadrian's Wall?'[12] Figures from the Office for National Statistics in 2018 revealed that the North East, with a population of 2.6 million, has a gross value added per head of £19,218 compared to an average for England of £27,108; in 2010–16, the regional economy only grew at an annual average rate of 0.7%, compared to an England average of 2.1%; and average wages, numbers of businesses and numbers of people in employment all tell a similarly anaemic story.[13] This is not for the want of effort: the traditions of Northumbrian Stakhanovism are as strong as ever on the lines at Nissan, where Unite union officials describe the job on the line as 'very hard, physically demanding,' for the men (and it is largely men) who spend eight hours on their feet machine-fitting engines, doors, dashboards and windscreens to an unrelenting assembly-line of car bodies.[14] As tough as it is, such employment is still much sought after, but there is a real sense that many of the men that work on these lines find it as alienating as Charlie Chaplin did in *Modern Times*.

After 61% of voters in Sunderland opted to leave the European Union, many commentators were baffled, and saw it as a grievous act of self-mutilation, not realising how dissatisfied such places were with being (as the Labour peer Lord Maurice Glasman put it) fobbed off with a 'a bicycle lane, a subsidised theatre/museum/Internet space, and a call centre.'[15] Such discontent was well-articulated by a fitness instructor who runs 'Made 4 The Cage Fight Academy' in the disadvantaged Wearside neighbourhood of Southwick. Steven France (a Remain voter himself) had some home truths for those who might think that Sunderland should have been grateful for the status quo. 'The truth is that people in Sunderland need more from life than hard-to-come-by work in car plants,' he wrote in *The New European*:

> Every week I watch as new lads come through the door, looking to prove themselves, to show that they are not hopeless, but strong men. This is an area where, historically, men were men, and where hard graft working down the pit was a badge of honour ... [Nissan is] a hard way to earn a living and it leaves many men bitter and disillusioned. Yet we are forced to cling to these jobs because, here in the North-East, it is all that we have. These jobs are prized, but they are inadequate to the task of keeping our communities alive.[16]

But do such male perspectives still dominate our understanding of North East England? Must we always take our reference points from maudlin songs like Jimmy Nail's 1996 hit 'Big River' and its lament for the demise of shipbuilding? It is now twenty-six years since Elaine Knox described how the 'economic marginalisation of women led to their social marginalisation,' and histories of the region perceived through the prism of male work have meant there being 'more words written on the geological formation of the Northern coalfield, than on women's part in regional life.'[17] This is changing, not least through a new and diverse generation of Northumbrian women in Parliament—from the trenchant Brexiteer Conservative MP for Berwick, Anne-Marie Trevelyan (who lives in the seventeenth century Netherwitton Hall, the ancestral seat of the Trevelyans, near Morpeth), to the Geordie-Nigerian former-engineer and Remain supporter Chi Onwurah, Labour MP for Newcastle upon Tyne Central. One of the most thoughtful of these women is Bridget Phillipson, a native of Washington who graduated in history from Oxford and managed 'Wearside Women in Need' for survivors of domestic abuse, before being elected as the Labour MP for Houghton and Sunderland South in 2010. Writing in the aftermath of the Brexit vote,

Philipson offered a clear-eyed take on the denialism and wishful thinking that characterises so much of what passes for political analysis in the Labour heartlands, and a certain impatience with a sentimental (and largely male) yearning for a world that is fast disappearing.

> We've seen various manifestations of communitarian reinvention, from 'community organising' to 'Blue Labour'—all variations on a common premise that it is possible to deal with cultural and industrial change by wishing it hadn't happened, an effort to pass off nostalgia as political strategy. Elegiac lyricism about a vanished world of large unionised workplaces full of men doing semiskilled jobs, shared cultural experiences, shared religious affiliation, and tight community links does not amount to a plausible programme for government. That world has gone, it isn't coming back, and hankering for the past isn't what any of us were elected to do.[18]

* * *

In the south aisle of Durham Cathedral, between the Neville Chantry and the Tomb of St Bede in the Galilee Chapel, is a monument to the miners of the county. A miner's lamp is suspended nearby, symbolising Christ's message in John 8:12: 'I am the light of the world. Whoever follows me will never walk in darkness.' On the monument itself is a more obscure Biblical reference, from the Book of Job (28:4) 'He breaketh open a shaft away from where he sojourns. They are forgotten of the foot that passes by.' Mining for precious metals in the ancient world was carried out by slave labour, but Biblical exegesis has shown that despite how alien this descent into the underworld seemed to the writers of the Old Testament, mining still was used in Job as a metaphor for the pursuit of wisdom.[19] For all the travails and tragedies of the Northumbrian working classes—which included some of the most arduous and heroic feats in the history of the British working class (in the 1930s George Orwell wrote of coalmining that it 'keeps us alive, and we are oblivious of its existence')—there is a sense in the North East that the region's contribution to the nation's story has been forgotten, and overlooked by those that pass it by. And this note of resentment still frames Northumbrian relationships with the rest of the country, especially the South of England.

As the two biggest centres of English population separated by the greatest geographical distance, London and Newcastle have long had a fascination with each other. Robert Colls has written that the connections between the North East and the metropolis 'was one of the most important creative relationships in the economic and social history of Britain, and indeed of the industrialised world.'[20] The associations are legion: from the Newcastle colliers in the 1700s who would gather in pubs near the Fleet river in London to mark the fifth Sunday in Lent—by eating grey peas, known as 'carlings,' fried in butter (to remember a siege of Newcastle when they were the only foodstuff to hand)—to the Kray twins' failed expeditions to swinging Newcastle in the 1960s. Even the British Museum's first home in Bloomsbury, Montagu House, at one time the grandest private residence in London, was paid for with Newcastle coal-money (Lady Elizabeth Montagu, 'the queen of the bluestockings,' called the Tyneside pitmen who toiled on her Northumberland estates, 'My sooty friends'); and the Museum's enormous hoard of Neolithic and Bronze Age antiquities were once the personal collection of the Lanchester-born Victorian cleric William Greenwell, a canon and Librarian of Durham Cathedral.

London has other ghosts of the Tyne and the Wear, although the City taverns where the colliers were known to gather—The Dog Inn, the Hole in the Wall or The George on Fleet Street—are long gone. Here in the 1790s, a homesick Thomas Bewick was teased as a 'Scotchman,' got into fights with the locals and complained that London was 'a world of itself' with 'extreme riches, extreme poverty, extreme grandeur & extreme wretchedness.'[21] Above the entrance to the old Lloyds Registry building on Fenchurch Street we can still see the 'three Castles triple towered Argent' from the arms of Newcastle upon Tyne, and, looking down from the Strand front of Somerset House is the glowering visage of the Tyne River God with writhing fish in its hair and crowned by a flaming corve of coal. These are now mere relics, but Northumbrian interests were once represented by more substantial embassies in the capital. From the Strand, the Royal Society of Arts is reached via Durham House Street, once the site of the palace of the Prince Bishops of Durham (until confiscated by Henry VIII); then half a mile further west is Northumberland Avenue where Northumberland House stood until the 1870s. This was the vast London townhouse of the eponymous dukes—and close to the famous street built by a seventeenth century Morpeth MP, Sir George Downing—but the straight-tailed Percy lion that once prowled the parapet overlooking Trafalgar Square has since relocated to the battlements of the Duke's other London home, Syon House which sits amid rolling Capability Brown-designed parkland across the Thames from Kew Gardens.

But the grandest lost consulate of Northumbria was the Coal Exchange on Thames Street. Opened by Prince Albert in 1849 and modelled on the Bourse de Commerce in Paris, its grand dome was decorated with Raphaelesque encaustic panels depicting coal-related themes—fossils, collieries and views of North Shields, Sunderland, Newcastle and Durham. It was tragically demolished in the 1960s in the teeth of opposition from Pevsner, Betjeman and others who all recognised its architectural and historical significance. For the 'Big Smoke' owes its nickname to the coal that warmed the hearths and choked the atmosphere of the capital for centuries. Most of this fuel came from the Great Northern Coalfield, and it made the Northumbrian coal-owners extremely wealthy. 'The burgesses of Newcastle waxed fat and proud, believing themselves to be citizens not only of the richest town in the North but soon of the richest in England,' wrote Anthony Eden's elder brother Sir Timothy Eden, in his 1953 history of Durham. 'They laughed and snapped their fingers at London herself [here quoting John Cleveland's satirical poem *News from Newcastle*]. "Our staithes their mortgaged streets will soon divide/ Blaydon their Cornhill, Stella [on the Tyne], share Cheapside."'[22]

This was not much of an exaggeration. London's prodigious growth would have been impossible without Tyne coal, and the Royal Navy at the turn of the seventeenth century became dependent on hardware and articles of war produced by Sir Ambrose Crowley's military-industrial complex at Winlaton. The re-financing of the government's debts to Crowley (through shares in the South Sea Company) was a key factor in the emergence of the City of London as a modern financial centre.[23] The North East coal trade became a vital source of tax revenue for a city where coal duties funded Sir Christopher Wren's great rebuilding project after the Great Fire of London in 1666, including St Paul's Cathedral itself and over fifty of his city churches. These coal duties were still being called upon to fund major capital projects in the Victorian metropolis, including the Thames Embankment itself.

But this relationship, once so fruitful, has now soured. UK-wide polling by YouGov in 2018 confirmed that the strongest anti-London sentiment can be found in the North East, which the pollsters adduced to a combination of small-C conservativism and a dislike of multiculturalism.[24] This latter point is telling, for I have certainly heard it said by some older Northumbrians that they find the diversity of London utterly bewildering (the absence of labour-hungry industries in the post-war North East had limited the appeal of the region to New Commonwealth immigrants). No doubt such views contain a large element of prejudice, even outright racism, but in the Northumbrian imagination the perceived atomisation and unfriendliness of London compared to the communitarianism of the North is as at least as disconcerting as the capital's demographics.

There are other sources of grievance. Northumbrians still pine for the return of the Lindisfarne Gospels, which were spirited away from Durham

Cathedral in the 1530s by Henry VIII's 'visitors' and now live in exile in London as the jewel of the British Library. But Westminster's continued uninterest has caused further estrangement. That the Conservative government's half-baked 'Northern Powerhouse' plans for regional economic development seem only to reach as far north as Leeds does not suggest an optimistic outlook. Nor does the pitifully small £20m budget for the new Mayor of the 'North of Tyne Combined Authority' (a collaboration between Newcastle, Northumberland and North Tyneside councils) who was elected in 2019; or a scarcely believable discrepancy in transport infrastructure spending—revealed by the Institute of Public Policy in 2014—of £2,500 per head in London compared with £5 per head in the North East. In this sense, London can feel like a remote imperial capital, where Westminster, the City and Whitehall elide into one mess of unaccountable power. In the nineteenth century and early twentieth centuries Sir W. G. Armstrong & Co had an office right in the heart of Westminster, directly opposite the headquarters of their main customer: HM Treasury. But now the closest that Northumbrian businesses get to the corridors of power is the aroma of steak bakes that waft in from the branch of Greggs the Bakers that opened in Westminster Tube Station in 2018; a development that caused the MP for Mid Sussex (and Churchill's grandson), Sir Nicholas Soames, to tweet disdainfully: '#disappointingsmells.'

If the North East has otherwise failed to kick up a stink in Parliament then the absence of a strong collective voice is not helping. Parochial rivalries have been a feature of Northumbrian politics since the Burgesses of Newcastle quarrelled with the Bishop of Durham over coal exports and the ownership of the Tyne Bridge (a jury in 1416 awarded one third of the famous structure to the bishopric). 'Tyneside, with its interdependent economy and its interwoven requirements and interests, becomes more and more a unit; as much a unit, for example, as Birmingham, which roughly covers the same area,' observed Henry Mess in the 1920s. 'Yet while Birmingham is governed by a single local authority, on Tyneside there are no less than sixteen.'[25] To remedy this fragmentation a Royal Commission in 1937 suggested a Northumberland Regional Council to extend south of the Tyne, but this was rejected; as were two attempts to create a single 'Tyneside' authority in the 1960s. But in 1974—and much to the dismay of county loyalists—the most populous parts of Northumberland and Durham were annexed into a short-lived Metropolitan County of Tyne and Wear, bringing the big cities and towns of Newcastle, Gateshead, Jarrow, Sunderland, South Shields, Wallsend, North Shields and Whitley Bay under a single jurisdiction for the first time.

215

All of these big Metropolitan authorities—from Greater Manchester to Greater London—were abolished by the Thatcher government in the 1980s, who saw them as municipal bastions of the 'loony left.' Some of Tyne and Wear's functions would continue, for example the Fire Service and Passenger Transport Executive (overseer of the Tyne and Wear Metro light rail system), but the political voice of the urban North East was again fractured. An attempt to build support for a so-called 'devolution deal,' whereby a new, single 'North East Combined Authority' would have been given greater powers by Westminster over transport, skills and economic development was supported by Newcastle, Northumberland and North Tyneside, but rejected by Sunderland, Gateshead, County Durham, and South Tyneside councils. This latter grouping all voiced concerns that the deal on offer was not well-enough defined or funded; but with Newcastle and Sunderland in separate camps it was hard to avoid the conclusion that traditional local rivalries had played their usual role in dividing the region.

Tyne-Wear antagonism has grown in intensity since the 1970s. What was once the sort of rivalry typical of neighbouring cities—think of Liverpool and Manchester, Glasgow and Edinburgh, Portsmouth and Southampton—has now become something nastier, unpleasant and tedious for anyone who lives here. The modern source of this enmity is football, especially as the decline of traditional industries has seen the sport become the main vehicle for local pride and identity. But there were other grievances, especially from Sunderland people who felt that Tyneside was unfairly favoured over Wearside when it came to public investment and support for local industries. The emergence of football hooliganism in the 1970s has made the two sets of supporters more bitterly tribal; before then it was commonplace for Northumbrians both north and south of the Tyne to go and watch whoever was playing at home that weekend; whether that was Sunderland or Newcastle it didn't really matter. Indeed, after Sunderland AFC won the FA Cup for the first time in 1937 the team was welcomed back to Newcastle Station with full civic honours and huge cheering crowds on Neville Street—and when Sunderland next won the Cup in 1973 their fans celebrated at Wembley by singing 'The Blaydon Races,' which concerns a horserace outside Newcastle.[26]

Such ecumenism is now almost unthinkable—but it needn't be. Writing in 1962, the Cambridge geographer Gus Caesar captured the intense bipolarity of the North East, but how in some contexts those same identities can dissolve:

> If a Wearsider visits a pub in Scotswood Road, Newcastle, on a Saturday evening, things may go hard with him, especially if by chance Sunderland have beaten Newcastle at soccer that same afternoon. But if a Wearsider meets a Geordie in

a more distant part of Britain, they may well linger over a drink together for they have many interests in common. These relationships epitomize much of the North-East with its intense local rivalries but strong regional unity.[27]

One of the most touching gestures that North East football supporters have ever made was the money raised by Sunderland fans in the aftermath of the deaths of John Alder and Liam Sweeney, two fans who were flying to New Zealand to watch Newcastle United play in a pre-season friendly when their flight was shot down over eastern Ukraine. 'There are things far more important than any football games' was the message on the fundraising site set up by Gary Ferguson, a red-and-whiter from South Shields, and although his plan was to raise money for a floral tribute, over £30,000 poured in which was then donated to local charities.

If the fans themselves can overcome these divisions at moments of crisis, why can't the politicians? As of 2019 there are now two 'combined authorities' divided by the River Tyne, but cleaving the North East in this way is surely unsustainable. Lying as it does between Newcastle and Sunderland, the borough of South Tyneside could play an important bridging role here. South Tynesiders are historically divided in their football allegiances between NUFC and SAFC, but the town of South Shields is home to one of the most sumptuous town halls in the country. 'The most convincing expression in the County of Edwardian prosperity' was Nikolaus Pevsner's view of Ernest Fetch's baroque extravaganza of 1910 on Westoe Road, where the 'Nymph of the Tyne' reclines alongside Neptune and Britannia on its pediment and the bas-relief around the portico shows how 'South Shields and Municipality Promotes Labour and Encourages the Arts.' If Newcastle will probably always be the region's commercial metropolis, and Durham City its ecclesiastical capital, then if Northumbrian politicians are ever able to agree a devolved administration South Shields would be a good compromise as the seat of government. The Hague of the North East.

It is not as if the region can afford much navel-gazing about its current circumstances. People here have the worst health outcomes, and the lowest *healthy* life expectancy of anywhere in England. What is more, the North East has the highest levels of opioid addiction in the country. In some astonishing recent analysis, it was shown that '95 per cent of authorities in the rest of the country don't reach even half the level of such prescriptions issued in the twelve local authorities in the North-East,' which the authors traced back to an excess of 'social trauma' caused by catastrophically high levels of domestic violence, abuse and adverse childhood experiences.[28] After almost a decade of government austerity the shrinking resources of local authorities in the region makes them ill-equipped to tackle such crises on their own. But not every arm of the state has become so withered. The NHS in the region remains a keystone in the region's public life: a huge employer and much-admired institution, it is also a flag-bearer for what the region can achieve. In a 2019 survey *Newsweek* magazine ranked the best 100 hospitals in the world, eight of which were in the UK—and of these eight, two were in Newcastle (The Royal Victoria Infirmary and the Freeman Hospital).[29] The NHS is now being asked to think more radically about how it can shift the wider determinants of health in the North East, and break the cycle of an over-reliance on hospitals which ties up resources that might be better spent on preventing ill-health. This is a common challenge for health systems around the world, but the enduring strength of the region's health service might give confidence—not least as the region has been the incubator for a generation of clinicians and NHS leaders which speaks to the esteemed place of the health service in the region, and that enduring Northumbrian dedication to big institutions. Indeed, when I began writing this book in 2018, the NHS in England was being run by Sir James Mackey from Hebburn, on secondment from Northumbria Healthcare Foundation Trust, and Simon Stevens, who had begun his NHS career at Shotley Bridge Hospital.

The North East cannot rely on the public sector alone to solve its problems, nor on new governmental structures and special commissions led by experts sent from London (an approach tried by Harold Macmillan in the 1960s when, to some derision, he appointed Lord Hailsham as 'Minister for the North-East,' who then toured the region in a cloth cap). If the North East is to revive its fortunes then any revival must be led from within the region itself. But from where might this come? Philip Blond has argued that the economic decline of Northern England is as much located in 'the loss of an active and engaged middle and upper class—highly educated, high status and heavily invested in the private as well as the public sector' as it is in the changing fortunes of heavy industry.[30] To support this claim he cites some depressing analysis that shows how this decline is 'mainly explained by selective outmigration of the educated and talented,' a process that had already begun in the 1800s.[31] Blond's argument is that the 'working-class monoculture' of parts of the North can only be diversified by doing more to make the North more attractive—through investing in cultural development as much as, say, transport infrastructure, to bring back the 'talented, technical, entrepreneurial and artistic classes.'[32] There is certainly a brain drain from the North East—which on some measures is the worst in the country at retaining graduates—and this continues to swell the ranks of Northumbrian exiles in London and elsewhere. But as any reader of the glossy business and lifestyle magazine *The North East Times* will soon notice there is no shortage of well-heeled Northumbrians gathering at their networking breakfasts and prize-days at the private schools of Durham and Newcastle.

The old aristocracy still maintains a visible presence in the public life of the region. Among other patronages, the Duke of Northumberland is the President of the Community Foundation, and his wife is the Lord Lieutenant of the county of which she is the Duchess. (There was even a charity football match at St James' Park in 2007 between the north and south of the region, where star players such as Alan Shearer, Niall Quinn and Peter Beardsley turned out under the respective colours of the Duke of Northumberland and the Earl of Durham to raise money for the Prince's Trust.) But in terms of political leadership the local middle and upper classes are conspicuous by their absence. Henry Mess made the pointed observation in the 1920s that there was, on Tyneside, an 'unhealthy segregation of the classes,' meaning that 'those in the pleasant suburbs escape their duties to their poorer neighbours.'[33] Not much has changed since then. The flight of the upper bourgeoisie from civic leadership is due partly to the declining prestige of local authorities, and the demise of the aldermanic bench in English local government. It was once expected that the leading citizens of any place would serve on the local authority (the industrialists Sir William Armstrong and Sir Mark Palmer were aldermen of Newcastle and Jarrow respectively). Although Newcastle had the rare distinction in the 2010s of having two peers on the council—in Lords Shipley and Beecham—the professional upper-middle classes are rarely if ever seen among the ranks of local authority councillors. This is in sharp contrast to the boards of local hospitals and the courts of the region's universities which benefit from the considerable talents and social capital of local high achievers. The political voice of the region will continue to be ignored unless and until the bourgeoisie of places like Corbridge and Jesmond, Low Fell and Durham City, Tynemouth, Cleadon and Seaburn take a more active part in Northumbrian political life.

The North of England is consistently described in terms of dearth, authenticity and pastness.[34] Maybe the last three hundred years were an aberration, for the North has always been poor and peripheral, and always will be. Dean Acheson's well-known remark from 1963 that 'Great Britain has lost an Empire and has not yet found a role' could be applied to North East England too. No longer the 'bulwark against the Scots,' or the 'hearth, that warmeth the south parts of this kingdom with fire' as William Camden described the region in 1577. Nor is it the arsenal and dockyard of an expanding world empire. As the playwright Lee Hall has said of one port on the North East Coast, which could be said of so many other Northumbrian towns, 'Hartlepool is there because it had a *raison d'etre*. The north-east had a *raison d'etre*. What is it now? Nobody knows.'[35] Only the Northumbrians can answer this. For although the mineral reserves and industrial capacity of North East England are now much depleted—in May 2019 the Prime Minister announced that the UK had gone for a fortnight without using coal to generate energy for the first time since the Industrial Revolution—if there is one resource that can be relied upon then that is surely the Northumbrians themselves.

The Northumbrian devotion to 'hyem' (home) is deep and enduring. The word itself is another relic of Northumbria's Anglo-Saxon past, derived from the Old English 'hām' (cognate with the German 'heim'), rather than the old Norse as is sometimes assumed on the basis of the Danish and Norwegian 'hjem.' But the word has a more profound meaning in the North East, speaking not just of the place where one lives, but of a bottomless longing for a homeland, for the familiar, for kith and kin. In some ways 'hyem' is closer to the Welsh term 'hiraeth,' or the Portuguese 'saudade,' that sense of longing for a missing time, an era, or a place, and 'hyem' retains a powerful grip on the Northumbrian imagination. John Tomaney once made the astute observation that the 'idiomatic use of "belong" is a notable feature of the North East dialect.' Quoting from the Rev. F. M. T. Palgrave's 1896 work *Words and Phrases in Everyday Use by the Natives of Hetton-le-Hole*—'a man, on being asked where he 'belongs,' says 'I belong Hetton"—Tomaney points out that 'You belong to a place, it does not belong to you.'[36] This emotion is still keenly felt by Northumbrians at home, and especially abroad. Writing to British fans in the 1950s from his beachfront apartment in Santa Monica, California, Stan Laurel would wax nostalgically about his Tyneside childhood—catching the 'ha'penny dodger' across the river, sucking 'black bullets' (boiled sweets), and even musing whether a new 'Wooden Dolly' (a statue of a North Shields fishwife) would look like Marilyn Monroe. As he was born in Ulverston, the North West likes to claim him as one of their own, but Stan himself dismissed this, confirming to a fan in 1955 that 'even tho' I was born in Lancashire, I've always felt I belong to Shields,'[37] But why do these places continue to possess us?

Despite making a new life for herself in the South of England, in part to escape a suffocating and at times traumatic childhood, Catherine Cookson never shook off the ties that bound her to North East England, nor did she ever write about anywhere else. Returning to the North East in the 1980s, she mused on what she found so compelling about the tight little Tyneside communities that she knew, and concluded that despite 'their narrowness,' and 'their bigotry,' what attracted her as a writer was

> the character of the people; the fact that work was their life's blood; their patience in the face of poverty; their perseverance that gave them the will to hang on; their kindness; [and] their open-handedness.[38]

This could stand for so many places in the North East of England, and for all their many shortcomings, the reason why they were—and are—so magnetic, so passionate, so *canny* was because of the generations of Northumbrians that made them.

* * *

In the summer of 2018 thousands of visitors came to Tyneside for The Great Exhibition of The North, a two-month series of events celebrating the art, culture and design of the North of England. The organisers stated that they intended to use the 'beautiful buildings and bustling businesses of NewcastleGateshead [the two places have been merging like Buda and Pest in tourism literature] as our display cabinet, and our beloved bridges and elegant streets as our canvas.' The Exhibition itself was a rather anaemic affair, funded with a paltry £5 million by the Conservative government, although Grey's Monument done up as a be-ribboned worker's maypole (as an echo of a Northumberland Miners banner from the 1920s) was visually stunning and, according to the designers, meant to evoke 'the accolades of society, health, education, science, art and fellowship for all; placing at the heart of civic space the shared principles that have been and remain significant to the communities of the North.'

But for those who visited Newcastle's Discovery Museum (in what was once the Victorian splendour of the Co-operative Wholesale Society's northern headquarters) there was an unforgettable sight. Next to Parson's Tyne-built 'Turbinia,' the first turbine-powered steamship in the world, stood Stephenson's famous 1829 locomotive 'The Rocket,' Here it was, back home; a mere half a mile from its birthplace, at Forth Banks behind the Central Station. Seeing these two side-by-side was a surprisingly moving experience. With the Lindisfarne Gospels' exile in London, the Rocket's enforced sojourn in the metropolis has turned them into Northumbria's Elgin Marbles. (There was even idle talk at the time, perhaps by me, about somehow preventing the

Rocket's return to captivity in the capital.) What it did remind those who saw them together of was the extraordinary ingenuity of North East England, and the symbiotic relationship between these two great innovations: for it was the Rocket's pistons that deposed the beam engine, and later Turbinia's turbine that overthrew the piston. Northumbria really did change the world.

The first Great Exhibition held in Newcastle actually took place in Queen Victoria's Golden Jubilee Year of 1887. The Royal Mining, Engineering, and Industrial Exhibition was a huge success, with over two million visitors drawn by star attractions that included a 110-ton Armstrong gun—described in the exhibition guide as being 'the largest gun ever made in this country and the most powerful piece of ordnance in the world'—and a full-size replica of the medieval Tyne Bridge. The local banker and historian Thomas Hodgkin was asked to compose an ode for the opening ceremony, and the reflections that it contains—on the lessons of history, and the place of Northumbria on its pages—could yet be an epitaph or an exhortation.

Upon a bleak Northumbrian moor
Behold a palace raised. Behold it filled
With all that fingers fashion, deftly skilled,
With all that strongest fibred brains have willed,
When they, like natures' self, have vowed to build
Structures that shall for centuries endure.

How came these marvels hither? By what power
Have all been gathered in the self-same hour
Upon a bleak Northumbrian moor?
Why should both East and West for ever pour
The willing tribute of their golden store
In ceaseless tide upon thy storm-swept shore?

...

Deep lies the answer. Endless is the chain
That binds the far-off ages with to-day.

NOTES

PREFACE

1. Adrian Green and A. J. Pollard, *Regional Identities in North-East England, 1300–2000* (Boydell, 2007), p. 183.
2. T. Hodgkin R.S. Watson, R.O. Heslop and R. Welford, *Lectures On Northumbrian History, Literature And Art. Lent Term 1898* (Newcastle-Upon-Tyne: Literary and Philosophical Society, 1898), p. 27.
3. Hernon, Jr., Joseph, M. (1976), 'The Last Whig Historian and Consensus History: George Macaulay Trevelyan, 1876–1962', *The American Historical Review*, 81(1), pp. 66–9.
4. Obituary of Frank Atkinson, *Daily Telegraph*, 11 January 2015.

1. UNDERSTANDING THE NORTHUMBRIANS

1. Lyn MacDonald, *1914: The Days of Hope* (Penguin, 1987), p. 345.
2. Paul J. Brown, '*Canny' Newcastle: Some Scattered Threads of a Romantic Story Collected and Tied in a Bunch* (Bealls, 1929), p. i.
3. 'Explained: 15 well-known "Geordie" words and where they originated', *Evening Chronicle*, 12 July 2016.
4. Jake Morris-Campbell, 'Marratide: William Martin's Chorography of County Durham', http://wildcourt.co.uk/features/2386/
5. Lynn Hunt, *Writing History in the Global Era* (Norton, 2014), p. 1.
6. Fernand Braudel, 'Histoire et Sciences sociales. La longue durée', *Annales. Histoire, Sciences sociales* 13 (1958), pp. 725–53.
7. Robert McManners, Gillian Wales, *The Quintessential Cornish: The Life and Work of Norman Cornish* (Gemini, 2009), p. 15.
8. Peter Davidson, *The Idea of North* (Reaktion, 2005), p. 30.
9. Procopius, *History of the Wars* VIII (Harvard University Press, Loeb, 1914), 20, pp. 42–48.
10. https://www.salon.com/2019/04/06/game-of-thrones-in-real-life-the-actual-history-is-just-as-epic-as-george-r-r-martins-tales/
11. Davidson, *The Idea of North*, p. 25.
12. Stuart Maconie, *Pies and Prejudice: In Search of the North* (Ebury Press, 2008), p. 291.

13. Henry Mess, *Industrial Tyneside: a Social Survey Made for the Bureau of Social Research for Tyneside* (Ernest Benn, 1928), p. 24.

14. John Ardagh, *A Tale of Five Cities: Life in Provincial Europe Today* (Secker & Warburg, 1979), pp. 201, 190, 192.

15. Robert Colls and Bill Lancaster, *Newcastle upon Tyne: A Modern History* (Phillimore, 2001), p. 320.

16. https://www.huffingtonpost.com/nataly-kelly/wampanoag-language_b_1107722.html?guccounter=1

17. David Simpson, *Aal Aboot Geordie* (My World, 2012), p. 5.

18. George MacDonald Fraser, *The Steel Bonnets: The Story of the Anglo-Scottish Border Reivers* (Harper Collins, 1989), pp. 72–3.

19. Ibid.

20. Norman McCord and Richard Thompson, *The Northern Counties From A.D. 1000* (Longman, 1998), pp. 40–1.

21. Alistair Moffat and George Rosie, *Tyneside: A History of Newcastle and Gateshead from Earliest Times* (Mainstream, 2006), pp. 68–9.

22. Frank Atkinson, *Life and Tradition in Northumberland and Durham* (Dalesman, 2006), p. 27.

23. Andrew Breeze, 'The Battle of Brunanburh and Cambridge', *Northern History* (2016), 53:1, pp. 138–145.

24. Symeon of Durham, *Libellus de Exordio atque Procursu istius, Hoc est Dunhelmensis, Ecclesie*, ed. and trans. D. Rollason (Oxford, 2000), pp. 156–7.

25. Henry J. Swallow, *The Battle of Neville's Cross* (Andrew Reid, 1885), p. 11; https://www.durhamcathedral.co.uk/worship-music/regular-services/sermon-archive/who-said-anything-about-safe-a-tale-of-two-cathedrals-durham-and-coventry; see also a tweet from Tom Holland, 20 March 2019 https://twitter.com/holland_tom/status/1108274248366391296

26. Helen M. Jewell, *The North-South Divide: The Origins of Northern Consciousness in England* (Manchester University Press, 1994), pp. 6–7.

27. Green and Pollard, *Regional Identities*, p. 224.

28. Sydney Middlebrook, *Newcastle-upon-Tyne: Its Growth and Its Achievements* (S.R. Publishing, 1950), p. 1.

29. See for example, Paul Morley, *The North and Almost Everything In It* (Bloomsbury, 2013); Maconie, *Pies and Prejudice*.

30. Stephen Broadberry, *British Economic Growth, 1270–1870* (Cambridge, 2014), p. 25.

31. R. Lomas, *County of Conflict: Northumberland from Conquest to Civil War* (Tuckwell Press, 1996), pp. 38–44.

32. D. J. Rowe, 'The north-east', in F.M.L. Thompson (ed.), *The Cambridge Social History of Britain 1750–1950 vol. 2: Regions and communities* (Cambridge, 1990), pp. 418–26.

33. S. Pollard, 'A new estimate of British coal production, 1750–1850', *The Economic History Review*, 33(2) (1980), p. 223.

34. C. B. Fawcett, *Provinces of England: A Study of Some Geographical Aspects of Devolution* (Charles Bungay, 1919), pp. 87–8.

35. Steven G. Ellis, 'Civilizing Northumberland: representations of Englishness in the Tudor state', *Journal of Historical Sociology*, xii (1999).

36. Fraser, *Steel Bonnets*, p. 43.

37. Colley, *Britons*, p. 314.

38. *The Northern Counties Magazine*, Vol. I (October 1900 to March 1901), https://www.gutenberg.org/files/11124/11124-h/11124-h.htm

39. McCord, *Northern Counties*, p. 51.

40. William Feaver, *The Art of John Martin* (Oxford, 1975), p. 7.

41. Robert Colls (ed.), *Northumbria: History and Identity 547–2000* (Phillimore, 2007), p. 169.

42. D. W. Rollason, *Northumbria, 500–1100: Creation and Destruction of a Kingdom* (Cambridge, 2008), pp. 287–90.

43. Joe Sharkey, *Akenside Syndrome: Scratching the Surface of Geordie Identity* (Jajoja, 2014), p. 5.

44. Robert Colls, *Identity of England* (Oxford, 2004), p. 46; Bill Williamson, 'Living the past differently: Historical memory in the North East', in Robert Colls and Bill Lancaster, *Geordies: Roots of Regionalism* (Northumbria University Press, 2005), p. 151.

45. Asa Briggs, 'Themes in Northern History', *Northern History*, 1 (1966); A. W. Purdue (2013), 'The History of the North-east in the Modern Period: Themes, Concerns, and Debates Since the 1960s', *Northern History*, 42:1, pp. 107–117.

46. Joseph Robinson, *Tommy Turnbull: A Miner's Life* (The History Press, 2007), p. 347.

47. Frank Atkinson, *The Man Who Made Beamish* (Northern Books, 1999), p. 87.

48. https://www.theguardian.com/travel/2014/nov/22/newcastle-travel-best-uk-city-galleries-restaurants

49. 'I'm in love with Newcastle and hope that wonderful city gets the football club it deserves', *The Herald*, 29 May 2019.

50. Maconie, *Pies and Prejudice*, p. 291.

51. David Olusoga, *Black and British: A Forgotten History* (Macmillan, 2016), pp. xv-xvi.

52. Tweet by @SFoodbanks, 2 March 2018.

53. Robert Colls, *The Collier's Rant: Song and Culture in the Industrial Village* (Routledge, 1977), pp. 11–12.

2. BLOOD AND IRON

1. *The New York Times*, 14 November 1984.

2. Basil Peacock, *The Royal Northumberland Fusiliers* (Leo Cooper, 1970), preface.

3. Neil R. Storey, *Northumberland's Military Heritage* (Amberley, 2017), p. 5.

4. David Hackett Fischer, *Albion's Seed: Four British Folkways in America* (Oxford University Press, 1991), p. 626.

5. Nolan Dalrymple, 'North East Childhoods: Regional Identity in Children's Novels of

the North East of England' (unpubld PhD thesis, Newcastle University, 2008), pp. 38–9.

6. Fraser, *Steel Bonnets*, pp. 3–4.

7. Thomas Bewick, *The Memoirs of Thomas Bewick* (Longman, Green, Longman, 1862), p. 10.

8. Fraser, *Steel Bonnets*, p. 6.

9. Helen M. Jewell, 'North and South: The Antiquity of the Great Divide', *Northern History*, XXVII, 1991, p18

10. Mess, *Tyneside*, pp. 25–6.

11. Matthew Miles, and Donald P. Haider-Markel, 'Personality and Genetic Associations With Military Service', *Armed Forces and Society*, 9 April 2018.

12. C. Tuvblad and L. A. Baker, 'Human Aggression Across the Lifespan: Genetic Propensities and Environmental Moderators', *Advances in Genetics* (2011), vol. 75, pp. 171–214.

13. M. Laucht, et al., 'Gene–Environment Interactions in the Etiology of Human Violence', in *Current Topics in Behavioral Neuroscience* (2014) Vol. 17, pp. 267–95; William Buckner, 'The Behavioral Ecology of Male Violence', *Quillette*, 24 February 2018, 17, pp. 267–95.

14. See for example, John Hope Franklin, *The Militant South, 1800–1861* (University of Illinois Press, 2002).

15. Robert Bartlett and Angus MacKay (eds), *Medieval Frontier Societies* (Clarendon Press, 1989), p. v.

16. William Stukely, *Itinerarium Curiosum; Or, An Account of the Antiquities, and Remarkable Curiosities observed in Nature and Art Observed in Travels Through Great Britain* (Baker and Leigh, 1776), p. 55; William Hutchinson, *The History and Antiquities of the County Palatine of Durham*, 3 vols (Newcastle, 1785–94), i, p. ii.

17. Vindolanda Tablets online: http://vindolanda.csad.ox.ac.uk/4DLink2/4DACTION/WebRequestQuery?searchTerm=164&searchType=number&searchField=TVII

18. John Sadler, *Battle for Northumbria* (Bridge Studios, 1988), pp. 2, 6–7.

19. J. D. Richards, *The Vikings: A Very Short Introduction* (Oxford, 2005), p. 75.

20. Richard Fletcher, *Bloodfeud: Murder and Revenge in Anglo-Saxon England* (Oxford University Press, 2004), p. 54.

21. Hackett Fischer, *Albion's Seed*, p. 623.

22. A. J. Pollard, *North-eastern England during the Wars of Roses: lay society, war, and politics, 1450–1500* (Oxford University Press, 1990), p. 86.

23. Anthony Goodman, 'Border Warfare and Hexhamshire in the Later Middle Ages', *Hexham Historian*, 13 (2003), pp. 50–1.

24. Derek Dodds, *Northumbria At War* (Casemate, 2005), pp. 138–9.

25. J. C. Appleby and P. Dalton, *Government, Religion and Society in Northern England 1100–1700* (Stroud, 1997), p. 52.

26. Jonathan Sumption, *Trial by Battle* (Faber and Faber, 1990), p. 504.

27. John Sadler, *Border Fury: England and Scotland at War 1296–1568* (Routledge, 2006), pp. 68–9.

28. Jeffrey Marcus Becker, 'Armed Conflict and Border Society, The East and Middle Marches 1536–60' (unpubld Durham University PhD thesis, 2006), p. 1.

29. Sadler, *Border Fury*, p. 123.

30. Becker, 'Armed Conflict', p. 188.

31. C. H. Hunter-Blair, 'Wardens and Deputy Wardens of the Marches of England towards Scotland in Northumberland', *Archaeologia Aeliana*, 4th ser., xxviii, 1950, p. 32.

32. Geoffrey Watson, *Northumberland Place Names: Goodwife Hot and Others* (Sandhill, 1995), p. 191.

33. Fraser, *Steel Bonnets*, pp. 55–65 passim.

34. Fraser, *Steel Bonnets*, p. 75.

35. Cecil Sharp to John Campbell, n.d., in Campbell, *The Southern Highlander and His Homeland* (New York, 1921), p. 70; see also Olive Campbell and Cecil J. Sharp, *English Folk Songs from the Southern Appalachians* (New York, 1917).

36. Hackett Fischer, *Albion's Seed*, p. 652.

37. Ibid., p. 654.

38. J.G. Rule, The Manifold Causes of Rural Crime: Sheep Stealing in England, *circa* 1740–1780', in J.G. Rule (ed.), *Outside the Law* (Exeter, 1983).

39. Joan Thirsk (ed.), *Agrarian History of England and Wales* (Cambridge University Press, 1967), IV, 49; Paul Brassley, 'Northumberland and Durham', in (Thirsk, ed.), *Agrarian History of England and Wales*, I, p. 49.

40. Hackett Fischer, *Albion's Seed*, p. 668.

41. Ibid., pp. 765, 769.

42. Ibid., p. 639.

43. Ibid., p. 647.

44. Colley, *Britons*, p. 16; Fraser, *Steel Bonnets*, p. 1.

45. Angus Calder, *Revolutionary Empire: The Rise of the English-Speaking Empires* (London, 1981), p. 376.

46. Sadler, *Battle for Northumbria*, p. 140.

47. Ibid., pp. 142–3.

48. P. M. Horsley, *Eighteenth-Century Newcastle* (Cengage, 1971), p. 7.

49. Moffat and Rosie, *Tyneside*, pp. 204–5.

50. Richard Pears, 'Image, identity and allusion: the Ridley monuments in St. Nicholas Cathedral, Newcastle upon Tyne', The School of Historical Studies Postgraduate Forum, E-Journal Edition 6, 2007/08.

51. E. Hughes, *North Country Life in the Eighteenth Century: The North East 1700–1750* (Oxford University Press, 1952), p. 16.

52. McCord, *Northern Counties*, p. 38.

53. Colley, *Britons*, p. 378.

54. Roger Finch, *Coals from Newcastle: The Story of the North East Coal Trade in the Days of Sail* (Terence Dalton, 1973), p. 176.

55. Andrew Griffin, *Cuthbert Collingwood: The Northumbrian Who Saved the Nation* (Mouth of the Tyne, 2004), pp. 86–7, 97.

56. Tony Barrow, *Trafalgar Geordies and North Country Seamen of Nelson's Navy 1793–1815* (North East History Press, 2005).

57. Keith Middlemas, *As They Really Were: The Citizens of Alnwick 1831* (Francis Lincoln, 2012), p. 79.

58. Jenny Uglow, *Nature's Engraver: A Life of Thomas Bewick* (Faber & Faber, 2007), p. 31.

59. John Gibson Lockhart, *The Life of Sir Walter Scott: Volume VI* (Edinburgh: Robert Cadell, 1839), p. 164.

60. Robert Colls, *The Pitmen of the Northern Coalfield: Work, Culture and Protest, 1790–1850* (Manchester University Press, 1987), p. 221.

61. Colls, *Pitmen*, p. 211.

62. Ibid., p. 232.

63. Michael W. Flinn, 'Sir Ambrose Crowley and the South Sea Scheme of 1711', *The Journal of Economic History* Vol. 20, No. 1 (March, 1960), pp. 51–66.

64. McCord, *Northern Counties*, p. 83.

65. Henrietta Heald, *William Armstrong: Magician of the North* (McNidder & Grace, 2012), p. 184.

66. David Dougan, *The Great Gun-Maker: The Life of Lord Armstrong* (Sandhill, 1971), pp. 67–68.

67. *Newcastle Daily Chronicle*, 27 December 1900.

68. Colls (ed.), *Northumbria*, p. 167.

69. Heald, *Armstrong*, p. 333.

70. Heather Streets, *Martial Races: The Military, Race and Masculinity in British Imperial Culture, 1857–1914* (Manchester University Press, 2004), p. 1.

71. Jan Morris, *Heaven's Command* (Faber & Faber, 2012), p. 240.

72. Peter Simkins, *Kitchener's Army: The Raising of the New Armies, 1914–1916* (Pen & Sword, 2007), p. 89.

73. Joseph Robinson, *Tommy Turnbull: A Miner's Life* (The History Press, 2007), p. 52.

74. Colls and Lancaster, *Geordies*, p. 128; Robinson, *Tommy Turnbull*, p. 91.

75. J. M. Winter, 'Military Fitness and Civilian Health in Britain during the First World War', *Journal of Contemporary History* (1980) 15(2), p. 238.

76. Neil Storey, *Newcastle Battalions in Action on the Somme* (Tyne Bridge Publishing, 2016), p. 29.

77. Ibid., p37

78. Jo Bath, *Great War Britain: Tyneside* (The History Press, 2015), pp. 47–8; Geoffrey Milburn and Stuart Miller (eds) *Sunderland: River, Town and People: A History from the 1780s to Present Day* (Sunderland Council, 1989), p. 189.

79. Simkins, *Kitchener's Army*, p. 120.

80. Adrian Gregory, *The Last Great War: British Society and the First World War* (Cambridge University Press, 2008), p. 188. The other figures cited in the speech were 10.5 in Nottingham, 7.6 in Swansea, 7.6 in Wakefield, 7.1 in Hull, 6.7 in Sheffield and Leeds, 5.2 in Derby, 4.1 in Bradford, 4 per cent in Oldham.

81. Bath, *Great War Britain: Tyneside*, p. 121.

82. Gregory, *The Last Great War*, p. 255.

83. Alan Allport, *Browned Off and Bloody Minded: The British Soldier Goes to War, 1939–1945* (Yale, 2015), p. 221.

84. Dennis Winter, *Death's Men: Soldiers of the Great War* (Penguin, 2014), p. 83.

85. C. H. Cooke, *Historical Records of the 9th (Service) Battalion, Northumberland Fusiliers* (Newcastle, 1928), p. 1.

86. Estimates of Scottish deaths in the Great War are difficult to estimate, but vary between 71,000 and over 100,000, from a population of around 4.7 million as recorded in the 1911 census; the combined population of Northumberland and Durham in 1911 was just under two million. See also https://www.scotsman.com/lifestyle-2–15039/great-war-worst-for-scots-troops-a-myth-1–3504582

87. Ibid., p. 75.

88. Armstrong, *Tyneside in the Second World War* (Phillimore, 2007), p. 76.

89. Allport, *Browned Off*, p. xix.

90. Ibid., p. 258.

91. Allan Converse, *Armies of Empire: The 9th Australian and 50th British Divisions in Battle 1939–1945* (Cambridge University Press, 2011), p. 80.

92. Ibid., p. 80.

93. William Moore, *The Durham Light Infantry* (Leo Cooper, 1975), p. 178.

94. Gavin John Purdon, *From Coalfield to Battlefield, the Road to Dunkirk Revisited* (G.J. Purdon, 1990), p. 72.

95. John McManners, *Fusilier: Recollections and Reflections* (Michael Russell, 2002), p. 68.

96. Converse, *Armies of Empire*, p. 16; Charles Jennings, *Up North: Travels Beyond the Watford Gap* (Abacus, 1995), pp. 117–19.

97. Peter Ford Mason, *The Pit Sinkers of Northumberland and Durham* (The History Press, 2012), p. 48; Moore, *Durham Light Infantry*, p. 45.

98. Ethan Rawls Williams, '50 Div in Normandy: A Critical Analysis of the British 50th (Northumbrian) Division on D-Day and in the Battle of Normandy' (A thesis presented to the Faculty of the U.S. Army Command and General Staff College in partial fulfilment of the requirements for the degree Master of Military Art and Science). US Naval Academy, Annapolis, Maryland, 1997, pp. 108–9.

99. Allport, *Browned Off*, p. 181.

100. Williams, '50 DIV IN NORMANDY', p. 35.

101. Patrick Delaforce, *Monty's Northern Legions: 50th Northumbrian and 15th Scottish Divisions at War, 1939–1945* (Fonthill, 2014), p. 86.

102. Ibid., p. 98.

103. Michael Chaplin, *Hame: My Durham* (Mayfly, 2016), p. 240.

104. Armstrong, *Tyneside in the Second World War*, pp. 28-9.

105. Ibid., p. 71.

106. Ibid., pp. 20, 25.

107. Ibid., p. vii.

108. David Edgerton, *The Rise and Fall of the British Nation* (Allen Lane, 2018), pp. 339–40.

109. Mike Morgan, *Geordie: SAS Fighting Hero* (The History Press, 2007), pp. 23, 101.

3. NORTHUMBRIAN ENLIGHTENMENT

1. Norman McCord (ed.), *Water under the Bridges: Newcastle's Twentieth Century* (Newcastle Libraries, 1999), p. 36.
2. Ford Mason, *Pit Sinkers*, p. 125.
3. E. A. Wrigley, *Continuity, Chance and Change: The Character of the Industrial Revolution in England* (Cambridge University Press, 1988), pp. 54–5.
4. Fawcett, *Provinces*, pp. 87–8.
5. W. B. Stephens, *Education, Literacy, and Society, 1830–70: The Geography of Diversity in Provincial England* (Manchester University Press, 1987), p. 16.
6. Colls, *Northumbria*, pp. 33–4.
7. F. Donald Logan, *A History of the Church in the Middle Ages* (London: Routledge, 2012), p. 61.
8. Alan Myers, *Myers' Literary Guide: The North East (Lives & Letters)* (Carcanet, 1995), p. 64.
9. Cuthbert Headlam (ed.), *The Three Northern Counties of England* (Northumberland Press, 1939), p. 139.
10. Report to the Secretary of State for the Home Department from the Poor Law Commissioners on the Training of Pauper Children, London, Stationery Office, 1841, p. 9; 'Levels and the profile of illiteracy in Lowland Scotland [were] extremely close to those for northern England … literacy over Lowland Scotland as a whole was not particularly high compared to northern England.' R. A. Houston, *Scottish Literacy and the Scottish Identity* (Cambridge, 1985), pp. 41, 34; see also 'Illiteracy in the Diocese of Durham, 1663–89 and 1750–62: The Evidence of Marriage Bonds,' NH 18 (1982), pp. 229–51.
11. Uglow, *Nature's Engraver*, pp. 27–9.
12. Middlemas, *As They Really Were*, p. 41. Colls and Lancaster, *Newcastle: A Modern History*, p. 296.
13. Colls, *Pitmen*, p. 91.
14. His full inventory of books can be viewed at https://corbettsbookshop.omeka.net
15. Headlam, *Three Northern Counties*, p. 166.
16. 'Collingwood, forgotten hero of Trafalgar', *Manchester Guardian*, 1 March 1910.
17. Harding, J.T. (1986), 'A History of the North of England Institute of Mining and Mechanical Engineers', *The Mining Engineer—Journal of the Institution of Mining Engineers*, 146: pp. 252–6.
18. Colls, *Pitmen*, pp. 127–8.
19. William Cobbett, *Cobbett's Tour in Scotland; and in the four northern countries of England: in the autumn of the year 1832* (Mills, Jowett and Mills, 1832), p. 23.
20. Nikolaus Pevsner, *Northumberland (The Buildings of England)* (Penguin, 1957), p. 84.
21. Horsley, *Newcastle in the Eighteenth Century*, p. 191.
22. https://scottishantiques.com/newcastle-light-baluster Accessed 20 December 2018
23. John Brown, *An Estimate of the Manners and Principles of the Times, Volume 1* (L. Davis and C. Reymers, 1757), p. 74.

24. Andrew Griffin, *Cuthbert Collingwood*, p. 104.

25. Middlemas, *As They Really Were*, p. 96.

26. A. S. G. Butler, *Portrait of Josephine Butler* (Faber & Faber, 1954), p. 34.

27. Judith R. Walkowitz, *Prostitution and Victorian Society: Women, Class, and the State* (Cambridge University Press, 1982), p. 118.

28. Myers, Literary Guide, p. 9.

29. Arthur Conan Doyle, 'On the geographical distribution of British intellect', *Nineteenth Century*, XXIV (1888), August, pp. 184–95.

30. Nicole Guenther Discenza, *Inhabited Spaces: Anglo-Saxon Constructions of Place* (Toronto University Press, 2011), pp. 34–5.

31. Bede, *The Reckoning of Time* (Liverpool University Press, 1999), p. 83.

32. Jane Brown, *The Omnipotent Magician: Lancelot 'Capability' Brown 1716–83* (Chatto, 2012), pp. 12–13, 15.

33. Simon Schama, *A History of Britain: 1776–2000. The fate of empire* (BBC, 2003), p. 96.

34. Uglow, *Nature's Engraver*, pp. 384, 353.

35. Heald, *William Armstrong*, p. 205.

36. Ibid., pp. 116–17,153.

37. Alastair Bonnett and Keith Armstrong (eds), *Thomas Spence: The Poor Man's Revolutionary* (Breviary, 2014), p. 42.

38. Heald, *Armstrong*, p. 9.

39. Thomas Frognall Dibdin, *A Bibliographical, Antiquarian and Picturesque Tour in the Northern Counties of England and in Scotland, Volume 1* (C. Richards, 1838), p. 365.

40. Heald, *Armstrong*, pp. 24–6.

41. Tom McGovern and Tom McLean (2017), 'The genesis of the electricity supply industry in Britain: A case study of NESCo from 1889 to 1914', *Business History*, 59:5, pp. 667–689.

42. http://www.twsitelines.info/industrial-period Accessed on 19 February 2019.

43. Colls and Lancaster, *Newcastle upon Tyne*, p. 269.

44. Max Adams, *The Prometheans: John Martin and the Generation that Stole the Future* (London: Quercus, 2010), p. 183.

45. Joseph Conrad, *Last Essays* (Dent, 1926), p. 22.

46. https://blog.twmuseums.org.uk/its-alive-riding-turbinia-1897/ Accessed 22 February 2019.

47. Hannah, L., *Electricity before Nationalisation: A Study of the Development of the Electricity Supply Industry in Britain to 1948* (Macmillan, 1979), p. 33.

48. Norman McCord (ed.), *Water under the Bridges: Newcastle's Twentieth Century* (Newcastle Libraries, 1999) p. 35.

49. https://www.nexus.org.uk/sites/default/files/Nexus%20Annual%20Report%20 2016.pdf

50. Mason, *Pit Sinkers*, p. 131.

51. Headlam, *Northern Counties*, p. 256.

52. Colls and Lancaster, *Geordies*, p. 164.

53. Colls, *Pitmen*, p. 194.

54. Percy, *Northern Counties*, p. 340.

55. Robinson, *Tommy Turnbull*, p. 86.

56. Jack Lawson, *A Man's Life* (London: Hodder & Stoughton, 1932), p. 77.

57. Frank Atkinson, *Victorian Britain: The North East* (Exeter: David & Charles, 1989), pp. 64–5.

58. Colls, *Colliers Rant*, p. 83.

59. Ibid., p. 89.

60. Heald, *Armstrong*, pp. 198–201.

61. Colls, *Colliers Rant*, pp. 92–3.

62. https://www.theguardian.com/stage/2007/sep/25/theatre1 Accessed 1 January 2019

63. Jonathan Rose, *The Intellectual Life of the British Working Classes* (Yale, 2002), p. 40.

64. Jack Common, *Kiddar's Luck* (Bloodaxe Books, 1990), p. 75; Keith Armstrong, 'From the 'freedom of the streets': a biographical study of culture and social change in the life and work of writer Jack Common (1903–1968)', p. 225. Unpubld PhD thesis, University of Durham, 2007.

65. Robert McManners and Gillian Wales, *The Quintessential Cornish: The Life and Work of Norman Cornish* (Gemini, 2009), p. 10.

66. Chaplin, *Hame*, p. 229–30.

67. Sharkey, *Akenside Syndrome*, p. 223.

68. John Lough and Elizabeth Merson, *John Graham Lough 1798–1876: A Northumbrian Sculptor* (London: Boydell, 1987), p. 48.

69. Ibid., pp. 3, 5, 7.

70. https://www.independent.co.uk/arts-entertainment/art/features/artist-norman-cornish-resented-being-lumped-together-with-the-other-pitman-painters-9652758.html Accessed 22 February 2019

71. Colls and Lancaster, *Newcastle upon Tyne*, p. 308.

72. Uglow, *Nature's Engraver*, p. 357.

73. Nolan Dalrymple, 'North East Childhoods', p. 82.

74. *Parliamentary Papers*, 1842 Commissioners Reports, vol. 16, p. 514.

75. Adams, *Prometheans*, p. 185.

76. Chaplin, *Hame*, pp. 55–6.

77. http://www.therecusant.org.uk/intrinsic-art-of-labour/4533430702

78. Colls, *Pitmen*, p. 125 fn.

79. Ibid., p. 159.

80. Fraser, *Steel Bonnets*, p. 79.

81. Joseph Robson, *The Song of Solomon: versified from the English translation of James of England, into the dialect of the colliers of Northumberland, but principally those dwelling on the banks of the Tyne* (George Barclay, 1860).

82. McCord, *Water under the Bridges*, p. 175.

83. McManners and Wales, *Quintessential Cornish*, p. 104.

84. Clark, G. and N. Cummins (2018), 'The big sort: Selective migration and the decline of Northern England, 1780–2018', CEPR, Discussion Paper 13023.

85. https://investnortheastengland.co.uk/sectors/it-and-digital/

86. https://www.thetimes.co.uk/article/tech-on-the-tyne-is-all-mine-hp9z8dfbr

87. https://supernetwork.org.uk/about/who-we-are/

88. https://www.chroniclelive.co.uk/business/business-news/newcastles-tech-sector-growing-huge-14835803

4. THE SPARTA OF THE NORTH

1. Pevsner, *Northumberland*, p. 11.

2. Colls and Lancaster, *Newcastle upon Tyne*, p. 247.

3. https://www.telegraph.co.uk/news/uknews/scottish-independence/11022110/Fifteen-things-I-love-about-England.html

4. Montesquieu, *The Spirit of the Laws*, trans. Anne Cohler, Basia Miller, and Harold Stone (Cambridge University Press, 1989), pp. 8–9.

5. Colls, *Identity of England*, p. 252.

6. Colls, *Colliers Rant*, p. 79.

7. Max Adams, 'John Martin and the Theatre of Subversion', *Public Domain Review* 7 December 1012 https://publicdomainreview.org/2012/07/12/john-martin-and-the-theatre-of-subversion/

8. W. Clark Russell, *The North East Ports and Bristol Channel: Sketches of the Towns, Docks, Ports, and Industries of Newcastle-upon-Tyne, Sunderland, the Hartlepools, Middlesbro', Bristol, Cardiff, Newport and Swansea* (Newcastle-upon-Tyne: Andrew Reid, 1883), quoted in Laura Tabili, *Global Migrants, Local Culture: Natives and Newcomers in Provincial England, 1841–1939* (Palgrave, 2011), p. 13.

9. Nikolaus Pevsner, *County Durham (The Buildings of England)* (Penguin, 1953), p. 139.

10. Michael Bracewell, *Roxy Music, 1953–1972: The Band That Invented an Era* (Faber & Faber, 2008), pp. 11–12.

11. Jeremy Black, *Culture in Eighteenth-Century England. A Subject for Taste* (Hambledon and London, 2005), p. 203.

12. Richard Pears, 'William Newton (1730–1798) and the development of the architectural profession in north-east England' (unpubld Newcastle University PhD thesis, 2013), p. 23.

13. Pevsner, *Northumberland*, p. 104.

14. Philip Walsh, *Brill's companion to the reception of Aristophanes* (Brill: 2016), p. 312, fn 20.

15. Pevsner, *Northumberland*, p. 56.

16. https://www.chroniclelive.co.uk/news/history/newcastles-grey-street-built-1830s-10260171

17. Owen Hatherley (ed.), *Nairn's Towns*, pp. 15–26.

18. Ibid.

19. http://www.jonestheplanner.co.uk/2015/08/superlative-newcastle.html
20. Thomas Faulkner and Andrew Greg, *John Dobson: Architect of the North East* (Newcastle Libraries, 2001), p. 95.
21. Pevsner, *Durham*, p. 73; *The Tyneside Classical Tradition. Classical Architecture in the North East, c. 1700–1850* (Tyne and Wear Museums, 1980), pp. 14–15.
22. Pevsner, *Northumberland*, p. 92.
23. Ian Ayris, *A City of Palaces: Richard Grainger and the Making of Newcastle Upon Tyne* (Newcastle Libraries, 1997).
24. Owen Hatherley, *The New Ruins of Great Britain* (Verso, 2011), p. 160.
25. Pevsner, *County Durham*, p. 20.
26. Jonathan Meades, *Museums Without Walls* (Unbound, 2013), p. 92.
27. Davidson, *The Idea of North*, p. 243.
28. Pollard, *North East England During the Wars of the Roses: Lay Society, War, and Politics, 1450–1500* (Oxford University Press, 1990), p. 2.
29. Pevsner *Northumberland* (1957), p. 15; and Pevsner, *Northumberland* (Yale, 1992), pp. 34–5.
30. Douglas L. W. Tough, *The Last Years of a Frontier: A History of the Borders During the Reign of Elizabeth* (Oxford University Press, 1928), p. 38.
31. Karl Marx and Friedrich Engels, *Capital: A Critical Analysis of Capitalist Production* (Swan Sonnenschein, 1887), p. 562.
32. A. W. Purdue, *Newcastle: The Biography* (Amberley, 2011), p. 213.
33. Milburn and Miller, *Sunderland*, p. 69.
34. F.M.L. Thompson, *The Cambridge Social History of Britain, 1750–1950, Volume 2: People and their Environment* (Cambridge University Press, 1990), pp. 215–16.
35. McCord, *Northern Counties*, p. 303.
36. Mess, *Industrial Tyneside*, p. 85.
37. McCord, *Northern Counties*, p. 379.
38. T. E Faulkner (ed.), *Northumbrian Panorama: Studies in the History and Culture of North East England* (Octavian, 1996), pp. 98–9.
39. Ibid.
40. Atkinson, *Life and Tradition*, p. 63.
41. Frank Atkinson, *Victorian Britain: The North East* (David & Charles, 1989), p. 62.
42. McCord, *Northern Counties*, p. 162.
43. P. J. Waller, *Town, City and Country: England 1850–1914* (Clarendon, 1992), p. 100.
44. Extract from Harold Heslop, 'From Tyne to Tone. A Journey' accessed at http://www.writinglives.org/haroldheslop/an-introduction-harold-heslop-1898–1983
45. Ian Nairn, *Britain's Changing Towns* (BBC, 1967), p. 22.
46. https://www.architectsjournal.co.uk/news/culture/nairns-towns/8658017.article
47. https://www.theguardian.com/travel/2018/dec/13/10-cool-shopping-districts-hamburg-st-petersburg-toronto-readers-travel-tips
48. https://laingartgallery.org.uk/sean-scully-1970; http://www.ianstephenson.net/is-library/uploads/2013/07/Sean-Scully.pdf

49. 'Compared with the rest of the country the North East spent more on flour, biscuits, bacon, fish and chips, lard, potatoes, sweets and chocolate; but less on breakfast cereals, wet fish, fresh milk and fruit', see McCord, *Water under the Bridges*, p. 4.
50. Colls, *Pitmen*, p. 134.
51. Mess, *Tyneside*, p. 24.
52. Fraser, *Steel Bonnets*, pp. 28–9.
53. Jack Lawson, *A Man's Life* (Hodder & Stoughton, 1932), p. 160.
54. *London Evening Standard*, 23 January 1862, p. 6.
55. Meades, *Museums Without Walls*, p. 91.
56. https://www.independent.co.uk/arts-entertainment/art/features/concrete-buildings-brutalist-beauty-9057223.

5. HARD WORK AND HEDONISM

1. Cecil J. Sharp, *Sword Dances of Northern England Together with the Horn Dance of Abbots Bromley* (Novello, 1912), p. 91.
2. https://noisey.vice.com/en_uk/article/r795a9/makina-the-youth-culture-phenomenon-taking-over-newcastle
3. http://www.factmag.com/2014/09/04/geordie-shore-this-aint-introducing-makina-the-northeast-scene-keeping-the-hardcore-flame-burning/
4. Colls, *Colliers Rant*, pp. 52–3.
5. https://www.chroniclelive.co.uk/news/north-east-news/newcastle-revealed-kindest-city-uk-12611829
6. http://news.bbc.co.uk/1/hi/england/west_midlands/4362442.stm
7. 'The Government research, compiled by Community Life, found that 84% of people say they chat to neighbours at least once a month', the highest in England. https://www.businesswire.com/news/home/20100420005158/en/Geordie-Accent-Rated-UK's-Friendly-Put-Good
8. David Levine and Keith Wrightson, *The Making of an Industrial Society: Whickham 1560–1765* (Oxford University Press, 1991).
9. Michael Pollard, *The Hardest Work Under Heaven: Life and Death of the British Coal Miner* (Hutchinson, 1986).
10. Colls and Lancaster, *Newcastle upon Tyne*, p. 14.
11. Davidson, *The Idea of North*, p. 242.
12. Colls, *Pitmen*, p. 11.
13. Middlemas, *As They Really Were*, p. 48.
14. Colls and Lancaster, *Geordies*, p. 24; McManners, *Quintessential Cornish*, p. 25.
15. Pollard, *The Hardest Work*, p. 49.
16. Mess, *Tyneside*, p. 72.
17. Eric Hobsbawm, *Industry and Empire: From 1750 to the Present* (Penguin, 1999), p. 70.
18. Adam Smith, *An Inquiry into the Nature and Causes of the Wealth of Nations, Volume 1* (Cooke & Hale, 1818), p. 72.

19. Colls, *Pitmen*, p. 125.

20. Cobbett, *Cobbett's tour in Scotland; and in the four Northern countries of England*, p. 68.

21. Bill Griffiths, *Pitmatic: Talk of the North East Coalfield* (Northumbria University Press, 2007), p. 156.

22. Colls and Lancaster, *Geordies*, pp. 104–5.

23. Griffiths, *Pitmatic*, p. 166.

24. Colls, *Pitmen*, p. 291.

25. Ibid., pp. 29–30.

26. Robinson, *Tommy Turnbull*, p. 212.

27. Colls, *Pitmen*, p. 125.

28. Pollard, *Hardest Work*, pp. 153–4.

29. Sharkey, *Akenside*, p. 33.

30. Atkinson, *Life and Tradition*, p. 95.

31. https://www.thenorthernecho.co.uk/news/4577747.Divvent_Gan_Doon_the_Pit___/

32. Chaplin, *Hame*, p. 20.

33. Moffat and Rosie, *Tyneside*, p. 192; Finch, *Coals from Newcastle*, p. 28.

34. Heald, *Armstrong*, p. 97.

35. Mess, *Tyneside*, p. 101; Colls and Lancaster, *Geordies*, p. 124.

36. Colls, *Pitmen*, p. 134.

37. Ibid., p. 135.

38. Griffiths, *Pitmatic*, p. 261.

39. Donald M. MacRaild and Daivd E. Martin, *Labour in British Society, 1830–1914* (Macmillan, 2000), p. 101.

40. Robinson, *Tommy Turnbull*, pp. 16, 18.

41. Ardagh, *Tale of Five Cities*, p. 246.

42. Pollard, *Hardest Work*, p. 79; Atkinson, *Victorian Britain*, p. 21.

43. Colls and Lancaster, *Geordies*, p. 108.

44. Just over 20 per cent of all occupied persons compared with about 30 per cent in England and Wales. *Water under the Bridges*, pp. 85, 87.

45. Mason, *Pit Sinkers*, p. 95; https://mininginstitute.org.uk/wp-content/uploads/2016/02/Mining-accidents-and-safety-Jan16.pdf

46. McCord, *Northern Counties*, p. 37.

47. Pollard, *Hardest Work*, pp. 104–6.

48. Review of Ken and Jean Smith, *The Great Northern Miners* (Tyne Bridge Publications, 2008), in *North East History*, 39 (2008), p. 253.

49. Lawson, *A Man's Life*, p. 160.

50. Colls and Lancaster, *Geordies*, p. 161.

51. Finch, *Coals to Newcastle*, p. 138.

52. Milburn and Miller, *Sunderland*, pp. 52–3.

53. Ibid.

54. Atkinson, *Victorian Britain*, p. 145.

55. Thomas, Gabe (1995), *MILAG: Merchant Navy prisoners of war*. Milag PoW Association, p. ix; data on South Shields merchant navy casualties passed to me by Janis Blower of the *Shields Gazette*.
56. Atkinson, *Life and Tradition*, p. 85.
57. A. L. Lloyd, *Folk Song in England* (Faber and Faber, 2008), p. 150.
58. Pevsner, *Northumberland*, p. 88.
59. R. Oliver Heslop, *Northumberland Words. A Glossary of Words Used in the County of Northumberland and on The Tyneside* (Oxford, 1893), p. 498.
60. Ralph Gardner, *England's Grievance Discovered* (1655) http://downloads.it.ox.ac.uk/ota-public/tcp/Texts-HTML/free/A42/A42371.html
61. A. Campos Matos, *Aquisições Queirosianas, Exposição Bibliográfica* (Lisboa: Biblioteca Nacional, 2007), p. 43; Alison Aiken (ed.) *Eça's English Letters* (Manchester: Carcanet, 2000), pp. xviii–xix.
62. Colls and Lancaster, *Newcastle upon Tyne*, p. 168.
63. Colls, *Colliers Rant*, p. 154.
64. Colls and Lancaster, *Newcastle upon Tyne*, p. 172; see also (Bean, 1971, p. 223): The North East has 'rarely been far from the top of the nation's drunkenness table'.
65. McCord, *Northern Counties*, pp. 186–7.
66. Heald, *Armstrong*, p. 218.
67. John Collingwood Bruce, *Reid's Handbook to Newcastle upon Tyne* (Andrew Reid, 1863), p. 89.
68. In 1920 Northumberland still topped the county drunkenness league, with Durham runner-up. See Colls and Lancaster, *Geordies*, p. 31.
69. Bath, *Great War Britain: Tyneside*, p. 88.
70. Ibid., p. 135.
71. R. Coffield, C. Borril, S. Marshall, *Growing Up at the Margins: Young Adults in the North East* (Open University Press, 1986), pp. 132–3.
72. Sharkey, *Akenside*, p. 69.
73. Uglow, *Nature's Engraver*, p. 11.
74. *The Spectator*, 27 July 1951.
75. Colls, *Colliers Rant*, p. 140.
76. Horsley, *Eighteenth-Century Newcastle*, p. 112; Sharkey, *Akenside*, p. 106.
77. Peter Winter, *Newcastle upon Tyne* (Northern Heritage, 1989), p. 65.
78. Dave Harker, 'The Making of the Tyneside Music Hall', *Popular Music*, Vol. 1 (1981), p. 31.
79. Atkinson, *Life and Tradition*, p. 145.
80. Hilary Fawcett (ed.), *Made in Newcastle: Visual Culture* (Northumbria University Press, 2007), p. 30.
81. https://www.rollingstone.com/music/music-album-reviews/back-in-black-5-185369/
82. Colls and Lancaster, *Newcastle upon Tyne*, p. 335.
83. Purdue, *Newcastle*, p. 220.
84. Faulkner, *Northumbrian Panorama*, p. 84.

85. Pollard, *Hardest Work*, p. 156.

86. Durham Miners Association, *Annual Report*, 1953.

87. Colls, *Colliers Rant*, pp. 54–5.

88. Middlebrook, *Newcastle*, p. 222.

89. Waller, *Town City and Country*, p. 103.

90. Colls and Lancaster, *Geordies*, p. 86.

91. Michael Walker, *Up There: The North East, Football, Boom & Bust* (De Coubertin, 2014), p. 2.

92. Horsley, *Eighteenth Century Newcastle*, pp. 55, 59, 63.

93. https://www.chroniclelive.co.uk/news/history/adults-began-wear-replica-football-15888886

94. Myers, *Literary Guide*, pp. 2–3.

95. E. Welbourne, *The Miners Unions of Northumberland and Durham* (Cambridge University Press, 1922), p. 18.

96. Pollard, *Hardest Work*, p. 128.

97. Colls and Lancaster, *Newcastle upon Tyne*, p. 327.

98. Fraser, *Steel Bonnets*, p. 47.

99. Waller, *Town, City and Country*, p. 199.

100. Pollard, *Hardest Work*, p. 70.

101. *Singing Histories: Sunderland* (Tyne and Wear Archives and Museums), nd, p. 21.

102. Helen Wood, 'The politics of hyperbole on Geordie Shore: Class, gender, youth and excess', *European Journal of Cultural Studies*, 20 (1), 2017.

103. Ronald Embleton, *Geordie Pride* (Frank Graham, 1974), p. 26.

104. William Brereton, *Travels in Holland, the United Provinces, England, Scotland, and Ireland, M.DC.XXXIV-M.DC.XXXV* (The Chetham Society, 1844), p. 85.

105. Daniel Defoe, Anthony J. Coulson (ed.), *A Tour Through the Whole Island of Great Britain* (Yale University Press, 1991), p. 282.

106. Purdue, *Newcastle*, p. 197.

107. Colls, *Pitmen*, p. 141; Colls, *Colliers Rant*, pp. 28–9.

108. *The Tyne Songster: A Choice Selection of Songs in the Newcastle Dialect* (W. & T. Fordyce, 1840), p. 123.

109. See: William Lancaster, *The Department Store: A Social History* (Leicester University Press, 1995).

110. Purdue, *Newcastle*, p. 198.

111. Ardagh, *Tale of Five Cities*, p. 197.

112. Tweeted by @LukeTurnerEsq on 11 November 2018.

114. Catherine Cookson, *Our Kate: An Autobiographical Memoir* (Corgi, 1993), p. 13.

115. Walker, *Up There*, p. 30.

116. Colls and Lancaster, *Geordies*, p. 162.

117. Anoop Nayak, 'Last of the 'Real Geordies'? White masculinities and the subcultural response to deindustrialisation', *Environment and Planning D: Society and Space* 2003, vol. 21, p, 13.

118. Ibid., p. 15.

6. COME LET US REASON TOGETHER

1. Ralph Robson. *The English Highland Clans: Tudor Responses to a Mediaeval Problem* (John Donald, 1989).
2. Hackett Fischer, *Albion's Seed*, p. 663.
3. https://peopleofthebritishisles.web.ox.ac.uk/::ognode-566::/files/newsletter6pdf
4. Colls, *Pitmen*, pp. 173, 53–4.
5. Pevsner, *County Durham*, p. 58.
6. William Cobbett, *Cobbett's Tour in Scotland; and in the Four Northern Countries of England* (Mills, Jowett and Mills, 1833), p. 84.
7. Colls, *Pitmen*, p. 43.
8. Richard Fynes, *The Miners of Northumberland and Durham* (John Robinson, 1873), p. 38.
9. Conall Boyle, 'Why Cavilling Worked: Exploring an evolved economic mechanism used in the Durham coalfield communities', University of Swansea, November 2005, p. 19. http://www.conallboyle.com/lottery/CavilseminarNov05.pdf
10. Atkinson, *Life and Tradition*, p. 65.
11. Alastair Bonnett, 'The Discovery of Thomas Spence's Lecture 'Property in Land Every One's Right' (1775)', *Labour History Review*, 2009, 74, 1, pp. 134–6.
12. Purdue, *Newcastle*, pp. 69–70.
13. Harvey, C., Maclean, M., Price, M. & Harizanova, V. (2018), 'Philanthropy—the North East Story', https://www.generosityfestival.co.uk/history. Accessed 16 January 2019.
14. Ibid.
15. https://grahamwyliefoundation.org.uk/about-the-foundation/
16. Finch, *Coals to Newcastle*, p. 33.
17. Purdue, *Newcastle*, p. 158.
18. Middlebrook, *Newcastle*, p. 158.
19. Horsley, *Eighteenth-Century Newcastle*, p. 59; John Daniels and Stafford M. Linsley, *The Real Northern Powerhouse: The Industrial Revolution in the North East* (Tyne Bridge Publishing, 2016), pp. 92,94.
20. Jonathan Rose, *The Intellectual History of the British Working Classes* (Yale University Press, 2010), p. 42.
21. Rev Henry Fletcher, 'Primitive Methodism and the Miners', The Christian Messenger (1921) accessed at https://www.myprimitivemethodists.org.uk/content/subjects-2/industry/primitive_methodism_and_the_miners
22. Mess, *Industrial Tyneside*, p. 82.
23. Alan Myers, 'Zamiatin in Newcastle: The Green Wall and The Pink Ticket', *The Slavonic and East European Review*, Vol. 71, No. 3 (July, 1993), p. 424.
24. Michael Higgins, *The Cambridge Companion to Modern British Culture* (Cambridge University Press, 2010), p. 87.

25. Middlebrook, *Newcastle*, p. 88; Colls, *Pitmen*, p. 36.

26. https://www.chroniclelive.co.uk/news/north-east-news/50-reasons-proud-youre-geordie-1738928

27. F. A. Flowers, Ian Ground (eds), *Portraits of Wittgenstein, Volume 2* (Bloomsbury, 2015), p. 730.

28. Ardagh, *Tales of Five Cities*, p. 201.

29. Atkinson, *Life and Tradition*, p. 149.

30. Pevsner, *Northumberland*, p. 98.

31. Ibid., p. 91.

32. Norman McCord, *The Regions's Development 1760–1960* (Batsford, 1979), pp. 89–90.

33. Common, *Kiddar's Luck*, p. 63.

34. https://www.independent.co.uk/arts-entertainment/books/features/martyn-waites-why-the-geordie-crime-writer-is-choosing-to-keep-it-real-769627.html

35. Sharkey, *Akenside*, p. 246.

36. Chris Donald, *The Inside Story of Viz: Rude Kids* (Harper Perennial, 2009), p. 6.

37. http://www.thedailymash.co.uk/news/society/geordie-with-posh-voice-baffles-workmates-20160428108414

38. Dave Russell, '"We All Agree, Name the Stand after Shankly": Cultures of Commemoration in Late Twentieth-Century English Football Culture', *Sport in History*, 26:1 (2006).

39. David Starkey interviewed by Damian Thompson, 'England has a terrible crisis of identity', 9 September 2005, https://www.telegraph.co.uk/culture/tvandra-dio/3646412/England-has-a-terrible-crisis-of-identity.html. See also Carol Stephenson and David Wray, 'Emotional Regeneration Through Community Action in Post-Industrial Mining Communities: The New Herington Banner partnership', *Capital and Class*, No. 87, (2005), 175–199; Huw Beynon and Terry Austrin, *Masters and Servants: Class and patronage in the making of a labour organisation* (London, 1994), p. 206.

40. McCord, *Water under the Bridges*, pp. 131–2.

41. Norman Dennis and George Erdos, *Families Without Fatherhood* (Institute for the Study of Civil Society, 2000), p. x.

42. Mess, *Industrial Tyneside*, p. 25.

43. Middlebrook, *Newcastle*, pp. 24–5.

44. R.R. Reid, *The King's Council in the North* (Longmans, 1921), pp. 15–16.

45. W. S. F. Pickering, *Social History of the Diocese of Newcastle, 1882–1982* (Oriel, 1981), p. 5.

46. McCord, *Northern Counties*, p. 213.

47. Alexander Rose, *Kings in the North: The House of Percy in British History* (Phoenix, 2002), p. 1.

48. https://www.theguardian.com/books/2002/nov/30/featuresreviews.guardianreview22

49. Pickering, *Diocese of Newcastle*, pp. 5–7.

50. Ibid., pp. 5–7.

51. Kynaston, *Austerity Britain*, pp. 66–7.

52. Winter, *Newcastle upon Tyne*, p. 86.

53. Horsley, *Eighteenth Century Newcastle*, p. 280.

54. Purdue, *Newcastle*, p. 74–5.

55. Waller, *Town, City and Country*, p. 293.

56. Purdue, *Newcastle*, p. 145.

57. Henry Pelling, *The Social Geography of British Elections, 1885–1910* (Macmillan, 1967), p. 345.

58. Finch, *Coals to Newcastle*, p. 81.

59. J. F. Clarke, 'The Shipwrights', *North East Group for the Study of Labour History*, Bulletin 1 (1967), pp. 21–40.

60. Samuel Smiles, *The Life of George Stephenson* (Murray, 1868), p. 3.

61. D. Levine and K. Wrightson, *The Making an Industrial Society: Whickham, 1650–1765* (Oxford University Press, 1991), p. 425.

62. Colls, *Pitmen*, p. 216.

63. Mason, *Pit Sinkers*, p. 146.

64. John Baillie, *An Impartial History of the Town and County of Newcastle Upon Tyne and Its Vicinity: Comprehending an Account of Its Origin, Population, Coal, Coasting, & Foreign Trade, Together with an Accurate Description of All Its Public Buildings, Manufactories, Coal Works, &c* (Vint & Anderson, 1801), p. 196.

65. Alastair Bonnett and Keith Armstrong (eds), *Thomas Spence: The Poor Man's Revolutionary* (Breviary, 2014), p. 38.

66. McCord, *Northern Counties*, p. 17.

67. Colls and Lancaster, *Newcastle upon Tyne*, p. 126.

68. T.P. McDermott, 'Charles Larkin, Radical Reformer', *Catholic History*, 28 (1988), p. 167.

69. Laura Tabili, *Global Migrants, Local Culture: Natives and Newcomers in Provincial England, 1841–1939* (Palgrave, 2011), p. 236.

70. https://jewishnews.timesofisrael.com/why-charedi-jews-are-flocking-to-the-gritty-town-of-gateshead/ *The Times of Israel*, 6 October 2017.

71. Purdue, *Newcastle*, p. 101.

72. G. M. Trevelyan, *British History in the Nineteenth Century* (Longmans & Green, 1922), p. 19.

73. Colls, *Pitmen*, p. 111.

74. R. M. Hodnett, *Politics and the Northumberland Miners: Liberals and Labour in Morpeth and Wansbeck, 1890–1922* (Teesside Paper in North Eastern History), 1 December 1994, pp. 10–11.

75. Ibid.

76. Aaron Watson, *A Great Labour Leader; Being a Life of the Right Hon. Thomas Burt* (Brown, Langhand & Co., 1908), p. 301.

77. Colls, *Colliers Rant*, p. 169.

78. John Tomaney, 'Economics, Democratisation and Localism: The Lost World of Peter Lee', *Renewal: A Journal of Social Democracy*, Vol. 26, No. 1, 2018.

79. John Saville, 'The Present Position and Prospects for Labour History', *North East Group for the Study of Labour History*, Bulletin 1 (1967), p. 5.

80. Mess, *Tyneside*, p. 73.

81. Hodnett, *Politics and the Northumberland Miners*, p. 33.

82. https://blogs.lse.ac.uk/politicsandpolicy/healing-a-broken-heartland-an-historical-perspective-on-labours-gathering-storm-in-the-north-east/

83. Robinson, *Tommy Turnbull*, p. 138.

84. McCord, *Northern Counties*, p. 370.

85. Ellen Wilkinson, *The Town That Was Murdered* (Gollancz, 1939), p. 193.

86. *The Times*, 10 May 1929.

87. A. J. P. Taylor, *English History 1914–1945* (Oxford University Press, 1965), p. 433.

88. Bew, *Citizen Clem*, pp. 126, 548.

89. Kynaston, *Austerity Britain*, p. 185.

90. 'Has the North-East lost its identity? asks Sir John Hall', *Northern Echo*, 6 August 2014.

91. Walker, *Up There*, p. 34.

92. https://www.telegraph.co.uk/news/obituaries/politics-obituaries/9260852/Lord-Glenamara.html

93. https://dominiccummings.com/2017/01/09/on-the-referendum-21-branching-histories-of-the-2016-referendum-and-the-frogs-before-the-storm-2/

7. UPON A BLEAK NORTHUMBRIAN MOOR

1. Venetia Newall (1974), 'The Allendale Fire Festival in Relation to its Contemporary Social Setting', *Folklore*, 85:2, p. 101.

2. https://www.roughguides.com/destinations/europe/england/the-northeast/newcastle-tyne/

3. https://www.sunderlandecho.com/lifestyle/retro/work-begins-on-the-new-1950-s-town-at-beamish-museum-1-8767903

4. https://medium.com/frankly-green-webb/why-dont-they-come-visitors-on-low-income-and-the-myths-around-admission-price-ebf8b1da1f69

5. https://www.nytimes.com/2019/01/30/sports/britain-premier-league-foodbanks.html

6. https://www.theguardian.com/tv-and-radio/2018/jan/21/geordie-shore-one-long-advert-drinking

7. https://www.vice.com/en_uk/article/wd7y39/the-curious-geordie-tradition-for-punching-horses-103

8. https://www.theguardian.com/uk-news/2018/sep/09/british-army-explicitly-targeting-working-class-recruits-say-critics

9. Sharkey, *Akenside Syndrome*, p. 247; House of Commons Library Briefing Paper, Number

05635, 7 December 2018 'Public sector employment by parliamentary constituency', p. 7.

10. https://www.chroniclelive.co.uk/business/business-news/test-facilities-make-north-east-12506275

11. https://northeasttechstories.com/2019/03/21/why-north-east-tech-desperately-needs-to-stop-shooting-at-the-storm/

12. Richard T. Kelly, *What's Left for the North East* (Newcastle: New Writing North, 2011).

13. Harari, D. and M. Ward (2018) *Regional and country economic indicators*, House of Commons Library Briefing Paper Number 06924, 15 June.

14. https://www.theguardian.com/news/2018/oct/04/will-nissan-stay-once-britain-leaves-sunderland-brexit-business-dilemma

15. https://www.thenation.com/article/brexit-britain-may-confidence-vote/

16. https://www.theneweuropean.co.uk/top-stories/steven-france-on-why-sunderland-should-be-given-another-say-on-brexit-1-5706366

17. Elaine Knox, '"Keep your feet still, Geordie hinnie": Women and work on Tyneside', in Colls and Lancaster, pp. 93–114, pp. 94–5.

18. *The New Statesman*, 18 November 2016.

19. Paul Lipowski, 'Who Is The "Miner"? A Brief Exegesis Of Job 28:4', *European Scientific Journal*, July 2015, pp. 204–16.

20. Colls, *Northumbria*, p. 150.

21. Uglow, *Nature's Engraver*, p. 103.

22. Timothy Eden, *Durham: Volume II* (Robert Hale, 1953), p. 569.

23. M. W. Flinn, *Men of Iron: The Crowleys in the Early Iron Industry* (Edinburgh University Press, 1962).

24. https://yougov.co.uk/topics/politics/articles-reports/2018/06/25/where-london-most-and-least-popular

25. Middlebrook, *Newcastle*, pp. 319–20.

26. Walker, *Up There*, pp. 79–80.

27. A.A.L. Caesar, 'North-East England' in *Great Britain: Geographical Essays*, J.B. Mitchell (ed.) (Cambridge University Press, 1962), p. 455.

28. https://members.tortoisemedia.com/2019/01/14/britains-everyday-drug-problem/content.htm

29. https://www.newsweek.com/best-hospitals-2019

30. https://unherd.com/2018/06/people-not-places-real-hope-northern-powerhouse/

31. Gregory Clark and Neil Cummins, 'The Big Sort: Selective Migration and the Decline of Northern England, 1800–2017', LSE, May 2017 http://eh.net/eha/wp-content/uploads/2017/08/Clark.pdf

32. https://unherd.com/2018/06/people-not-places-real-hope-northern-powerhouse/

33. Henry A. Mess, 'The Social Survey of Tyneside: An English Regional Social Survey', *American Journal of Sociology*, Vol. 33, No. 3 (Nov., 1927), p. 428.

34. Davidson, *The Idea of North*, p. 215.

35. Walker, *Up There*, p. 35.

36. https://twitter.com/john_tomaney/status/1094518821757571072

37. http://www.lettersfromstan.com/stan-1955-11.html

38. https://www.independent.co.uk/arts-entertainment/obituary-dame-catherine-cookson-1164344.html

INDEX

INDEX

INDEX

INDEX

INDEX

INDEX

INDEX

Graham, Billy, evangelist, 41

Grainger, Richard, Newcastle builder, 78, 104

Grant, Ulysses S., President of the United States, 78

Gray, Professor John, Philosopher, 3, 85

Gray, William, antiquary, 162, 179

Great Exhibition of the North (2018), 221

Green, John and Benjamin, Newcastle architects, 101, 104, 115

Green, Robson, actor, 138

Greenwell, Jack, football manager, 158

Greenwell, William, Canon of Durham Cathedral, 213

Greggs the Bakers, 94, 171, 215

Gresford, 'The Miners Hymn', 148

Grey, Charles, 2nd Earl, Prime Minister, 71, 190–1

Gurney, Bobby, footballer, 158

Gurney, Ivor, poet, 164

Guthred, King of Northumbria, 12, 101

Ha'way/Howay, definition of, 6

Hackett Fischer, David, historian, 33, 38–41

Hacky, definition of, 7

Hadaway, Tom, playwright, 88

Hadrian, Emperor, 4, 29, 110, 122

Hadrian's Wall, 4, 8, 9, 27, 98, 133

Hailsham, Viscount, 'Minister for the North East', 218

Hall, Lee, playwright, 88, 91, 165, 220

Hall, Sir John, businessman, 200, 209

Halsey, A. H., sociologist, 108

Hancock, Albany, naturalist, 77

Handle, Johnny, folk singer, 152, 154

Hankinson, Andrew, writer, 208

Harbottle Castle, 39

Hard work of, 89

Harrying of the North, 32

Hartlepool, County Durham, vii, 53, 170, 208, 220

Hartley, Sir Charles, civil engineer, 76

Hatherley, Owen, architectural writer, 105

Havelock, General Sir Henry, 51

Heaton, suburb of Newcastle, 88, 116, 176

Heaton Hall, Northumberland, 102

Heavenfield, Battle of (633), 9, 30

Hebburn, County Durham, 76, 83, 121, 128, 148, 158, 218

Heddon-on-the-Wall, Northumberland, 21

Hedley, Ralph, painter, 147

Hedley, William, locomotive engineer, 80

Henderson, Arthur, Labour politician, 198

Henderson, Jordan, footballer, 159

Henderson, Tony, journalist, 128

Henry III, King of England, 12, 33

Henry IV, Part 1 play, 13

Henry VIII, King of England, 1, 36, 107, 117, 192, 213–4

Hepburn, Tommy, Durham miners' union leader

Heslop, Harold, working-class writer, 109

Heslop, Richard, lexicographer, 90

Hetton Colliery, County Durham, 81

Hexham and Hexhamshire, Northumberland, 10, 12, 17, 30, 43, 100, 171, 205

Hexham, Massacre (1761), 43

Higgs, Professor Peter, 94

Hilda, saint and abbess, 10

Hinny, definition of, 7

Hodges, Mike, film director 102

Hoare, Sir Samuel, ambassador to Paris, 14

Hobsbawm, Eric, historian, 136

Hockey, David, artist, 126

Hodgkin, Thomas, historian, 222

INDEX

Holden, Charles, architect, 115

Holland, Abraham, poet, 65

Holmes, John Henry, electrical inventor of the electrical switch, 83

Holmes, Professor Arthur, geologist, 76

Holmes, Sherlock, fictional detective, 50

Holywell, Northumberland, 124

Homer, Winslow, painter, 119, 142

Hopper, Joseph, miner, 85

Hoppings, Newcastle funfair, 154

Horce-racing, 154

Horrocks, General Sir Brian, 26, 56

Hotspur, Harry, more formally known as Sir Henry Percy, 8, 13, 19, 34, 56, 182, 345

Houghton-le-Spring, County Durham, 109, 211

Humber, river 13, 14

Hutchinson, William, sailor and inventor, 68, 138

Hutton, Charles, mathematician, 67

I, Daniel Blake (2016 Ken Loach film), 206

India, 51, 57, 139, 183

Industrial Revolution, 3, 15, 136, 220

Industrial unrest in 1820s and 1830s, 47, 48

Invasions and raid by Scots on North East England, 14, 15, 26, 31, 35, 42

Irish immigrants to North East England, 14, 53, 87, 109, 126, 153, 174, 191

Iron and iron making, 19, 21, 48, 61, 79–81, 100, 114, 138–9, 156

Italian Navy, links to Tyneside, 49

Ive, Sir Jony, Apple designer, 94

Jackson, Andrew, President of the United States, 40

Jacobite Rebellion (1745), 43, 69

Jacobites, 42, 43, 102

James IV, King of Scots, 36

James II, King of England (VII of Scotland), 193

Japanese Navy, links to Tyneside, 49

Jarrow, County Durham, 19, 22, 28, 48, 50, 53, 55, 57, 62, 81, 113, 143, 171, 176, 185, 215, 219

Jarrow March (1936), 199–201

Jewish immigrants, 192

Jobling, William, hanged for murder in 1832, 48

Joblings, Sunderland glass-making company, 79

John, King of England, 33

Johns, W. E., author of Biggles, 60

Johnson, Brian, Gateshead-born singer, 153

Johnson, Lyndon, President of the United States, 41

Joicey, Sir James, coal-owner, 183

Jones, Adrian, architectural writer, 104

Kearney, Fr Francis, Catholic priest, 174

Keel Row Book Shop, North Shields, x, 112

Keel Row, folk song, 51, 83, 160

Keelmen, 45, 47, 139, 149, 160, 161, 171–2, 186

Kelly, Gene, dancer, 132

Kelly, Richard T., novelist, 210

Kemp, Lindsay, dancer, 132

Kendall, Howard, football manager, 158

Kennedy, Ray, footballer, 158

Kennedy, Alan, footballer, 158

Khaldun, Ibn, 2

Kielder Water, Northumberland, 105

Kilbourn, Oliver, pitman painter, 200

Killingworth, Northumberland, 11, 78, 80, 86, 110, 123–4

King, Dr Martin Luther, 189

King's Council in the North, 13

Kipling, Rudyard, 30, 51

Kirkharle, Northumberland, 37, 74

INDEX

INDEX

INDEX

INDEX

INDEX